SHOW ME THE PRISONER
And I'll show you a young man

Patricia Farren (signature)

Patricia Farren
A Memoir

Matador
9 Priory Business Park,
Wistow Road,
Kibworth Beauchamp
Leicester LE8 0RX, UK
Tel. (+44) 116 279 2299
Fax: (+44) 116 279 2277
Email: books@troubador.co.uk
Web: www.troubador.co.uk/matador

ISBN 978 1780880 518

British Library Cataloguing in Publication Data.
A catalogue record for this book is available from the British Library.

Typeset in 10pt Bembo by Troubador Publishing Ltd, Leicester, UK

Matador is an imprint of Troubador Publishing Ltd

Printed and bound in the UK by TJ International, Padstow, Cornwall

Show me the prison
Show me the jail
Show me the prisoner
Whose life has gone stale
And I'll show you a young man
With so many reasons why
There but for fortune
Go you or I
                                    Phil Ochs

For
Sean Conlon in Belfast
&
Charles Eason in Arkansas

AUTHOR'S NOTE

Although I have taken liberties by changing names, sometimes making composite characters, relocating events, dates and scenes, or compressing incidents for the sake of lively reading, my aim in this book is to bring to life events within two prison establishments during my fifteen-year tenure. Apart from the protagonist's family and my immediate family, those deceased, or those who have already achieved fame or notoriety through public life and the media, all other names used are fictitious.

Usage of the term 'the governor' does not imply the number one governor in any establishment. It may refer to deputies, duty governors, or the several house, security or special-interest governors, who operate within the service with principal officers, senior officers, and ordinary-rank officers. They, along with others who work in the Prison Service, are characterised for their temperament, character, outlook, wit and, on occasion, their sense of the absurd.

ACKNOWLEDGEMENTS

I owe an enormous debt of gratitude to Carlo Gébler, Writer in Residence to the Prison Service of Northern Ireland, for his continuous encouragement and support during the writing of this book. Carlo loves a good story, and when I brought this one to his attention thinking he would write it up himself, he told me to go away and write it myself. He has been with me every step of the way since.

Thanks also to Claire Keegan who read my scribble at the Listowel Writers Week and told me I could write. To Michael Harding who accepted me on to his extra-curricular creative writing programme when he was Writer in Residence at Trinity College Dublin. To Antonia Logue who encouraged me to keep going, as did Mary Murphy, Stephen Price and Robert Welch. And to Bernie Magill who conducted Flowerfield Arts Centre creative writing group, Heather Newcombe of Ballycastle creative writers group for the weekend on Rathlin island, and the members of Portstewart U3A reading group.

I want to pay tribute to the teachers, board members and staff I met during my fifteen years association with the prison service. You may recognise yourself in here someplace, so watch out. I remember with affection the many prisoners who sought my help in sorting out problems, and especially one rascal who came to my classes.

I would like to mention by name a dear friend Justin Gorman who served with me in Maghaberry and passed away during that time. Betty Chambers who read the ms. at an early stage and told me she laughed her legs off. And Sophy Bryson who was appointed to the Board of Visitors of Maghaberry prison around the same time I was. We soldiered through together.

Finally I want to thank my husband Seán, and my four children for their love and support in bringing this work to publication. They all have walk-on parts. My sons-in-law Alex and Paul, and my three little grandchildren, Nora, Anna and Oona.

In memory of Charlie Conlon, proceeds from publication of this book will be donated to Extern.

Patricia Farren

ABBREVIATIONS

BOV	Board of Visitors – a panel of lay members appointed by the Sectary of State
INLA	Irish National Liberation Army – breakaway group from IRA
IRA	Irish Republican Army – an illegal paramilitary organisation
LVF	Loyalist Volunteer Force – an illegal paramilitary organisation
NIO	Northern Ireland Office, based in Dundonald House. Headquarters to the Prison Service of Northern Ireland
ODC	Ordinary decent criminal
PO	Principal officer
POA	Prison Officers Association
Provo	Member of Provisional IRA – its full title
PSNI	Prison Service of Northern Ireland
PSU	Prison secure unit
RA	Abbreviation of IRA
RUC	Royal Ulster Constabulary
SO	Senior officer
SSU	Special secure unit
UDA	Ulster Defence Association – an illegal loyalist paramilitary group
UDR	Ulster Defence Regiment – an infantry regiment of the British army
UFF	Ulster Freedom Fighters – formed to carry out terrorist attacks for loyalists
UVF	Ulster Volunteer Force – an illegal loyalist paramilitary group
YO	Young offender

PART ONE

MAGILLIGAN

1

The first time I went through the gates of Her Majesty's top-security prison, HMP Maghaberry, I tried to visualise the world beyond. With the exception of young Ramsey down the town, who had stolen an Ulsterbus and driven it into a stone wall before stealing a barrowful of eggs from the local bakery and firing them at the same wall, I knew hardly anybody who'd been inside.

Today I am staring at the headline dominating the front page of the *Belfast Telegraph* declaring another young man 'Ulster's Most Feared Prisoner'. They show his photograph and tell how he has spent the past two years of his life in solitary confinement, judging him more threatening than any terrorist of our time.

I examine the fuzzy dark image of the feared and dangerous 'time bomb'. Then, as directed, I turn the page for more 'sensational revelations'. Here it is revealed that the prison authorities have constructed a specially fortified cell to contain this 17-stone flesh-biting inmate, dubbed Hannibal, whom they deem too dangerous to handle by conventional means; so dangerous in fact that all the furniture in his cell has to be bolted to the floor. Prison officers will only approach in teams of four, kitted out in riot helmets and wearing protective clothing, including steel mesh gloves. 'In case he bites some of them', they say.

His name is Charlie, and in a roundabout way, the story I tell started in a bank.

Northern Ireland in 1990, and the Troubles were at their height. I was standing in the bank in my home town of Coleraine, preoccupied with my own troubles. One moment I was having a quiet chat across the counter with Jeremy; the next, a raised finger was directing me towards a secluded booth in Customer Services.

'As you were saying?' Jeremy, obviously more at ease out of other customers' earshot, continued.

'As I was saying, Jeremy,' my eye was directed at the sterling/dollar exchange rate on the display board behind his head, 'perhaps the time has come to pull the shutters down on the business.'

Jeremy shrugged away any such notion, and reached to a batch of brochures labelled *We're Here To Help*.

'You're well set up in that wee craft shop over there in New Row,' said he, pulling on an earlobe. 'It would be a hell of a damned pity to see her go, wouldn't it?'

He had the solution. I needed to diversify. To look beyond the narrow confines of cottage industry, beyond my nose and see the wider horizon. I needed to open up new markets, develop new products, break new ground. Drawing up a business plan, I assured him, would be no problem.

In the process of pulling on my gloves the doubts emerged. 'You know, Jeremy, this is very big money we're looking at here. A loan that size?'

'You always have the wee house down there in Portstewart, haven't you?' said he. 'If I'm right, the bank is holding the deeds.'

'Our home?' My ears pricked up. 'Like...'

'Collateral,' said Jeremy.

'Collateral? Like risk the family home on this venture?'

'How would himself feel?' enquired the all-obliging bank official.

'About losing the roof over our heads, you mean?'

Jeremy never blinked.

'Ecstatic, Jeremy,' I said. 'In raptures actually, particularly if he believed the bank was rowing in with me.'

And on that note, I departed the bank.

In the end I did not take the plunge. The lease on the workshop in New Row was not renewed, and the family home remained secure, at least for the time being. Having bid goodbye to the cutting table and the scissors, it was time to close up shop, and the account with the bank.

Best take a sabbatical, I thought. A breather.

I was happy at home, minding the house, until I saw the advertisement in the *Coleraine Chronicle*: 'Teachers Wanted to teach in Her Majesty's Prison Service'.

I applied for the job, and was called for interview, which took place in an upper room in the Job Centre in Coleraine. I must be first up, I thought, seeing only self and a row of empty chairs along a wall. On entering the interview chamber two grey-suited gentlemen rose as one from behind a desk.

'Governor Grogan,' one said, introducing the other.

Goodness! I thought. A governor! I am impressed. With mayhem raging on the streets of Northern Ireland the last person I'd expected to be shaking hands with in Coleraine Job Centre was a prison governor. Who's minding the shop while he's away? I wondered.

As I settled into the hot seat, the governor's classy suit kept drawing my eyes his way. Italian cut, I reckoned. But it was his moustache that distracted me the most. I thought it spoiled his face. I had a compelling urge to tell him to shave it off.

We talked through my qualifications. Then it was my work experience. I had a degree in arts, and a post-graduate diploma in social administration. I had certificates and diplomas in business studies, accounting, computer skills, secretarial skills ... and some temporary teaching experience, but no teacher-training qualification. I had a wide range of hobbies: could knit jumpers, sew patchwork quilts, make cuddly toys, weave baskets, punch and thong leather...

There was a six weeks' maternity leave pending at Magilligan prison. 'How would you feel about covering for the arts and crafts teacher, working six to eight, three evenings a week?'

'Fine.'

'How would you feel about working with offenders?'

'Fine.'

'How comfortable would you feel sitting in the same room as hardened criminals – men who have murdered, men found guilty of raping and abusing women and children, men who have...'

'As comfortable,' I said, 'as I am sitting here with you two guys.'

Fortunately for me, they both smiled. My next test: how would I perform under pressure? The governor took over. I sat up.

'Place yourself in this situation, Mrs Farren,' he said, tossing his biro onto the desk and swiping his index finger across the narrow band of moustache above his upper lip.

'Yes.' I waited expectantly.

'You are in your classroom. You are conducting a class, using an overhead projector, the light focused on a spot below. A prisoner walks up to the top of the class and, in full view of all the other prisoners, places a leather-bound wallet underneath the spotlight, and says: "Here is a present for you Mrs Farren. I made this especially for you in handicrafts, and I want you to have it from me as a gift." How would you react were you to find yourself in that situation?'

'Anyone,' I said, again without giving the question sufficient thought, 'who would go to such lengths to craft a gift especially for me, well, I think I'd probably give him a hug.'

It was the wrong answer. I should explain to the prisoner why I was not at liberty to take anything other than essentials in or out of class, show myself to be a law-abiding citizen who played by the rules. But as I had never read the prison rulebook – which I like to believe law-abiding citizens do not normally read – all I could do was endeavour to convey something to the above effect during the remainder of the interview.

The interview concluded, and with smiles all round we shook hands. They did say, however, that it was nice meeting me, and would be in touch; me thinking, heading for the door, I've blown it. Others will be lined up on those chairs outside, all clamouring to teach in Her Majesty's Prison Service. I haven't a chance after that performance.

But nobody was waiting outside.

Later on the letter arrived, offering me employment in HMP Magilligan, and so commenced my prison career. To begin with, I substituted for the arts and crafts teacher three evenings each week, but when the baby was born and the mother returned to work my time was my own again. A few months passed before the offer of daytime work arrived: business studies and social studies, four hours allocated to each subject, classes twice weekly. And that was when this story really started.

Two years from the day when I first shook hands with a prison governor in the Job Centre in Coleraine, I was parked outside Magilligan prison, waiting to be allowed inside to conduct my business studies class. Absentmindedly, I stared up at a watchtower high above me, cameras high on the walls holding me in their sights. Cars pulled in behind me. Cattle and sheep grazed the surrounding fields, fenced in by barbed wire. Barbed wire spread along the prison walls ensured the prisoners, too, stayed in their place. I listened to music on the car radio, tapping the steering wheel to the beat, an eye fixed on the dashboard clock.

Five minutes, eight minutes ... the beep of a horn behind me. The door in the perimeter wall was opening. We were on the move. In the car park, among a sea of lustrous limousines, I searched for a parking space for my battered Honda Civic.

My next port of call was a Portakabin. I was pushing my car keys through a narrow slit in a large plate-glass partition. The officer was on the telephone, his feet resting on the desk, a cigarette smouldering in an ashtray at his elbow. I rattled the glass. He reached for the cigarette, flicked a curl of ash to the floor, and returned the cigarette to the ashtray. I withdrew my keys and tapped again. His eyes were focused on a girlie calendar on the wall opposite. The year: 1992. A blond maiden in a tutu was hung out to dry on a clothesline, pegged by her bra straps, her legs spreadeagled above a cannonball. I wasn't surprised the poor girl's tongue was hanging out, the position she was dangling in.

'Cheers, Geordie, cheers, mate.' The conversation was finally drawing to an end. But Geordie would not let go. Heavy officer boots pounding the floor behind me gave the man on the phone the excuse he needed to disconnect.

I pushed my keys through again, and was handed a pass. I moved to the next barrier. An officer reached to his side and jangled forth a chain with a ring of keys. He selected one and inserted it in the lock. Chained to the gate, he held his boot against it while I walked through.

I said hello at the Education Office, picked up my class list and joined Louise, a teacher colleague, for the fifteen-minute trek to our classrooms. Together we approached our next high fence, the inner-perimeter wall. We buzzed a buzzer but nobody came. We banged and shouted to attract attention. Still nobody came. We jumped up and down trying to reach a slat high above our heads.

'Ach, ladies,' said an officer, coming up behind us, 'will nobody let yous in?' He hollered through the slat and got an instant response.

Next we were in Searches, being told that the female searchers were delayed in Visits. We would have to wait. A stream of officers sailed by, lifting their arms for the male searchers, until finally someone came to peer into our bags and give us a rubdown.

We were on our way again, exchanging passes at the next plate-glass window, clanking after each other through a metal turnstile, passing Portakabins, prefabs and Nissen huts (a legacy of a British Armed Forces' presence during the Second World War, now used as prison workshops). Open space. Green grass. Rabbits scurrying in and out of burrows. An officer walking towards us with an Alsatian on a lead. The dog ignoring the rabbits, the officer ignoring us. The blocks still five minutes away.

A short-term facility, Magilligan housed those serving maximum three-year sentences, or serving the last three years of longer sentences. Prisoners were housed in blocks – B1, B2 and B3.

The education facility was wire-fenced into its own private enclosure, and comprised an arts unit, three classrooms, a library, toilets and a cubbyhole – the nerve centre of operations in education. It held anything that had to be nailed down, such as keys to cupboards, an extra supply of tea, toilet rolls ... and a telephone for emergencies. The officer on duty remained in the library throughout. He guarded the kettle and the key to the cubbyhole.

A glass-partitioned corridor for surveillance led to the classrooms. When I arrived the prisoners had yet to come across from the blocks. I glanced down my class list, noting two new additions.

A formation of yellow pockmarked Formica-topped tables created a centrepiece in the classroom. A battered bin surrounded by cigarette ends, soggy teabags and scrunched-up balls of paper stood in a corner. Fixed to the wall behind my head was a silicone blackboard, to my right a padlocked metal cabinet, the key locked in the cubbyhole. Overhead a fluorescent tube suspended from two chains hissed at a lofty height on all below. I sat down to await the arrival of my students.

'Paul Martin Delaney, sweetheart,' the laughing eyes behind the outstretched hand twinkled with mischief. 'But, never worry your head about names, everyone calls me Pablo.'

While the accent was vintage Belfast, his honeyed skin tones hinted at more exotic lands.

'I was a professional footballer,' he explained, unzipping a glitzy jacket with a jazzy lining that sported a designer label. He was an absolute dazzle of colour. There were numerous pockets concealed beneath studs and flaps, and he searched each one meticulously before removing the jacket and draping it over a chair. Brushing a speck of cigarette ash from the eye of the crocodile on his crested Lacoste T-shirt, he added, 'Before a bullet put a stop to my career. You're Mrs Farren, aren't you?' he continued on the same breath. 'The teacher who does business? You know, you come highly recommended by the lads on the block, sweetheart.'

'That makes my day,' I deadpanned back.

'We're on the same wavelength, kiddo,' he laughed. 'You and me, we're going to hit it off.'

'Delaney?' I glanced down the class list. A moment later he was leaning over my shoulder, his finger stabbing at number 1762 Delaney, checking on my accent. My southern brogue? Was I originally from the Free State?

'Yes,' I acknowledged I was originally from the Republic.

He expected that a lady such as me would have a husband, and forgave me when I told him I had.

He needed to get his business transacted before the others arrived, he explained. 'Lead by example,' being his motto. It had to do with his niece Kerry-Marie. He adored kids. 'Been drumming it into that wee girl's head how important education is. Know what I mean? She's clever. Let me tell you that wee girl is one clever wee girl. It's my hope that one day she'll redeem the Delaney name. Last year she went to America. One of your junkets. Yous ones would know all about them carry-ons for ones that has been hit worst by the Troubles. From deprived areas, know what I mean? The family in America wanted her to stay, wanted to send her to school, university, the lot. But she missed her ma and her wee brothers, and wanted to get back to Belfast and see all her pals again. The family still keeps in touch with her. They'd do anything for her. Her father's inside,' he added, almost as an aside. 'He's not half wise, know what I mean?'

'Is any of you?' I ventured, guessing he could cope with a wisecrack.

'Look into that eye.' He raised his eyelid. 'Do you see that brown speck?'

I looked into his eye and saw it.

'My maternal grandfather was a black man, an American airman billeted in Northern Ireland while serving with the American forces during the war.'

Here followed the story of lovely Molly from Dungloe coming across the border to a dance in Derry. The dashing airman was billeted with his troops not far from where we sat, a few miles up the road at Ballykelly, the old RAF base used by the Americans during the Second World War. The airman was enamoured by the beautiful Molly and when she fell pregnant, her family – which, by the way, was full of priests and nuns and owned shops and land and what-have-you in and around Dungloe – was none too keen on having the offspring of the union come to live in those parts. The outcome was that his 'gorgeous wee ma' was put into a Barnardo's home, where she remained until she could leave at sixteen. By seventeen she'd married his father, a Belfast docker: a tough, heavy-drinking man, a boxer in his day, who made a hell on earth of her and her twelve children's lives.

But enough of all of that. If Kerry-Marie was to listen to his advice, he had to clean up his act. And that was where I came in.

'Why have you chosen business studies?' I asked.

'Not to worry!' He had it all figured out. 'I'm a late beginner,' he accepted, 'but what odds! What the hell!' He needed to make an honest living instead of robbing banks, and to do that he needed to understand how business operated from the inside out, not the outside in. I would be the conduit of that information, and he would lap at my fountain of knowledge. He was determined to pay tax and National Insurance, anything they looked for. We would make a fantastic team. Me and him. He couldn't wait for us to get started.

'Check if Joe McCoy's on that list of yours,' he said, a tin of Golden Virginia tobacco landing on the table.

'Number 1874 McCoy?' But on raising my head I found myself talking to thin air.

He was away, yelling up the corridor.

'You're OK, Joe. Get yourself down here, kiddo. Mrs Farren's dead on. You don't mind, do you?' over his shoulder to me. 'I got Joe to come along for the craic.'

Fists jammed like two cocked pistols into the pockets of a cropped denim jacket, McCoy stood in the doorway. 'Isn't she a babe?' said Delaney to McCoy.

'Aye. Stickin' out, boy. How's about you, darlin'?' Belly straining against a red polo shirt, all five foot of him rocked on his heels as he eyed me up and down.

In dribs and drabs others arrived, sweeping McCoy through with them. I ticked off names as they entered. Everybody knew Paul Delaney.

He knew them all, called everyone 'mate'. He wanted tea. Somebody had a packet of chocolate biscuits; he'd have some of them. He discovered I had a jar of coffee in my bag. He changed his mind. He'd have coffee instead of tea. There was no milk; milk was found. He had no jotter, no pen. I called for a prison officer to come and open the padlocked cabinet. I produced a jotter, and a choice of pens.

'Bic biros, red or black?'

He confiscated both. Then gave a potted version of his life story. Belfast, the flats, St Pat's, football, dope, robberies, jail. 'Happy days. I'm a thirty-year-old *mon,* and I'm virtually as innocent as a child,' he lamented to the assembled group. 'Every time they let me out I revert to the age I was before I went in. The world's left me behind and I can't catch up.' He begged someone to come to his rescue.

'Well, let's start right now,' I suggested, grasping the opportunity to get the class underway. But first, a cigarette was needed before he could become fully operational. It was McCoy's signal to slide cigarette papers across the table. Without raising his eyes Delaney reached out and the papers were there. He laid his line of tobacco, dusted it down, rolled and shaped, then licked and moistened. A tap on the lid of the tin brought McCoy's lighter to his elbow.

Only then could he inhale his first satisfying breath of the day.

'Fire ahead everyone,' he commanded.

We heard not another squeak from him until a conversation developed about my social studies class. His ears pricked up.

Social studies would interest him greatly. Just what was needed for the final polish.

'Sign me up, Skipper,' he directed the education officer.

2

'What's got into everyone? Why are officers crawling all over the place this morning?' I remarked to Susan, a colleague, as we walked through the library on our way to our classrooms. The scene inside had changed little since I had last been there. It was just another day, another few months down the line, and another business studies class. Anxious to get to work I dispatched a prisoner, Terry Maguire, to round up the stragglers, Pablo Delancy included, and turned my back on the semicircle chatting at the table to write up some figures on the blackboard.

I paused, a presence by my side causing me to glance sideways. A faded grey hood screened his eyes as he took a step backwards, while my eyes swivelled between him and the blackboard. You're not impressed, I thought. 'What?' I asked, glancing back to the board. It was then I realised I had slotted a set of figures into a company account the wrong way round.

'You want to get your balance right,' I was told.

I was expecting no newcomers that day, but prisoners often wandered into classrooms for a word with a mate. Or, perhaps he was interested in joining the class? I was at the point of enquiry when Terry rushed back in, having located Pablo chatting up Susan in the classroom next door. They were followed by Eugene McQuillan bearing a mug of tea as if it were a mine detector sweeping the floor before him. Eugene booted the door shut with a backward kick, unfastened the fag from the side of his mouth, sat down and raised his two feet on to the table, alongside the mug of tea. An officer passed by and looked in.

Already Pablo had turned his attention to the fellow beside me, now in the process of yanking his anorak over his head. 'Have you told her who you are?' Pablo enquired while doing the honors himself. 'Charlie Conlon. Mate of mine. Comrades in arms. Right kiddo?'

A slight crinkling at the corners of Conlon's eyes hinted at a history between the pair. The anorak was rolled into a ball, and flung at a chair in the far corner of the room. Another chair lifted. It was while he was moving towards the table to join us that he glanced towards the partition. The officer was back, peering in, another with him. Conlon froze, his grip tightening on the chair in his hand. The room froze with him.

The officer had his face right up against the glass.

All eyes were riveted on the man gripping the chair, its four legs suspended a foot off the floor. Eyeball to eyeball, officer and prisoner stared one another down, the tension in the room mounting. Eventually the two officers moved away.

Conlon placed the chair at the table and sat down. Pablo dived into his stockpile of pens and handed one to his comrade. Conlon placed the biro behind his ear.

Could I teach him mathematics?

'No,' I said. I couldn't.

He hadn't thought so.

'I'm not a maths teacher.'

'I know.'

'So why are you sitting in business studies if it's maths you want? I don't see your name on my list. Have you come to the wrong class?'

'I put my name down,' he said. 'I was in the maths class yesterday and the teacher transferred me to you.'

'Well, your name didn't come up on my list today.'

'That doesn't surprise me.'

'Why are you transferring?'

'Because the teacher told me that my maths was too advanced for what she was dealing with, and she pointed me in your direction.'

'I don't understand why, when she knows it is business studies I teach.'

'Try to,' he said, glancing at the blackboard.

'You must remind me to thank the maths teacher for sending you my way,' I returned his glance.

Charlie Conlon, for whatever reason, was joining some tough guys in that business studies class, if I could believe a word anyone told me. At least one murderer, a sprinkling of robbers, diesel-launderers, car thieves, joyriders ... we had them all. There were those who came to class to learn, and those who came to kill time: fellows who could hardly read or write, and fellows who could buy and sell you. And, maybe now and then, the odd innocent man. It being Northern Ireland, we had our share of freedom-fighters too. Loyalists and Republicans, Protestants and Catholics, all creeds and no creeds, passed through the classroom, and eventually out the prison gates; with luck to a better life. The last thing worrying me at that precise moment was whether or not Charlie Conlon would fit in.

Conscious that time was ticking by I told the class we'd better get rolling. Although I wanted to ask Eugene McQuillan to take his feet off the table, Terry to take his hands out of his pockets, and Pablo to take things seriously, I was itching to see what would transpire since I could not teach Charlie Conlon mathematics.

'Fire ahead,' Pablo directed, and of course, we obeyed.

'Some business people,' I began, developing the theme of the previous lesson, 'will actually read company accounts the way a musician might read sheet music. Figures can virtually sing for some of your big business moguls.' I liked to spice up my lessons with examples of wealth and achievement, and talked about the kick some businesspeople get when they read a balance sheet. Heads dropped to jotters in search of the buzz.

While I had their attention I kept up the pressure. 'Let's say that you're the financial adviser to the chairman of this company on the blackboard. You're being asked to do an analysis of the company's health. What tests would you employ?'

I wanted textbook responses. And, to be fair, some did open books. Charlie Conlon's eye was on the pile at my elbow. 'Page 140,' I said, sliding one along to him. He took the biro from behind his ear and started to read.

I then turned to Terry. 'It is difficult, I know, Terry,' I said. 'But remember the formulas you noted last time? All I'm asking is that you apply them to these figures.'

Terry searched his jotter for evidence of the previous week's work. I tried another ploy. 'Think of it this way, Terry. Imagine you've just won a million pounds on the lottery, or the pools, whichever, and here you are looking to invest your winnings in some shares. Would you invest in this company? Look at their price/earnings relationship. Remember?'

'Invest a million? Holy Jaysus, woman,' McQuillan's feet left the table, 'has the world gone wallop. You wouldn't see me out of the pub til the last penny was spent.' And so saying Eugene reached for his mug of tea and cradled it in his two hands like he ached to cradle a pint in the pub on a Friday night. 'Invest a million pounds? Jaysus Christ, Missus, would you wind your neck in.'

'OK, then,' I rephrased the question. 'Let's say it's two million you've won. You've been to the pub, you've had the holiday, bought the car, seen to your mates, and now you want to speculate, invest the second million for a rainy day. Think of it as a day at the races, a visit to the bookie. You're testing form.'

They warmed to the notion, and the lesson progressed. Calculations completed, Charlie Conlon leafed beyond page 140.

From where I sat, I figured he was mid-to late-twenties, and like Pablo Delaney, he was of mixed race, although much more pronounced. There was the jagged evidence of a scar that circled one ear. Another ran halfway across his cheek, the outline of the stitches clearly visible. I imagined this was the result of a recent encounter. His eyes were brown, dark and alert, his matt black hair threaded with wires of grey. His muscles were flexed at the knuckles and the neck, allowing his head to dart like a boxer's fist. He had the form and physique of a gladiator: head high, eyes focused, shoulders set as if permanently squared for action. There were no tattoos, no tribal emblems, tricolours or Union flags. No IRA, UVF, Celtic crosses, Red Hands of Ulster. No dragons or spider's webs. Nor were the letters LOVE etched on his knuckles.

While work was in progress, I decided to take a trip up the corridor to make a coffee. Waiting for the kettle to boil, I was approached by the prison officer who had earlier peered through the partition.

'Do you see your big fellow, Conlon?' he said, removing his cap to wipe a sleeve across a weary brow. 'Him that went into your class early on?'

'Yes, I see him,' I said, watching the steam start to rise from the kettle spout. The officer sat down and stretched his legs. I put a spoon of coffee into my cup.

'I'm going to give you a bit of advice for your own good,' he said.

'You are?' I glanced up, all ears.

'That is one dangerous individual, that boy Conlon. One dangerous individual. Let you be warned.'

'How do you mean "dangerous"?'

'I said dangerous, ma'am. And if you take my advice you'll steer clear of the same fellow.'

If the officer was waiting for encouragement to reveal the juicier bits, I obliged. 'What's the fellow in for anyway?'

'*What's Conlon in for?* Ask me what Conlon is *not* in for.'

It was now dawning on me why everyone had been so tense earlier.

I fumbled with the kettle for a few more moments, waiting. Officers were normally friendly, chatty and open with teachers, more than willing to share titbits of information about prisoners, particularly about 'the worst sorts'. Why should now be any different? I poured water on the coffee granules and watched them dissolve.

'I've only just met him,' I offered, 'and all I can say so far is that he's studious.'

'Hah,' said the officer. 'If you take my advice ma'am, you shouldn't plan on meeting that boy for the second time because, let me tell you, he might be studious about a lot else than his work. *One day that fellow will kill somebody.*'

'Good grief, and how do you know that?'

'You heard what I said, ma'am. You mark my words.'

And with his word marked, I lifted my cup and carried it gingerly back to the classroom.

'They seem to know you quite well out there,' I said to Charlie Conlon on entering.

'Not half as well' he replied, drawing a line underneath his finished work and handing it to me, *'as I know them.'*

The spell of activity could not sustain itself, and a tea break was declared. Pablo, taking possession of the coffee jar, dispatched Joe McCoy to the kettle with his order, while one of my regulars, Mickie 'The Mountain' Doherty, saw his chance and edged nearer to me.

'Joe's my commanding officer in here, but keep that under your hat, miss.' Mickie's eyes followed the departing Joe.

'Provo' Joe McCoy?' I looked at Mickie askance. 'Commanding officer of *what?*'

'Joe's high up in the Provies. He's my CO. While I'm in here I'm under his orders.'

I put that piece of classified information under my hat, and assured Mickie that my lips were sealed. Mickie was serving three years. A terrorist charge. 'Caught red-handed by the peelers with two creamery cans full of Semtex outside his kitchen door,' Eugene McQuillan informed.

'Mickie? A terrorist? He's no more a terrorist than Joe McCoy is a commanding officer!' I said to Eugene.

'It's true, about the Semtex. Obliged a few boys late one night when they dropped by asking if he could do them a turn. Mind you, seeing the barrel of a gun between his two eyes probably helped persuade auld Mickie.'

'I keep a lookout for Mickie,' said a prison officer on another occasion. 'I know Mickie, going back years. Comes from the same neck of the woods as myself. Since the mother died he's lived on nothing but bread and tea. Never knew how to look after himself the best o' times, when to wash or anything. When she went he threw in the towel completely. He thinks he's on his holidays here.'

'He's very respectful to everybody, isn't he?' I replied.

'He'll soon change his tune, like the rest of them.'

'Tell me why you want to study maths,' I asked Charlie Conlon, Joe handing him a mug of tea, and me another coffee.

'I done maths with a teacher in Maghaberry last time I was in. I didn't take the exams because I got out. The teacher thought I was doing well enough though, and said I should continue.'

'When were you in Maghaberry prison?' I asked, and was told it had been in the recent past. While we talked he leafed through another of my textbooks.

'How did you get yourself into prison this time?'

'With the help of my co-accused,' he replied, his co-accused was sitting beside him. PJ's sheepish grin suggested that therein lay a story best kept for another day. Tea finished, I had difficulty getting their attention. Another prisoner had joined us, and was in a huddle with Pablo. Susan put her head round the door asking for the coffee jar. 'We'll get no more work out of this lot today,' she predicted.

'What's up?' I asked.

'Have you to ask?'

'I take two sugars, sweetheart,' Pablo called after the departing Susan. Next, there was a rattle of keys coming down the corridor, heavy footsteps. A kerfuffle amongst the prisoners. Heads shooting sideways towards the door.

'Shit!' Hands holding lighted cigarettes disappeared under the table. An officer was approaching.

The officer opened the door. You could hear a pin drop. He looked in; then withdrew. Hands sneaked out from under the table. I took off my glasses, and rubbed my eyes. Like the officer, I saw nothing out of the ordinary going on all around me.

'Right, fellows.' The officer had put his head round the door again, this time to call time on the class.

'Last drinks, lads,' roared Eugene McQuillan.

'You know what you have to read up on for the next day,' I reminded everyone as the room began to empty.

'No problem.'

'Will we see you again?' I asked Charlie Conlon. He had stopped to enquire if he could take the textbook back to his cell.

'Yes.' He would be across on Thursday.

'Well then, I will make sure your name is on the list for Thursday.'

He placed his biro behind his ear, grabbed hold of his anorak, and was gone.

'Come here, you.' I beckoned Pablo as he was about to disappear out the door after his mate – by now he had established a position as something of a teacher's pet. 'Will someone enlighten me? Why are people around here so afraid of Charlie Conlon?'

Before answering, he yelled up the corridor after the escorting officer. 'Be with you in a tick, mate. Mrs Farren needs to consult me,' and closed the classroom door.

'What are you on about? You and Charlie Conlon?' "Comrades in arms?" What in God's name have the pair of you been up to? I have just been warned that I am about to be murdered.'

'Never mind them ones out there,' he consoled me. 'We'll look after you in here.'

'That, my friend,' I said, 'is what's scary.'

3

Within the week Charlie Conlon had registered for social studies, and now that he had a double-vested interest in me, I figured I'd live a while longer.

Louise and I were on our way to class and within sight of the blocks when an armoured vehicle raced past, dispatching rabbits down burrows and us to the grass verge. A second one followed, rear doors open, uniformed officers inside. They screeched to a halt farther up, officers spilling out on to the gravelled area in front of one of the blocks.

'It's the riot squad,' said Louise. 'There's been an incident somewhere.'

The vehicles stood nose to the wall on the gritted area in front of B1. Helmetted officers in boiler suits milled about, visors lowered. They carried Perspex shields and thick truncheons and stomped the ground in their high-laced boots.

'Conlon's in B1,' Louise remembered, as we drew closer to the block.

'The Charlie Conlon I have in my class?'

'I think I'm right,' she said. 'I'm sure it was B1 the officer mentioned last week. Said they were expecting trouble; for teachers to be on the lookout.'

I told her I'd had a similar health warning.

'If it's bad, the whole place will lock down and we'll be here for God knows how long.' Louise had a daughter to take to piano, a son to ferry to football, and, she was convinced, there would be no getting out of that prison for any of us. 'There's always something, isn't there?'

'But what should we do meantime?' I asked.

'I suppose we just keep going until someone turns us back,' was Louise's best advice.

So that was what we did. Closer to the block, we realised what the commotion was about. A training exercise was in operation, a dress rehearsal for the real thing. It was nothing more ominous than the testing of brakes, the flexing of muscle and the wielding of hardware.

Due to the activity out front, prisoner movement had been completed earlier than usual. Inside, they awaited our arrival. The majority had not advanced beyond the kettle in the library. Handing my jar of coffee to Joe, I remarked: 'When I saw the riot squad out there I thought some of you fellows had killed somebody.'

'If we had,' said Charlie Conlon, following me down the corridor, 'we wouldn't have licked the practice off the ground, let me tell you.'

'Meaning?' I was toying with the notion that this might be an opportune way to kickstart discussion for the lesson I was about to deliver, if and when I got the remaining few away from the kettle and into the classroom.

'Don't you think we're in the right training camp for it, Patricia?' Charlie asked, putting his mug of tea down on the table and pulling a chair forward.

'And you all know how you got yourselves in here,' I said, unzipping my bag of books. Charlie pulled his chair closer to the table, took my *Irish Times* from under his arm – I had left it with him earlier on – and rolled it into a cudgel. We were set for battle.

The theme of the lesson was law, order and delinquency. I was expecting a lively and wide-ranging discussion, if not a heated one, as I turned to write up some lyrics from a Sex Pistols album on the blackboard. The passage I selected spoke of chaos and lawlessness, of not knowing what you want, but knowing how to get it. Of wanting to 'destroy the passers-by' so as not to be anybody's 'dogsbody'.

'Well?' I turned to the class to be met by blank stares. 'Have none of you got tongues in your heads?'

Charlie Conlon had, and plenty to say with it. Government policy at that particular time was the catalyst for anarchy on the streets of Britain. Government was responsible for demonising a handful of disadvantaged youths who had got caught up in a global economic recession. 'Teenagers,' he claimed, 'who had nothing more to answer for except that they wouldn't conform, were targeted. The Pistols caught on because they struck a chord with disaffected young rebels. They were telling the people not to give in to the authorities but make the authorities give in to you.'

'And this is your philosophy as well?' I asked. 'Make the authorities give in to you?'

'If it's a case where governments are prepared to squeeze the disadvantaged harder and harder in the interest of their capitalist paymasters, if it's naked personal politics, then I'm an anarchist.'

The entire focus of the British election that had brought Margaret Thatcher to power, he believed, was based on one issue alone: law and order. 'Nothing whatsoever about justice and equality.'

'What age were you when she came to power?'

'Twelve, thirteen. Check your list. If they haven't given you my date of birth already it's about the only thing they've kept from you.'

I intended to pinpoint what he might contribute to the discussion. I knew Charlie had been in care because he'd told me so earlier. Eight he'd said he was when he went to the children's home, although he had had a perfectly good home of his own and a perfectly adequate mother to look after him. He had remained in care until he was twelve or thirteen. Although tempted to explore the reason behind removing a child from the care of a parent and placing him in a state institution, I knew such questions could wait. For the moment, I was determined to keep the focus of the class on my class notes.

'So, did that experience make you angry?' I asked. 'Make you want to "destroy the passers-by"?'

'Whether it did or not, it qualified me to have opinions on related issues.' His argument today was that pragmatism always came before idealism. He claimed he had been put into care to satisfy a quota.

'Don't be ridiculous,' I snapped, brushing the suggestion aside. However, I conceded, that on the question of lawlessness, Margaret Thatcher's election was influenced by the pragmatic argument. Her policies, I suggested, were a reaction against the violence of the times. It was frightening for law-abiding citizen to be confronted with muggings, attacks on the elderly and the police, wanton acts of thuggery, terrorism and football hooliganism.

'And the despair of a generation of out-of-work youths who had nothing more to do with their time than walk about the streets with spiked hair, and a few safety pins stuck in their noses. Those weren't signs of the times too? Come on, Patricia, you'll have to do better.'

'But law and order were the issues that touched the popular nerve,' I persisted, almost as if I were single-handedly responsible for organising the British Conservative Party's entire election campaign thirteen years before. 'Surely it was a time when people were frightened by the confrontational society they saw emerging.' I focused on the sharp rise in juvenile delinquency, and the fear that moral authority was breaking down.

'Are you telling me people like you were scared by the sight of a few punk rockers walking the streets listening to a bit of punk music on transistors?'

'If the transistors were blaring out lyrics like "I am an anarchist" then I was scared.'

'A few punk songs would have that much effect on you? Come on! And what did the middle classes think when the Pistols topped the British charts with 'God Save the Queen', despite it being banned by the BBC? Did that upset you too?'

'Was it supposed to? I thought music was meant to be uplifting. Forgive me for asking, but had the Sex Pistols some profound message for me back then?'

Obviously familiar with the lyrics of the Pistols' version of "God Save the Queen", Charlie advised me not to be told what I wanted, since, according to the Pistols, there was no future for any of us.

'What a wonderful outlook on life,' I said, and his mates guffawed.

'When police arrest a few musicians for getting into a boat on the river Thames and blaring a bit of punk music back at Parliament, you know something's rocking the boat,' said Charlie. 'But, let me ask you this, Patricia. Maybe you agreed with the Government and the BBC when they banned the Pistols. Maybe you thought that the people shouldn't be allowed to listen to messages about moral authority?'

And so the discussion continued, Charlie perhaps the only one in the group who did not assume I had put the Pistols lyrics on the blackboard so as we could all sing karaoke.

It was both challenging and refreshing to have someone like Charlie in class. Discussions were lively, sometimes too much so: the walls were thin and voices carried up the corridor. Eddie 'Red' McFarlane, one of our class regulars, frequently got on his soapbox. Mention Margaret Thatcher and he really did see red. 'Look what she done to the striking miners,' he reminded.

'And what she done to Bobby Sands!' Provo Joe was on his as well. 'Think about the ten hunger strikers, Patricia. Ten dead men! Know what I mean? All of us ones wouldn't be wearing our own clothes if it wasn't for them ones.' A wake-up call for Mickie: his commanding officer was telling it how it was. While Mickie hung on Joe's every word, I hung on to my patience.

'Look, Joe,' Charlie said, finally putting a stop to Joe's tirade. 'My family have been Nationalists all our lives. Still are. My grandfather, John Conlon, toiled every day of his working life driving a Belfast city bus. I have relations married to British army personnel. All my people are working people. And they're all better Irish Nationalists, and prouder Irish Republicans today without killing or condoning the killing of anybody. I have no time for the 'RA, or their claptrap about men dying for the sake of a shirt and a pair of trousers.

It was break time, the question of juvenile delinquency still unresolved. Neither of us was prepared to concede an inch. I'd declined Joe's offer to roll me a spliff that would calm me down, and was still arguing that government policy was a reaction to the perceived failure of detention centres – or holiday camps, as they were popularly known – to address the problem of young offenders.

And *did* Charlie Conlon know his criminal justice?

'If detention centres were about care, what's supposed to stimulate kids and make them into achievers, how come a percentage of them didn't end up in university? Do you know anyone who became a teacher like yourself, or a trade-union leader, or went into business and became a captain of industry?'

'The point being?'

'I'll put it another way to you. How many holiday-camp kids got the chance to be high-profile trade-union militants during Thatcher's time in office? How many of them became international terrorists? How many have since gone bankrupt? Were those not the questions that should have been looked at before worrying about a few punk rockers on the streets, and deciding to change the model for state care?'

'So, are you telling me I'm wrong in my belief that the system encouraged staff in these detention centres to make a real effort to find out what was wrong with the young people in their care? Did nobody ever try to help *you?*'

'Never mind what anything is supposed to do,' answered Charlie. 'The only thing important to any government is what's *seen* to be done.' He argued that bringing youngsters before the courts kept the liberal lobby happy despite the fact that custodial sentences were being handed down for mitching from school, simply because the courts now had the power to include younger, and, eventually, less delinquent children. They could lift youngsters of eight out of their homes, he claimed, and have them put away for years. 'And everybody was happy because they were sold the notion that the kids were all heading off to *holiday camps!* The more youngsters were taken off the streets, the better it showed how well the system was performing.'

When I suggested that children must have been taken into care for valid reasons, his response showed profound pain. His was the impassioned argument of someone speaking from deep personal experience. I admired his tenacity, the way he mounted such a defiant and heated challenge to my arguments. And although I did not want to have the last word for its own sake, I still went for the final throw of the dice.

'You're talking about the establishment of detention centres during a period dominated politically by a Labour government, not the Tories.'

'Labour could have a clear conscience, couldn't they?'

'I'm not with you.'

'Labour put youngsters into *holiday camps*, remember? That kept everyone happy. It was the social workers' word that counted in the courts then.'

'And later?'

'The Tories' way forward was, "Never mind why things failed in the past, that's not important, we have our own solutions. Let's introduce another experiment. We'll have the short, sharp shock. We'll turn these *holiday camps* into *boot camps.*"'

Charlie claimed that the detention of children was an ongoing experiment depending on who was in power. Labour wanted a liberal alternative to prison. The Tories sold a harsh deterrent. 'The whole thing was nothing more than a public-relations exercise based on statistics.'

'It's difficult to argue on the basis of statistics when we haven't got the figures before us,' I complained.

'If you open your eyes, you have three statistics sitting across the table from you,' he reminded me. 'Joe, Pablo and me.'

'Another good day's work done, Alfie,' I remarked to the officer holding open the gate for me to leave the education centre.

'Some job you teachers have,' he said, turning the key in the lock. His shift was finished and we walked together towards the front gate.

'It's all in a good cause,' I ventured.

'I see you have Conlon with you.'

'You know Charlie Conlon?'

'I know him only too well.'

'He seems to have a bit of a reputation around the place.'

'He has more than a reputation, let me tell you. Same boy left an officer in such a state he'll never work again. And that's a fact.'

'When did that happen?'

'A while back.'

'He doesn't appear that bad to me.'

'You wait.'

Conversation was sporadic. A gale was blowing in from the Atlantic, causing my skirt to rise, to the amusement of a coltish group of prisoners returning to the blocks from an afternoon session in the gym, hungry for their next meal and hungry for amusement. Whoops of glee rode each gust. The hilarity subsided as we drew closer, their escorting officer and Alfie stopping to exchange a few words.

I spotted one fellow among the group.

'Why haven't you been over to class? You were doing so well. They tell me you have a job as an orderly now, and you've packed in education.'

Gareth was serving a short sentence for manslaughter. A group from the North on a social trip South had been denied admission to a nightclub. A brick was thrown at a window, missing its target, and hitting a young person in the queue, killing him. Gareth, and perhaps others, took fright and fled back across the border. It was only a matter of days before the Royal Ulster Constabulary (RUC) were knocking on his door.

Opting for work brought Gareth additional pocket money each week. Opting for education carried no incentive beyond self-improvement.

'Pity that young fellow gave up on his studies. He seems a decent type,' I remarked to Alfie when we were on our way again.

'You'll hear many's the sob story in this place. If I had a pound note in my coat pocket for every one I've listened to, I'd be a millionaire th'day.'

'But still, I wish he had something to show when he gets out and starts looking for work. A certificate to prove he'd made some use of his time in prison wouldn't go amiss.'

'Some folk think they can transform these boys,' Alfie had tilted his cap against the prevailing wind, 'and education is going to solve everything, but c'me'ere till I tell you something, I've seen where things are at in Her Majesty's Prison Service and you mark my words, Mrs MacFarren, we're at a stage where a degree is the least these boys 'ill settle for. But if a few more of your so-called politicians out there saw things like prison officers see them inside it might be a different story. I've done my stint in the Maze and, believe you me, there's not a lot anyone can tell me about education after that experience.'

'How long were you there, Alfie?'

'Long enough to watch murderers walk through the gates one day and out the next waving degrees, all paid for by the state. "Bring back capital punishment" is my motto!'

'Still and all, it's a pity to see intelligence wasted.'

We had arrived in the car park and Alfie drew himself to full height, the better to spot his own vehicle amongst the competition. 'I'll give you a good example of intelligence,' he said, his hand reaching inside his pocket for his keys. 'Young lad of mine, no interest whatsoever in the books. His mother was the one pushing. Couldn't wait to leave school, first day he could he was away. Th'day the same fellow's working to McGarvey's Engineering the other side of Coleraine, drawing close on two hundred a week, and that's after full deductions. Talking there last week, the same bloke, about changing the car. Did he need a university degree to get on? Now, did he?' At which point I was silent on the benefits of education.

'Oh, don't get me wrong. Education in its own place is one thing, but prison should be about putting manners on a few people. If you want my opinion, it's the victims, women like yourself should be doing something about.'

Alfie clicked the remote control in his hand and an Alfa Romeo lit up like a Christmas tree.

'Conlon,' he said, 'is going nowhere.'

4

Ethnicity and race was the theme of the day's lesson, with Charlie describing himself as 'a black Celt.' I already knew a little of his background. That his father, an African-American GI, had been killed in Vietnam. That his mother, originally a mill worker from Belfast, had met the young serviceman in Germany when based there with the American troops. She and a friend had been recruited to work with Grundig in their Stuttgart plant. Charlie was at pains to point out that his parents had wed.

'The sixties, Charlie.' I joked. 'We were all hippies back then.'

'With Vietnam the Achilles' heel,' he cut me short.

During the latter part of the sixties I lived in Sierra Leone, and had come to some understanding of the terrors of that war when I saw the anxiety generated among American Peace Corps volunteers serving there. For young Americans it was a terrible time. Fear of the dreaded draft was ever present. Volunteering for a stint of overseas development work granted a short respite before the arrival of the draft papers that would surely await many on their return to the United States after their tour of duty.

And so, over the break I encouraged Charlie to talk. What did he know of his father?

'Not a terrible lot,' he said. 'I do know he was the love of my mother's life. She goes balmy when she talks about him.'

'How sad, to die in Vietnam.'

'Sacrificed, more like,' he corrected me. 'Just one more of the sixty-thousand American GIs slaughtered alongside their black brothers in the rice paddies of Asia.'

His mother, I discovered, was my own age. Charlie was born in 1966. He had a brother, Sean, born the following year. And I had a daughter, Orla, born in Africa in 1968.

We chatted about family, about Africa, about America and Vietnam until it was time to get back to work.

Around this time application forms for the Open University were circulated to teachers. As one of its graduates I was enthusiastic about this accommodating and relatively inexpensive way to earn a degree.

'Here's an opportunity for some of you fellows to play to your intellectual strengths,' I said, as I handed round the forms. I asked for a show of interest, knowing well that many lacked the grounding to study at OU level.

Charlie indicated an interest, at least in answering the questions on the form.

'Why don't you fill it in and we'll see how far you get.' I suggested. 'Acceptance on a foundation maths course, and you could finally achieve your ambition to study at a higher level.'

Acceptance was one problem. Finance, another. Charlie was dependent on the prison service for funding. Headquarters, based in the Northern Ireland Office (NIO) in Dundonald House, made those decisions. To justify outlay there were certain stipulations: the prisoner must write an accompanying letter to the NIO outlining career to date, and reasons to justify financial support. He must also have two or more years to serve.

Charlie being the mathematician, I accepted his calculations of 'time to serve'. The form was duly filled out, and the letter written.

I read both. "Charles John Conlon. Address: HMP Magilligan. Born: Stuttgart, Germany, 26 February 1966. Nationality: Irish". I was happy with what I read. But I was more than impressed by the accompanying letter. He made his case by stating how previous attempts to study A-Level maths came to nothing because of long periods of incarceration, then focused on a period when he had gone straight for almost two years.

'Tell me how all these attempts to study maths were frustrated,' I asked. 'You weren't a wet week in this establishment and already people were finding ways to help you. I'm not vain enough to imagine I'm the first teacher to notice that you had ability. Margaret, next door, was trying to help when she sent you to me, believing I could push for the higher level with business studies, whereas she couldn't concentrate solely on one maths student at your level.'

A priest had looked over his work when he was in care, he told me, and recommended he go to an outside school and sit his 11+ exam (grammar school entry qualification).

'And?'

'And they made arrangements to get me out to another school during the day.'

'And how did you get on at the other school?'

'I ran away.'

'And they found you, I presume.'

'I hid out in my old granny's house. I did the exam but no one ever found out if I passed or not. Anyway, who'd know what to do about it if I had?'

'So in all the prisons and in all the other places you've been, you have to walk into my prison before you meet anyone else who thinks you should be studying for something?'

'Well, there was Joan, the teacher I mentioned before, in Maghaberry. Joan was giving me as much help as she could.'

'Great. And, how far did you and her get?'

'I got out.'

'So, just explain to me in simple English, Charlie. Why, if your ambition was to study mathematics and Joan had you to a certain level, didn't you try to complete the course at one of the colleges of further education when you were released?'

'I did think about that.'

'Well, good for you. So, tell me what happened.'

'I got lifted.'

I handed the OU application form with accompanying letter to the appropriate authority and awaited the outcome. Meantime, lessons proceeded as normal.

Eugene McQuillan sat with his feet on the table, scratching his inner ear with the cap of a biro, tracking my attempts to focus a faulty projector on the wall.

'She's gone wallop,' he dismissed my efforts, recommending 'a good boot up the arse,' as a remedy.

Pablo could be of no assistance. Technology was beyond him, once having had a bad experience with a camera.

'Have I ever told yous ones,' he asked, reaching for his Golden Virginia, 'about the Monday morning I hit Shaftesbury Square intent on robbing three banks?'

With McQuillan still calculating the best angle for that threatened kick, Pablo took the floor. 'Things got off to a flying start,' he told us.

'That reassures everyone,' said Charlie Conlon, lifting his head out of my *Irish Times*.

'And a flying finish, I'll guarantee,' I muttered at my faulty projector.

'Few days beforehand, mate of mine, Mackie McDonald, dropped by the bank. Yous all know big Mac, over in B3. Didn't mind leaving the few quid with them ones. Knew I'd be in to collect in a day or so.'

'Jaysus, you're the boy to pick them,' complimented McQuillan, taking his eye off the projector to lick his biro cap, '"Big Mac" McDonald. The double burger.'

'*Happy days*, mate,' Pablo accepted all tributes to his genius.

One recollection suddenly triggered another. Had he ever told us about the butcher's shop job, also on Shaftesbury Square? He hadn't.

Seems, the robbers entered the premises demanding the day's takings. Lining the counter inside stood three burly butcher boys, necks thick as the bullocks adorning the walls behind them. The butchers took one look at the robbers; the robbers likewise at the butchers. 'No contest,' conceded Pablo, as the butchers leaned back to pick up three meat cleavers.

Traffic outside ground to a halt as, coat tails flying, the butchers pursued the robbers through the square, egged on by the cheering masses.

But, don't distract him. Back to the bank heist, or rather, a holding cell in the police station, courtesy of the RUC.

'I'm lying in this cell staring into a po-full of piss. In the throes of despair. Asking the bloody po why I'm such a mug. I had just done three years for another bank robbery that went haywire. Next thing the cell door opens, and this peeler boy has his head stuck in inviting me out to watch a video.

'Didn't know yous ones were laying on entertainment since the last time I dropped by, I told the ones outside. Feckin Martin "Bloody" Scorsese, sitting one side of me focusing a projector, just like that outfit of yours there, on a wall. Another cowboy with his feet up on the table beside the pile of good clean notes I'd just rescued from the bank. Hadn't a ruddy notion what would come out of the hat, when up popped my own big mug. And then it slowly began to dawn on me how they caught me; cameras! *In the bloody bank; cameras!* And I never twigged!'

Joe, anticipating the finale, had a roll-up at the ready.

Wanting the yarn wound up I had my class notes waiting.

Pablo sent a perfect circle of blue smoke my way. 'All blown away. My life blown away for another three years.'

'If the police didn't catch you leaving the bank,' I quizzed, 'how did they know to come knocking on your door?'

'Look at me, Patricia. Take a good gape. How many friggin' niggers do you think there was on the streets of Belfast in the early eighties, robbing banks?'

On another occasion, when the prisoners were delayed coming across to class, I strolled up to the library to chat with Davy, the officer on duty. Tommy, an orderly, was running a dry mop over the floor.

With the arrival of the first batch of prisoners Davy stood up to collect identification.

Charlie Conlon was first through. Head high, books under the arm, ballpoint behind the ear, ignoring the officer he nodded to me as he proceeded purposefully towards the classroom. Provo Joe followed, Mickie attached to his CO like a suck-calf. Joe winked at me, and saluted Davy in Gaelic.

'God Almighty, miss,' said Mickie, shivering in unlaced shoes, 'it's great to be inside on such a cauld day?'

'You'll be all right, Mickie,' said the officer kindly.

'Yes sir,' said Mickie, touching his forelock and continuing on his way.

Last, but not least came Pablo. Head pulsating, limbs gyrating, he boogied his way towards us. '*How's a-bout y-a, kiddo?*'

In two seconds Tommy was relieved of his mop; me of my scarf. The mop was up-ended, scarf draped over the head, before Pablo took his lady-mop in his arms and serenaded her past the kettle, around the bookshelves, into the toilet and out again, swaying and swerving to the music in his mind.

The eyes of the three bystanders, orderly, officer and teacher never left him. Instinctively he knew when the woman in his arms had had her fill. Puckering his lips and smack-kissing the air he upended his lady-love, waving her back into the safekeeping of the orderly.

Reunited with my scarf, I pronounced: 'That fellow is nuts,'

Tommy, testing his mop on the floor, tittered. 'Delaney's nuts alright. But he's a good laugh all the same. Isn't he!'

'Who's laughing most, Tommy? Him or us?' I asked, winding my scarf round my neck.

'Who's laughing?' echoed Davy, his gaze following Pablo as he disappeared in fits of giggles into someone else's classroom. Alas, my students awaited me, but the officer's eyes boring into the orderly signalled I wait. Tommy got the message and took himself and his mop off to another area.

Out of earshot, the officer would talk. 'Do people realise,' he said, 'that that fellow threw away the opportunity of a brilliant career in football? Maybe we were looking at another Georgie Best. Time won't tell, but by Jove did he have talent.' Davy's words carried all the thrills of a game I knew little about, save for my young son's enthusiasm for soccer. In that voice was the potential of the man, the loss of the game, the disappointment of the day.

'I had an inkling, Davy,' I started. 'But, like ,,, I don't know much about football, and I take most things Pablo tells me with a pinch of salt...'

'The waste! The sheer, sheer waste of talent.' Davy shuffled the pack of prisoner-identity cards in his hand, and dealt himself the Joker: Paul Martin Delaney.

'He spun me this yarn, Davy, about a talent scout spotting him and bringing him to America. Maybe it was England first, and America later. But there was a world tour involved, and a stopover in Belfast.'

Davy was only half listening, his mind in another world. *Should I reveal more about that Belfast stopover?* About Pablo heading out on the town with his mates? The pile of dollar bills left sitting behind a statue of the Infant of Prague on his mother's mantelpiece? And coming in later to find the money missing?

'The New York Cosmos? The LA Aztecs?' Team names came to mind. 'Are there such teams, Davy?'

'The New York Cosmos!' The LA...'

I should not have played *away games* with Davy.

Should I now tell him about the solution to the missing dollar bills? How his mates consoled Pablo: said they'd head out later and have the money back in no time. And that unfortunately he headed out with them. About, when the army shot him.

I thought better of it.

'The talent was there. The speed. Could have made it to the top. Downright squandered his genius, if you want my opinion. Had the pick of any of the top clubs on the mainland. Liverpool, United ... you name it. They were watching back then. They were all watching.'

Davy had eyes only for the Joker lying on the table.

'Drugs,' he said. 'Drugs destroyed him.

5

The classroom, on occasion, was akin to a circus ring, except I had no idea what my role in the performance was. Whether I should play the tightrope walker or the clown.

'Just go with the flow,' a prisoner advised. 'That's how you get your time done.'

'That place is bugged,' I was warned by well-meaning friends on the outside.

'What are they like, the prisoners?' asked others.

'Are you not frightened?'

Of whom? One asked oneself. Of Pablo? The rascal in him made me laugh when, really, I should have cried. Then again, would life be as colourful without its rascals? And no, the name Pablo had nothing to do with his mother's devotion to a Spanish saint, but to her son's prowess on the football pitch.

With his football career in shreds, what might he do to make an honest living when released? The class sat back to hear my advice.

'My first suggestion would centre on training younger players. Failing that, since it's a business studies class we're in, perhaps set up in business. Start small. Get a market stall. A van. Sell ice cream on the beach. Burgers, T-shirts, sports gear. Sell anything, but do it legally. You have the blarney. Exploit your talents.'

My advice was well received. It was the offer from his mates to stock him up that worried me.

Stories abounded of lives lived for the moment, no sense of direction other than the gratification of the impetuous deed.

Terry Maguire and his mate, Brendan, the joyriding duo from Belfast, caught doing wheelies on a roundabout, and still high on the thrill of those screeching brakes. It was all a great laugh. The pair in the back ran away and weren't caught. Well, wasn't that just another great laugh! We were expected to laugh yet more when told how they hotwired the BMW.

Hughie, a true tragedy of the Troubles if ever there was one, was from Derry. From a large, Catholic, working-class family in a polarized community. Few of his generation entered white-collar employment.

Brothers, cousins, friends, neighbours, had seen *active service* in our time. He listed the dead. Hughie was the brains in the family. He got out. Got married. Bought a house. Incurred debts.

The proposition was tempting. 'I was transport manager and the RA needed information.' The sweetener being the mortgage and his Credit Union loan. Everything would be taken care of.

'A date and a time was all they wanted. It was for Irene and the children I done it.' He talked of his precious family, his wife, young daughters and little son. How he cleared his mortgage.

'Was Irene in to see you last Thursday?' I asked, because, waiting for the main gates to open that day, I had noticed a young woman with three children approach the visitor entrance. The pretty mother with eyes only for her children caught my eye. Two lovely blond-haired girls in navy coats and frilly white ankle-socks, and the little dark-haired boy who kept scarpering off. The girl's long hair bouncing when they ran to take his little hands.

My description pleased Hughie. 'Yes that would be Irene sure enough.'

Hughie wanted to do things for his family; things never done for him. Package holidays. Disneyland. Computers. Take young Fergal to matches across the water when he was older. Irene to have her own run-around car. He wanted out of debt. He wanted to show his love for them all by how well he provided. All this, he was promised, could be achieved if he would supply that vital scrap of information. Clearing the mortgage in one go gave the game away.

Men pretend not to cry. Hughie did not. 'But Hughie,' I said, 'now they are showing their love for you. And the time will pass sooner than you think, and you're a decent man, and you are still young enough to make a fresh start somewhere else, and everything will be all right.'

I like to believe now that my words came true.

It was in arts and crafts that I came face to face with my own past. Vincent Duffy his name. He asked me what part of the country I originally hailed from.

'I thought so,' he smiled, pleased as punch. 'What part of Cavan?' I told him.

'I think I know who you are,' he claimed, saying he remembered dancing with me in a popular ballroom, years before.

Only very vaguely could I recollect my ex-dancing partner. But as we recalled times and events of more than thirty years before, memories resurfaced. 'What are you doing with yourself, living in the North?' he asked.

I explained, and asked him where he himself resided, when at home. 'Armagh,' he said.

'You won't believe this,' I said to my husband later that evening. 'I have this guy in class who remembers me from years back. He was an old admirer.'

Seán had heard of other *old admirers* – possibly why he didn't bother to lift his head out of the newspaper. 'I wonder what landed a fellow like that in prison,' I mused.

'Armagh, you said. Worked with the Department of Agriculture when you knew him. Probably got involved in smuggling along the border.'

Now, why hadn't I thought of that? We border folk have an affinity. Tend to understand the movement of livestock from one field to another. OK, it's smuggling, but I could live with that. I was looking forward to my next chat with Vince, my admirer of old.

Basket-weaving the following week, Vince and I revisited the scenes of our youth. Memory lane took us all over the countryside. The ballrooms, the marquees, the big bands, and the magic of dancing the nights away. Class time just flew. Had I really declined Vince's offer to buy me a mineral in that carnival tent?

'Work it out for yourself,' I said to Seán later that evening. 'You expect me to walk into the mineral tent in front of all the local fellows, escorted by a *bull-with-a-hat?*' Artificial insemination of livestock was a new phenomenon back then: an occupation this Cavan girl found difficult to accept as an attractive occupation for a suitor.

Later, an opportunity for further research arose. 'See the prisoner I was chatting to just then?' I asked the officer helping me tidy up after class.

'Duffy? Why?' he asked.

'What's he in for?'

'Attempted rape.'

Charlie Conlon rarely spoke about his criminal past. It was as if the punishment, once administered, washed clean all traces of guilt.

On the other hand, he could be very vocal about assaults he claimed were perpetrated against him by police and prison officers. They were the aggressors. They were the ones with questions to answer. Not him. He detested the RUC. He despised prison officers. They were all tainted with the one brush. Whatever wrong he had done, and he admitted he had done wrong, paled into insignificance compared to what others had done to him. His head was high. Address the injustices done to him, I was told.

'And, just how are you addressing these grievances yourself? Languishing in prison, perpetuating the problem? Get your life together first, and then deal with the injustices.'

His lawyer might understand the charges against him. I could make neither head nor tail of anything. Sentences overlapped sentences. Frequent court appearances, cases deferred, bail applications ... certain charges had yet to come to trial. Two of his co-accused sat with him in class.

'How you land yourselves in such scrapes beats me,' I remarked.

I was about to be told.

Few guys walking home late one evening, Charlie one of them. Up the road there is a disco, and at the disco there is a lady. One of the guys has an interest in the lady, not Charlie. Fellow feels he can't go the night without her. Nobody has any money. Passing a doorway, dejected guy remembers a *wee job* planned some time back. Charlie advises: not a good time. But to help a friend in need, and against his better judgement, he is persuaded.

They got under a thousand for their efforts, split four ways. Charlie also got three years. Loverboy got one. The other two got off.

The scar at his ear? That happened while he was on remand in Crumlin Road prison. Later I would locate a cutting from the *Irish News*, dated September 1991:

Four prison officers were hurt and a few prisoners received minor injuries when trouble broke out at Crumlin Road jail in Belfast yesterday. The incident occurred in the Chapel when a number of Catholic prisoners attending Mass began smashing furniture and barricading themselves in. The incident was the third flare-up in the prison around the time, but this time the violence was not coming from hard-core paramilitary prisoners who had been involved over the past days in rioting and setting off fires to highlight their demand for segregation, but from ordinary inmates from B and D wings.

'I admit, I was milling about like everyone else,' explained Charlie. He turned his head sideways pointing to his ear, and to a deeper scar in his scalp. 'Does that look to you like the result of "minor injuries"?'

His co-accused on that occasion – a class-mate in social studies – was Rab McConville. Rab was the orphaned son of the widowed mother of ten, Jean McConville, who, years earlier, was taken from her home just before Christmas 1972 and "disappeared" by the IRA. Her children were subsequently dispersed into care. Jean McConville was an East Belfast Protestant woman who had married a West Belfast Catholic. Reportedly she had angered the IRA when she comforted a seriously wounded British soldier shot by a sniper outside her front door. Charlie gave this somewhat bizarre explanation for his participation alongside Rab in that riot.

Prison officers, he claimed, were engaged in a charade by pretending to enforce a mixed regime in the remand prison – mixing Protestant and Catholics during recreation – when it was obvious that they were doing no such thing. 'What they *were* doing,' he claimed, 'was allowing Loyalist and Republicans to control recreation on alternate evenings: an arrangement which suited both paramilitary groupings, and made for an easier life for the officers, until the media became aware of the cosy arrangement.'

Charlie was not involved with the IRA. He was black, hated by officers, vulnerable. 'They picked on those in weak positions,' he said, 'knowing they'd get away with it. Made scapegoats of us by scheduling our recreation for a time when Loyalists were in control. Giving legitimacy to the NIO claim that segregation was not operating in the Crumb.'

He had no quarrel with Loyalists so long as they had no quarrel with him, but that was not to say he was willing to socialise with them during recreation. He had his principles. He was approached by prisoners from B and D wings wanting to make a stand. Charlie joined the protest planned for the chapel. Nobody contemplated violence.

'Of course, I was prancing around like everyone else. That's what you do.' The riot squad storming the chapel. (It is conceivable the authorities had information, and were waiting in the wings.) According to Charlie, 'they broke through, screaming, "*Get the nigger! Get the nigger!*" They made directly for me, and pinned me between the seating, before laying into me. I was hospitalised for two weeks as a result.'

There was a court case pending; deferred month on month, because Rab, his co-accused, when let out on compassionate leave to attend his sister's funeral, had gone AWOL. Without his co-accused Charlie's case kept being deferred.

'Do you know where Rab is?' I enquired.

Charlie knew.

'And are you telling anybody?'

He was telling nobody.

Best of all was, he was now taking the NIO to court himself, for injuries sustained.

'Charlie,' I said, 'the way your life is progressing, it would not surprise me if one day you walk out of Magilligan prison, PhD in hand'

It was 1993, a bad year in the North's troubled history. Massive explosions and horrific murders dominated the news. John Hume, leader of the Social Democratic and Labour Party (SDLP), had several talks with the Sinn Féin leader, Gerry Adams with a view to searching for a way to end the conflict. Loyalist paramilitaries were incensed at reports of such discussions and random murders of Catholics became more frequent.

My husband, an active member of the SDLP and the party's representative for the constituency of North Antrim, had been involved in earlier exploratory talks between Hume and Adams, which led to later negotiations. Because of his political activity I was very much aware of the realities of political life in the North; the biases, the prejudices and the sectarianism that fuelled the conflict. I found I was also in the firing line when political views were expounded in class. Incidents in October and November on the Shankill Road in Belfast and at Greysteel in County Derry shocked everybody. Peace rallies took place all over Northern Ireland.

The classroom buzzed with views. For me, paramilitarism was leading us nowhere. It was futile. Violence was wrong. A resolution could only be found through peaceful means. A united Ireland could only be achieved by consent.

'Isn't it great craic getting her wound up?' The remark followed a heated argument with Provo Joe.

'Grow up,' I told Joe. 'Gerry Adams? President of Ireland? Would you give my head peace?'

A lift home from work with an officer, and I really did put my foot in it:

'The last time I laid eyes on Conlon,' said Harry, inserting the key in ignition, 'was in the Maze prison. Him covered in shit.'

'I never had Charlie down as a dirty protestor,' I said, reaching for the seatbelt. I genuinely did not think he played any role in the IRA campaign; particularly as the protest escalated into prisoners smearing their bodies with excrement and refusing to clean out their cells. 'That's very much at odds with the picture I have formed of Conlon.'

'Conlon's some picture, let me tell you!' Harry fired his engine. 'The teachers must be very short of things to admire,' he added, tilting the rearview mirror and checking his profile while edging the car out of the parking lot.

On many occasions Charlie had been my political ally in class, so I thought it only right that I should defend him, believing that given similar circumstances Charlie would jump to my defence.

'I suppose if you're surrounded by shit, Harry,' I said, 'you might as well cover yourself in it.'

Was that his hand stiffened on the steering? A muscle twitching in his jaw? I rearranged my handbag on my lap.

The car inched forward, Harry's eyes set steady on the straight road ahead.

'When I joined the service back in the early eighties,' he said, 'us *men* were on the brink of going in and sorting a few of them boys out. Others thought they knew better, of course. But, by Jove, let ME tell YOU, if a few of them boys had been put in their places back then...'

In political debate, I might be a match for prisoners in the classroom, but come prison officers? I knew my limitations. I was also sitting in the man's car.

'This is some impressive motor, Harry,' I changed the subject glancing round the luxury interior.

Harry's knuckles relaxed.

'How long have you got her?'

'Three months. Very latest model.'

Harry inserted a tape in the deck. 'You're a Dolly Parton fan like myself,' I observed. And while 'Jolene' sang the blues, we talked zero to sixty acceleration rates, fuel injection systems and engine capacity until we arrived in Portstewart.

'Forget it,' Harry said, when I attempted to thank him for the ride home.

6

The NIO turned down Charlie's application for OU funding. Grounds for rejection: 'insufficient time to serve'.

'They must truly believe they are seeing the back of you quite soon.' It was my attempt to take the bitter edge off the rejection.

Although disappointed, there was a philosophical edge to his reaction. 'If they could find a reason to say no, they would find it. Know what I mean, Patricia?'

'Need I remind you,' I said, 'you are in litigation with the NIO. Know what *I* mean, Charlie?'

It was back to the drawing board. 'Look,' I proposed a compromise. 'There are other avenues to third-level education. Why not take the traditional A-Level (General Certificate of Education) or RSA (Royal Society of Arts) route? Should you, in the future, reapply to the OU, or approach a conventional university as a mature student, you'd have something to show. Other penniless students put themselves through college on meagre funding. Why not you?'

Perhaps some things were possible. He talked of being 'in pocket', should his claim for compensation from the NIO succeed.

'Well, if you do win your case,' I said, without a trace of irony, 'I'm sure the NIO will be delighted to see their money put to good use.'

My concerns were not about his ability, or his dedication to study. He was a consummate worker. But I had so little teaching experience, never having taught beyond O Level. It would be an uphill struggle.

As luck would have it, into the classroom walked my saviour: Winston Fullbright, an accountant – or more correctly, an ex-accountant.

An easy-going and friendly lad, Winston was serving a short sentence for embezzlement. His career in shreds, the young man had turned his thoughts to God. And on discovering the Good Lord, Winston soon found the truth, the light, and the way. A criminal record would have professional repercussions for Winston. He needed to change course, and teaching in higher education was one possibility. His entry into accountancy had not taken the traditional GCSE, or RSA route, necessary qualifications for acceptance on a professional teaching course.

While he talked, a plan was forming in my mind. Had God's way led my way? Perhaps Winston could be teacher's little helper? Might he and Charlie Conlon study together?

'Delighted,' said Winston.

That was half my problem sorted. Winston was no Celt, he was Protestant, Charlie, Catholic. The prison was two separate ghettos. Coupling them was now the test.

Winston had no hang-ups about whom he socialised with in prison, and was doing his time secure in the knowledge that he would not be harassed or set upon. Indeed, I suspected a degree of admiration amongst his fellow inmates, some believing they might learn a thing or two by association.

Charlie's reaction was guarded. He had reservations, he told me, about aligning himself with 'a dodgy accountant. Know what I mean, Patricia.'

'Oh, for God's sake, Charlie,' I pleaded, 'would you just give us all a break?'

Winston's unassuming manner won Charlie over, and soon the pair had their heads locked in common purpose.

And with the Good Lord on our side, I had nothing but high hopes for the future.

'I doubt if we'll have any more across,' said the officer as I passed by. 'The POA's called a snap meeting for ten. There's a few already here from B3, but nowhere else is moving.'

I carried on to the classroom, walking in on a conversation.

'Your boy from Londonderry? What-you-may-call-him?'

'Lynch, Billy. Seamus Lynch.'

'Jaysus, me head's a strainer, Francie. It won't hold a fucking name.'

'Sure, never worry, Billy, things'll start to look up, so they will, know what I'm saying?'

Billy looked unsure.

Francie, the younger of the two, was perched on the edge of the table, legs swinging like a child on a garden swing.

Billy sat brooding, eyes riveted on his companion.

'By Jaysus, Francie, if thon boy, what-you-may-call-him, Lynch, had'a got his hands on my case, I'll tell you one thing for certain, you wouldn't be fucking sitting there looking at me now, boy, so you wouldn't.'

'That's what I'm saying Billy.'

'That's where I got it wrong, Francie.'

I turned, duster in hand, to wipe the blackboard. The conversation continued behind my back.

'When my case came before auld Moses Black in the Crown Court, I swear to God, Francie, if only I'd'a fucking knew. I'd'a had your boy, what-you-may ... Lynch, acting for me, no problem! Jaysus, if only I'd'a fucking talked to you beforehand.'

'Like I say, Billy. Shamie Lynch was your man. If you're a Prod, have a Taig for your brief, know what I'm saying? A Taig! Get someone of the calibre of big Bob McCartney. Any Provie'll tell you as much. Judges'll take them boy's word when they're representing the other side. But, com'ere Billy. One would'a thought that yous Belfast boys would'a knew? Know what I'm saying?'

I turned from the blackboard, and offering to fetch me a coffee, Francie swung down off the table, taking the coffee jar and himself off to the kettle.

'How are things, Billy?' I ventured, ticking numbers 8672 Patterson, and 8451 O'Kane off my class list.

'Well you might ask, Pat,' Billy sighed, rising from his chair and throwing his eyes to the heavens.

'Nothing can be that bad.'

Twenty Silk Cut lay on the table. Billy reached for the pack, gazed into it long and hard before offering it to me.

I shook my head. 'I'm still off, Billy.'

Drawing a cigarette from the pack with his teeth, he bent a knee to search for his lighter.

'As a matter of fact,' he said, directing a stream of smoke at the bulb above our heads, 'I was just talking over my case with young O'Kane, as you may well have heard.' He flicked his cigarette towards the door through which Francie had departed. 'And, by Jaysus, Pat, but you learn something new every day in this trade.'

'I gathered something was troubling you.'

'Trouble? You don't know the start of it.'

'How long have you left?'

'What?'

'In for? Still to serve?'

In his confusion he couldn't think straight. 'Three ... three years. Aye, three years.'

'Look, Billy,' I tried my usual line. 'It will pass. Think positive. Paroles. Remission. You'll be out before you know what's hit you.'

Billy shook his head, took a longer drag on his cigarette, and inhaled deeply. 'I should never have got jail,' he stated.

'Time does pass,' I repeated my reassurance. 'Believe me.'

'I'll say this much straight to you, Pat. Bad as things wur, I thought I was settled. Thought I'd hack it, until young O'Kane put me straight on a few matters. You'll forgive the language, Pat, but, by Jaysus, if only I'd'a fucking knew before my case was heard. If only I'd'a fucking knew what I know th'day.'

It was Billy's second outing to education. Presenting himself as, 'an electrician by trade, two men working to me', he chose the class for practical reasons, he told me the week before. VAT and Income Tax were an enigma to Billy. He needed a hand with the books. 'Them boys above in the tax office, let me tell you, they won't be too long til they're after you for their money. Herself saw to that end of affairs, but God knows how things'll stand in that direction when I'm out.'

Ruling out embezzlement, I speculated on other possible reasons for incarceration. A three-year sentence? Manslaughter? A possibility.

Billy cultivated the cowboy image: jeans, plaid shirts; all that was missing was spurs on the sides of his boots and he'd have been the full 'yee haw'. Line dancing was his great passion. But I'm afraid his fondness for fags, fish suppers and the proverbial few cans had taken their toll.

'Are you a dancer yourself, Pat?' he enquired.

'I've had my day, Billy,' I admitted, without venturing down that road again.

Now, a week later, seeing Billy pace the floor, his beergut straining his plaid shirt, I feared his dancing days were numbered.

'This looks like it's it,' announced Francie, returning with the coffee, two prisoners from B3 following. 'The screw up above says B1 and B2 is on lockdown.'

'You pair are showing tremendous interest in your work, I must say.' I ticked off Terry and Brendan for loitering in the library. 'If we intend to cover the syllabus in the short time remaining, you had better get your act together, boys.'

'Never worry your head,' I was told.

'I'm paid to do a job,' I reminded them, 'and I'm depending on you fellows to produce some results to show I'm earning my keep.'

'Earning her keep in here?' They fell about in stitches, splitting their sides. That was just about the greatest laugh anyone had in years.

'You expect some employer is going to offer the pair of you jobs when you leave here?'

Catch myself on, I was told. Kuwait was only around the corner.

'Come again, Terry?'

'The Gulf War.'

'You intend enlisting with the Armed Forces? They'll be thrilled to get you.'

Terry had no such plans. What was obvious to him, if not to me, was that in the aftermath of the Gulf war, when the dust settled on the Middle East, Kuwait would need rebuilding. And no better boys for the job than Terry and his mates. Aeroplane-loads of them were planning to head out from Belfast to rebuild Kuwait, 'brick by fucking brick'.

'Might it not be helpful, Terry,' I suggested, 'if you could distinguish between inches and centimetres on a slide rule before heading on to any building site, at home or abroad?'

'Never you worry your head about things like that, Tricia. Sure that'll be no bother to us on the day.'

Terry and the boys just could not wait to get on that aeroplane and *hit up* Kuwait.

'*Here we go, here we go, here we go.*'

Still pacing the floor, Billy's mood had not improved. Thrusting a hand between his legs, he drew in a chair and sat down at the table, stubbing out one cigarette and lighting another. Francie set a mug of tea before him. He was continuously glancing my way, willing me to ask him something. I could no longer ignore the pleading in his eyes.

'It can't be all that bad, Billy.'

'Bad?' he flinched.

'A problem shared is a problem halved,' I counselled, meaning he now had his new friend, Francie, as adviser.

'Have you a month?' he asked, not quite on the same wave length.

'Well, until I finish this coffee.' I picked up the cup.

'Jaysus, Pat. If I'd to fucking do it over again.'

'Couldn't we all say the same, Billy.'

'Never set foot in a jail in my life. No, nor anyone belonging to me. I'm a working man. Never out of work a day, so I wasn't. My missus was never left short. You may have read something of my case in the papers? It was splashed all over the front page of the *News Letter*.'

'I must have missed it, Billy,' I said. 'What was the case about anyway?'

'I was done for attempted rape. Three-year conviction.'

And so the floodgates opened.

Auld Mosie Black, the judge, should be done for contempt of his own court. Then it was the turn of the barrister. The way that boy conducted the case he deserved to be taken out and shot. The class agreed. All had had similar experiences with barristers. Billy's big mistake was not consulting Francie O'Kane before the trial. If he had done so, there would be a very different tale to tell.

While my better judgement was urging me to move this class on, my silence served to encourage Billy.

'At the time, the arrangement with the wife was not exactly a hundred percent, if you get my meaning. Relegated to the wee lad's room, I was. Banished from my own bed after the last wee'un came along. A year's rough on a man, no matter what.'

'Was your wife suffering from post-natal depression, Billy?'

'No. No. The trouble started way before. Threw the head, Myrtle did, when she fell pregnant. I hadn't got the *wee job* done you see, like she believed.'

'Job? Billy? Job? I don't ...'

'It was the surgeon's knife if ever I was to lie in me own bed again. She gave me my ultimatum.' Billy's lips tightened. 'See, a fellow like me, Pat. We're not too fond of the knife in particular regions, if you see what I mean.'

We all shuddered at the very notion, but the spark was back in Billy's eye as he recounted how one problem led to the next: a row between neighbours.

'Months earlier, this young lassie moved in across the street. Just her and a wee'un; ne'r sight nor light of any man about the place. At the start there was nobody like Tracey Fagan with Myrtle. It was Tracey Fagan this, Tracey Fagan that. No separating the two weemen. Your lassie had this wee dog, Marilyn she called her. Our back porch catches the sun from early on, and the wee bitch would throw itself down on the step. There for the day. Ne'r bothered nobody. Your lassie was backward and forward so often, it was hardly worth the dog's while going home. As a matter of fact I doubt if it knew where it lived anymore.'

'It's a dog's life,' commented the class comedian.

Billy continued. 'If I was working nearby I'd slip home for the bite a' dinner. She'd be there. We'd have a bit of an auld yarn. I kept a wee sweetie in my pocket for the youngster. Wasn't one word of complaint out of Myrtle about the dog while the two weemen were on terms. Then the row rises. The auld dog keeps coming over, and your lassie won't venture next-nor-near the place to take it home. I arrive in. Myrtle's in the kitchen, the head gone: wants rid of the dog. I slip the finger under the dog's collar on my way out and bring her across the road. Have the usual auld yarn with the lassie, pulling her leg; the youngster searching my pockets looking for his wee sweetie. And, well, to be honest with you Pat, I knew I was getting the green light, for when I was leaving that particular Friday she reminded the youngster, "Now, don't forget to give Billy his good-bye kiss." I always got a wee kiss from the youngster.'

'Got me wee kiss, and then the youngster started telling your woman, "Now, you give Billy a kiss as well".'

'"Sure Billy'll be back th'night and I'll give him a kiss then. Won't you Billy?" She's looking at me, and, well, what was I to think, Pat? You know what I mean? What's a bloke to think?'

Francie caught my eye, his finger poised above his tobacco pouch, framing a question. I shook my head.

'To cut a long story short,' Billy continued, 'that Friday I went down to the pub. Heading home with a few pints in me, I says to myself, the youngster'll be asleep be-now, I might as well drop in on her across the road, and see what's the craic. Place in total darkness. Tried the back door. It was on the latch. Right enough, I says, she's expecting me. Groped me way down the hall and put the head round the door.

'"It's me. It's Billy", I whispered in. "I won't turn on the light in case it wakes the wee'un." At this turn n'er a word of complaint. So I throw the trousers on the end of the bed, and pulled back the quilt intending on putting in an hour or two in the bed with her.'

'"Who's that?" she jumps up out of her sleep.'

'"Billy. Remember? Early on?"'

'"Billy who?" She whipped the sheet round her.'

'"Billy, who? Billy me," I tell her.

"Oh my God! Oh my God! Help me! Help me!" She's screaming at the top of her voice, battering me with her fists, roaring: "It's Joanne Patterson's daddy."

Who was in your lassie's bed, but young Hannah, one of my wee girl's friends from school, babysitting the youngster while the other one was out flying her kite. Naturally, I was every bit as shocked as her. All I feared was that the youngster in the next room would hear the commotion and arrive in, so I put my hand over her mouth to stop her bringing the house down.'

'Good God Billy,' I said, 'you must have got an awful gunk.'

'Don't be talking, Pat. Next thing, the headlights of a car flashes on the window. I let go. She's away. Out in her nightdress screaming for the whole neighbourhood to hear: "Help! Help! He tried to rape me. Joanne Patterson's daddy tried to rape me!" Who do you think jumps out of the car but your lassie, and this bloke with her.'

Francie signalled a second time. Would I change my mind about the roll-up?

'Oh, go on, Francie.'

'When I saw your boyo, I decided to make myself scarce, so I did.'

Fast thinking boy was writ large on Francie's face as he handed across the roll-up.

'She'll clear things up with young Hannah, I was thinking. She'll know the score. It'll get sorted now she's back. Slipped on the trousers, I did, and out the back with me, way I came in.

'Next thing: sirens screeching in the street, the Constabulary battering down my front door! Me down in the station giving my end; her standing there, you won't believe, the bloke with her, admitting nothing. Said she had no idea why I thought she was interested. She'd issued no invitation.'

'And why do you think she took that line, Billy?'

'By Jaysus, Pat, if I'd'a but knew the type of her at the start. It was Him, your boyo. The fancy boy! She didn't want her chances there spoiled. But let me tell you something for nothing. They're well matched, the pair of them, so they are. If I'd'a only fucking listened to my own missus in the first place. She was right all along. By Jaysus, Myrtle had the measure of that one from the start.'

'Women have certain instincts, Billy,' I agreed.

'You'd want to be up early of a morning to be clever enough for some weemen these days. Oh aye! Everyone could tell me afterwards, about your bucko. She had her cap set there for a while. Her game was clean documentation when her chance came.'

'A clean sheet is right,' offered one sympathetic listener. 'You'd'a been safer had you stuck with auld Marilyn, Billy.'

'And your family, Billy,' I enquired, 'how are they coping with you inside?'

'Myrtle's standing by me. As-a-matter-of-fact,' he added, 'this whole carry on brought me and Myrtle closer nor ever we wur.'

7

Over the coming weeks my classroom was a hub of activity. Charlie and Winston diligently working through the syllabus, my input consisting of little more than trips to outside resource centres in search of material. Everything was going swimmingly, until the morning I looked around to find no Charlie Conlon in the room.

'Where's Charlie?' I looked to Winston.

Winston dared not speak for anyone outside his own camp.

I turned to Pablo.

'Where's Charlie?'

'You're all right,' Pablo brushed my question aside. 'Never worry your head, he'll be along any minute.'

I got the impression Pablo was overdoing the business-as-normal routine, fussing over biscuits, shouting orders everywhere. Something was not quite right. He buried his head in a book, no longer able to avoid the evidence of the missing Charlie.

'He's down on the boards,' he finally conceded. But not to worry, he would be along to class any minute. (The boards being the prisoner's euphemism for the prison segregation unit, the PSU – generally referred as the punishment unit.)

According to Joe, being there was no big deal. Pablo and he had checked with the screws before leaving the block. Got them to phone down to the PSU. Charlie would be out by ten. Prisoners knew the rules. The PSU could not hold a prisoner beyond forty-eight hours without the consent of the Board of Visitors (BOV). That consent had not been sought. They had double-checked with the screw in the library. It was confirmed, Charlie was on his way.

'So, is nobody going to tell me why he's in the punishment unit?'

Best wait; hear it straight from the horse's mouth.

'I can't wait,' I said, lifting the duster.

Ten minutes later a very sober Charlie limped in, a shoe on one foot, a carpet slipper on the other.

'What wars have you been through?' I asked, watching him hobble towards a chair.

He nodded a respectful good morning to me, pulled his chair in beside Winston, and grimacing towards the others. It was a stoic performance.

'What happened to the foot?' I asked.

'My foot?' he said, as if at a loss to know what I was talking about.

'The slipper?'

'There was an accident.' He glanced down as if just discovering his foot was attached to his leg.

'Take off the slipper and show me.' It was an order.

He took off the slipper and held out the injured foot for inspection. It was red, raw and swollen, the instep one massive angry white blister.

I expressed concern. 'What on earth happened?'

'It got scalded.' He glanced down, pursing his lips.

'It couldn't have just scalded itself? Could it? Should it not be bandaged?'

'It'll do,' he said, edging the slipper back over the angry flesh.

'Did you walk all the way from the block?'

'I was told that I should have a crutch,' he grimaced as he forced his heel down, 'but they won't give me one.'

'And why not?'

'Because they fear I might use it on some of them.'

'Whoever said you should have one, should see to it you get one.' I asked had he seen the doctor?

'It was him said I should have a crutch.'

'Well, insist you see the doctor again.'

'I have *written* to one. To Dr Joe Hendron, Member of Parliament for West Belfast. That should move some of them.'

'Whatever about your MP, Charlie. What about painkillers? Did the doctor prescribe anything?'

'I wouldn't let on I was in pain. I wouldn't give them the satisfaction.'

'You appear like someone in shock. Are you thinking straight?'

'I'm thinking straight, Patricia. Straighter than a lot of them here realise.'

'But why suffer?' I was still at a loss. 'That's not very straight thinking in my book. Why make things so hard on yourself?'

'I'm used to it,' he said, making a valiant effort not to grimace again.

Before long I had a version of the incident that led to his foot being scalded, why he had spent three days in solitary confinement, and why he was prepared to endure whatever it took rather than display weakness.

It happened in the refectory. There was a grievance, and his mates agreed Charlie should act as spokesman. Charlie made, what he considered, was a reasonable complaint to an officer.

'I assume you were courteous, not aggressive or demanding?'

He was businesslike. Spoke to the officer in a civil tongue. The officer acknowledged there was, indeed, a problem. One easily sorted on the spot, were they not inside prison walls where no prison officer will jump to the demands of any prisoner.

Charlie expected that the matter would be rectified there and then, but the officer did not move fast enough.

Charlie brought matters a stage further. He issued an ultimatum.

'If you don't move yourself and do what you said you'd do half an hour ago, I'll rip this place apart.'

'Suit yourself,' said the officer.

'I'll give you ten seconds,' threatened Charlie, 'and if I don't see action fast I'll start by ripping that water geyser off that wall.'

'Away you go,' said the officer. 'It's no skin off my nose what you do.'

Charlie miscalculated. When he made his threat he did so presuming the geyser contained cold water. Too late, he realised it was switched on, the water boiling. Backing down would mean losing face in front of mates, and more important, in front of prison staff. He had to go through with it. Given his physical strength, the first hard chuck brought the geyser off the wall. With it came gallons of scalding water cascading down on his right foot.

Off went the alarm bells. In came the riot squad. And off went Charlie to the punishment block to cool down.

I searched my bag while Pablo did a scout around; returning with an assortment of painkillers produced from teachers' handbags. Water was fetched, and Charlie was made to swallow a cocktail of pills.

The colour returned to his face. Soon he and Winston retired to a quiet corner and got down to work.

Just how would I feel if this were my son? With the injured foot resting on a chair, Charlie and I chatted during the break.

'Does your mother come to see you?'

He hadn't seen any of his family in over a year.

'Not even your brother?'

'Nope.'

'Is it the journey?'

'No.' It wasn't that.

'So what is it then?'

'They've *give up* on me.'

'And why should that surprise me?'

Communication had ceased some time back. The family had not written, and he had not written to them.

'Not even a Christmas card?'

From his brother Sean's children, yes.

'Well, maybe they are telling you something. That they want to maintain contact, however tenuous.'

As far as his mother was concerned, he had no intention of ever seeing the woman or speaking to her for the rest of her life.

'Does she despair of you that much?'

'Other way round, more like!'

Somehow Charlie did not sound totally convincing when he pronounced so emphatically on his family. I was curious. I asked about his brother. Had Sean ever been in trouble with the law?

'Yes,' Charlie said, 'Sean ran up against the police like any of us in the area where we grew up.' But, apart from those early skirmishes, Sean was not like him. (Later I would learn of Charlie giving Sean's name to cover his own crime. He felt some shame about involving his brother, but whether Sean took the rap or not, I was not told.)

'Sean *wised* up,' Charlie explained, and was now head barman in a popular Belfast pub-restaurant, the Elbow. Sean was pursuing study in his leisure time, with a mind to a university course somewhere down the line.

'I've frequented the Elbow,' I remarked 'Next time I'm in Belfast I must pop in, keep an eye out for Sean. Will I recognise him? Are you alike? Maybe I could bring him your regards?'

'Sean is a hard-working, law-abiding, family man. A respectable citizen like yourself, Patricia. I think the two of you would get on.'

Easing his foot on to the floor, Charlie signalled it was time to get back to work.

Following lunch, he returned wielding a crutch.

'Good Grief!' I exclaimed. 'Your MP has worked a miracle.'

Charlie, unable to conceal his satisfaction, explained that it was putting a letter to an MP through the system, ensuring officers were fully aware of exactly what he was up to, that activated matters. He knew which buttons to press. Some people at the top might not be too comfortable about him communicating with his Member of Parliament.

One month to the day, the crutch long discarded and the foot healed, a delegation arrived in class. Charlie: spokesman, Provo Joe: organist. Dr Joe Hendron had not acknowledged receipt of Charlie's letter. MPs always replied to letters! Always! Without fail! Hendron had not!

'Right, well ...' I said, searching for a reason why Joe, a political colleague of my husband's, might have overlooked responding.

What did that tell Provo Joe about my defence of the SDLP? What had I got to say for myself? Charlie was on the brink of changing political allegiance. 'Know what I mean, Patricia! A letter to your MP! And your MP doesn't bother to answer!'

To save face, when I got home I phoned Joe Hendron's constituency office, asking his assistant, Brendan, about the delay in responding. Brendan had no record of ever seeing such a letter come through the office. Joe phoned later. He was most, most concerned. A letter from a prisoner – any prisoner – would be given immediate attention, investigated, a phone call made to the NIO. But nobody – and he had checked with Sally, his wife – had any knowledge of any letter ever arriving at either address. And yes, the prisoners were absolutely correct. MPs always replied to letters. Always. Joe was upset. 'This is very serious, Patricia.'

I reported this conversation to Charlie.

'This is a very serious matter, Patricia. A letter to an MP: withheld?'

'And, your vote?' I doorstepped Charlie.

The vote was safe for the time being. He believed Hendron.

'So do I, Charlie.' And I left it to him to convince Provo Joe.

'You know,' an officer once said to me, 'they give Conlon a bad reputation, but I know Charlie Conlon from way back, and I don't believe he's half the way so bad as they make out. I had him when he was in Young Offenders, and I thought he was a decent type of young fellow, and that things would turn out for him. Always felt he was a cut above average.'

'I'm surprised they sent him back here after the last time,' piped up another officer, which was my opening to ask a question I'd been wanting to ask for some time.

'Did any officer here ever spit on Charlie Conlon because of his colour?'

'The Trevi Fountain,' guffawed the first speaker, describing an infamous officer with a habit of invading the space of the person opposite, spraying spittle all over them. Unaware of the man's unfortunate habit, Charlie took a drenching while being given an order to clean a floor.

He took offence.

Repeating the order, the officer directed his eyes and his spout towards the floor.

Spitting on his person, then spitting on the floor he was being ordered to clean, was one step too far for Charlie Conlon. He refused. This was one spat-upon black man who would not get down on his knees and clean up a white man's spit.

Words led to actions. A punch-up followed. Officers intervened to separate the two. Charlie sustained injuries, as did the officer. I gathered from those telling the tale that they did not believe Charlie bore full responsibility. There was more than a hint that things may have gone far too far.

The officer retired from the service soon afterwards. And from that day on, I was led to believe, it was open house on Charlie Conlon.

8

How much did Charlie remember of his formative years? It was another tea break. Another of our chats.

He had no bad childhood recollections. Life was happy and carefree. Neighbours in and out. Uncles and aunts coming and going. His granny's house in Serpentine Gardens. His mother's in Queen's Gardens. Someone knit him an Aran sweater once. Things like that. He was as happy as the next kid.

The family moved out of his grandmother's house when he was around four. He and his brother frequently dropped by his mother's workplace after school; played football on open ground out the back. Neighbours kept an eye on them. His mother might not be the greatest of housekeepers, but they always had plenty to eat. There was no violence or abuse in his home. His mother wasn't the type to go out to pubs with men. It was work, and chatting with her neighbours, reading and smoking fags and drinking tea. She was a talker. If she wasn't talking she was reading. Always reading something. The cornflakes box if there was nothing else.

School was all right. He couldn't remember if it was regular attendance or not, but he reckoned it was because there was nothing to keep him away. He had loads of friends, schoolwork no problem. The dark side came with a change of teacher.

'She had this black look on her face every time she looked at me. I knew she didn't like me. Some of it may have been because I got my work done quickly, and was probably fidgeting, distracting others. Wee Johnny McCann, my best friend, sat beside me, and Johnny wasn't a great speller. Naturally you want to help your friend, so I'd whisper all the answers. Whenever she caught me she'd slap me. Harder than anyone else.'

'Stop and think, Patricia. If it was your Ronan down at his school, and his friend didn't know something, wouldn't you expect Ronan to keep him out of bother with the teacher?'

He spelled out the miss-spelt word. Still remembered. He was told to hold out his hand to be slapped.

Charlie had had it. Enough was enough. He held out his hand, but when she reached out to hit him with the cane he grabbed her hand. Then he bit her.

Next memory. Social workers. 'My mother swallowed everything fed her. Putting a kid into care? Would you think that was helping?'

'I was eight when I was sent to Fallowfield,' he continued. 'The place was sold to my mother like they were putting me into some private school, when in fact it was your classic borstal.' Which was his home for the next number of years. (Researching Fallowfield, Co Armagh, for the purposes of this book, one person from the area recalled: 'It's long closed down. But I remember well as a kid us being threatened by our parents that if we misbehaved we'd be sent up the road to *"the bad boys' home"*.')

Charlie recalled arriving, the size of the building, number of windows. His first thoughts: how great to live in a place like that. 'I pictured myself running wild and climbing trees, and doing things boys did in storybooks.'

'You talked about your mother working. About leaving you boys to your own devices? As a war widow, was she not entitled to a pension from the American Government?'

In fact it wasn't until they were into their teens that he and Sean actually discovered the true facts about their parents' relationship. 'In them days,' Charlie explained, 'there was a stigma attached to being an unmarried mother, and especially an unmarried mother with two black kids.'

Conlon, was his mother's maiden name. Charles Eason, his father's name. 'I was called Charlie after him.' At pains to point out that it had been his parents' intention to wed, but for the intervention of the Vietnam posting, he apologised for misleading me earlier. His father dying before Sean was born put an end to those plans.

Still curious, I asked him whether he had relatives in the US.

Initially, he told me, his mother corresponded with his father's mother, but such correspondence had long ceased. Letters, photographs, addresses, everything was lost when his family were intimidated out of Queen's Garden as a result of the 1970's riots. During the move to the Bawnmore estate, belongings were hastily thrown into the back of a coal lorry. Much was destroyed. And that was another bone of contention Charlie had in relation to his mother. 'She never claimed a penny in compensation for anything lost as a consequence of being forced to move home. Not,' he added, 'that she owned anything of great value. But, still, that was the type of her. She wouldn't claim.'

'Still and all, Charlie,' I said, 'I would have thought that even without a marriage certificate your mother would still qualify for some form of assistance, provided she could establish paternity. And from what you've told me I don't think that should have been a problem.'

He had told his mother so. But trying to get his mother to take any action! He just gave up.

I made some vague comment about American citizenship rights. Would he, or his brother, be interested in establishing citizenship?

'I would be very sceptical,' he replied.

'About being an American?'

'About the system there.'

'You mean, compared with here. Compared with living in Northern Ireland at the present time?'

He passed on that one.

'And well you might be, Charlie. Judging by what we read about conditions in American jails, particularly if you're black. By comparison, our prisons are first-class hotels.'

Charlie did not disabuse me, of either my assessment of the US justice system, or conditions for prisoners in Northern Ireland.

9

Glorious weather arrived in May and class attendance suffered. Francie O'Kane – legal eagle adviser to Billy Patterson – first to depart. The message from the wings: Francie had decided to throw in education in favour of the great outdoors.

'Can't some of you fellows coax him back?' They shook their heads. He and a mate had been fixed up with a set of wheels, assigned to grounds duty and out all day collecting bins around the estate. I conceded defeat.

My class was further depleted when I lost Billy Patterson to Magilligan strand. Driving through the prison gates one morning I met Billy riding out on a bicycle. I rolled down the car window and asked him where he thought he was off to.

'I'm heading for the beach for the day, Pat,' said Billy, his lunch in a brown paper bag swinging from the handlebars of his bicycle.

Another prisoner peddled up behind and put a foot to the ground, set for a chat. They were working on an outdoor work scheme: a project to provide benches for beach-goers.

'When the weather turns,' Billy made a promise to return to class. 'Keep the seat warm for me, Pat,' he called over his shoulder as he cycled off in the direction of the sand dunes and the sea. True to his word, when the project finished, Billy returned. He had some better news. Myrtle had been up to the beach. They took advantage of the sand dunes. Asked about his need for further bookkeeping help, he was cagy. 'I'll spread my bets, Pat' he said, 'for one never knows the day nur the hour.' And I couldn't agree more.

Billy was fortunate that his account of the whole sorry business with the babysitter was accepted by fellow inmates. Others with similar convictions would not be so fortunate.

'Kill, maim, rob, vandalise property, blow up towns and cities, terrorise communities? You were a prisoner like everyone else. Sex offend? You were a marked man.

Just how scary a sex offender's lot might be was brought home the day one man skulked through the classroom door. Your proverbial loner, casting furtive glances around, 'scared shitless' as his fellow inmates wanted, unsure whether to sit or stand. '*Root!*' I heard someone mutter, twitching his nose like the man was a skunk.

He never contributed to discussion. Was he ashamed in front of a woman? No. He was terrified to open his mouth in front of his fellow inmates, his views as unwelcome as himself.

He had barely eaten a bite for two weeks, he told me. Petrified to run the gauntlet to the food servers to pick up his meal. Afraid to go to the showers to have a wash. Scared to leave his cell for any reason, and equally so of someone coming in during unlock periods. His few hours in education, where he determined to stay within sight of a teacher or officer, were his only respite from constant harassment on the wings. But even in education, opportunities were seldom ignored. A boiling kettle could be a fearsome weapon.

Twice he came to class. Then I learned he had sustained a number of broken ribs and would not be returning.

Paedophiles were particularly vulnerable. Stories abounded of heads smashed against billiard tables, bodies battered to pulp, bones broken. Serious efforts were made by management to guard those at risk, particularly during times of heightened media attention. It was policy to offer work opportunities in areas not prone to violent outbreaks. But however well meaning, and however well officers looked out for the vulnerable, nobody could be expected to have eyes in the backs of their heads.

Yet some did slip through the net unscathed.

The sixty-seven-year-old Norbertine, Fr Brendan Smyth, whose sex abuse case stirred a political storm, leading to the collapse of the Irish government, was serving four years for child molestation in Magilligan during my time. He was pointed out to me when he enquired about education classes. Nothing materialized.

Unaware of his brewing notoriety south of the border, nobody North took any special notice of him. Later on, officers spoke of escorting him to court. How he became aroused when he sighted young girls outside Loreto College gates as they drove past. Talk was that he celebrated 'dry' masses in his cell.

Whether Brendan Smyth *took his medicine* at the start, I was never told, but time in the end tended to do everyone a favour, the focus invariably shifting to the next new committal.

Arts and crafts, where I encountered my old dancing partner, Vince

Duffy, was a refuge for many. Basket-weaving or toy-making were hardly macho activities, so the hard men stayed away, allowing the classroom to become a haven for the more vulnerable, if only for a few short hours each week.

Day-time education? Now, that was the preserve of the elite. One message the sex offender must learn. And fast. Some did not learn fast enough.

As time passed, I firmly believed I could spot a sex offender miles off. So imagine my surprise when one day someone piped up in class, 'I'm here on a rape charge,' claiming he was stitched.

'How were you stitched, Philip?' I asked, if for no other reason than to cover the silence. Surely he would realise nobody was buying his *innocent victim* line.

Or, was it possible we were about to take another trip down the Billy and the Babysitter road?

His was a widely reported case. A cocky, self-assured young man, Philip did not fit my image of the classic rapist. It was fairly obvious he believed so himself, and had no hesitation telling us why.

He was on duty, doubling as barman and night-porter for a wedding reception, guests booked to stay overnight. During the day, a guest, an attractive young woman, caught his fancy. According to him, mild flirtation developed. There were smiles, and some banter when he served drinks to her party; indications only that everyone was happy. Later that evening there was a disco. Philip was on duty in the bar, and the smiles kept coming. The disco ended. The young woman remained unattached at the end of the evening.

Bedtime! He was last off duty. Still smiling as before, she collected her room key from the desk and went off to bed. He read something else into those smiles. He held the master-key to all bedrooms.

The classroom had fallen deadly silent; expressions indicating that Philip was digging his own grave, deeper and deeper with every word coming from his mouth. I would put a bet on it. Some of those men at the table would know the party involved, or, know someone who knew '*that wee girl,*' and that before too many more hours had passed, one or other of those fellows would feel duty bound *to kick Philip's head in.* Heedless of the effect his words were having on his audience, Philip ploughed on regardless. The signals were clear. He wasn't a fool. He could tell a come-on as well as the next bloke. 'Look,' he postured, arching his shoulders, 'blokes know. Some of us are, well, not exactly desperate, are we?' A broad grin to his fellow inmates; but he was the only one grinning.

'And it never crossed your mind, Philip, that you could have misjudged those "signals"?' I intervened.

'What do you mean, *misjudged*?' It was ludicrous to suggest he could misjudge anything.

'I'm talking about you misinterpreting a friendly smile. I'm talking about a bit of innocent banter a few friends were engaging in on a happy occasion. Is it not possible for a woman, especially if surrounded by her friends, to have a joke or a laugh with the barman or the waiter serving the table without him thinking she is giving him the come on?'

I should have put a stop to the conversation there and then. I should have acted professionally and got on with my lesson, but something inside of me was not prepared to let him away unchallenged.

'She made no attempt to fight me off when I went into the room and sat on the bed,' he said.

'Maybe she thought that the best method of getting rid of you was to talk to you. I cannot even begin to imagine how any woman in such a frightening situation would react: seeing a man sitting on the side of her bed in a hotel bedroom in the early hours of the morning? But if it were me, although terrified, talking might be one ploy.'

Had the circumstances been otherwise, I might have told him that from where I was standing he was not a bad-looking fellow. Not someone, you would expect to go forcing unwanted attentions on girls. 'Is this what you do when every other pretty woman smiles at you, Philip? Respond to every smile coming your way as you did on that occasion?'

'I'm talking about women giving the lead.'

'You're talking about a girl who smiled at you.'

'Yes, but why? They pretend. Blokes know.'

'This woman wasn't pretending, either before or after. She told you emphatically she was not interested.'

'She was saying one thing, but I knew different ...'

'You knew what?'

He knew where eye contact with women led. When she left the disco unattached, he knew where that was leading. He had been watching all day. He had been keeping track all evening, and he knew where it was all leading ...

My unease had become obvious when Pablo rowed in. He lifted Philip's hand and placed it on his own knee. Then, ever so gently, he lifted Philip's hand off his knee and placed it back on the table. All eyes following the gesture.

'If a girl does that, she is saying no. NO.' His voice rose. 'Do you hear me? And that is all it should take for any bloke to know that n, o, spells *NO*. And if he doesn't get that message clear and simple, then he deserves to be here.'

Philip, bare-faced in his assumption that his explanation found favour, brazened it back to class once more.

And then Philip wasn't there any more.

I was alone in the classroom when a terrified man rushed through the door, his eyes out like a startled deer. He crouched in a corner, trembling in fear.

Was someone following? I glanced through the partition.

An officer outside had just warned he was 'in for a *doing-over* from prisoners', he panted.

Ross had already talked with the teachers about his conviction, requesting we say nothing to other prisoners. He had been convicted in the Scottish courts of molesting his partner's daughter, and now the case was under appeal in Northern Ireland. The charges, he claimed, were unfounded. Vital evidence had not been produced in court. He believed it was a malicious attempt by his ex-partner to gain possession of the home. His lawyer was confident that on appeal the sentence would be rescinded.

The previous day, a prisoner out to court had noticed the court listing for the following week, and Ross's secret was out.

With quaking voice he identified the group who were *out to get him*. The ringleaders were in the classroom next door.

I went next door and talked to Margaret. She talked to the men. Ross, she told them, had confided in us, and we felt he should be given a chance to prove his innocence.

They considered. Perhaps the teachers had a point? And pulled back.

Ross joined the group for the remainder of class. And the following week, on appeal, the case was squashed.

'Were you gearing up to attack some sex offender on the wings a few days ago?' I asked Charlie.

He looked at me quizzically, brow quivering.

'A little bird told me.'

'I never have anything to do with that lot. If they're bothering no one I have no business with them.'

'I was told you were seen going into the showers after a fellow, twisting a towel. Why would you do that, Charlie?'

I assume he guessed at the source of my information. A prison officer. Charlie twisted his hands as if wringing the neck of a chicken. 'Yes,' he said, 'maybe I twist the towel into a rope going into the showers. Maybe I'm flexing my muscles. You're walking into a shower, Patricia. You're loosening up. Does whoever's watching me expect me to get down on my hands and knees and crawl in? Would that keep them all happy?'

Were motives misunderstood? I was not around to witness. But I was around for an incident in my own classroom.

A social studies class was underway without the usual raised feet on the table, and Maxie Mitchell took advantage, inching his backside on to a corner.

He asked me a question, and I turned to the blackboard to highlight a point.

When I turned back Maxie was stretched out on the table, head cupped in his palm, nodding towards the blackboard, forcing me to turn back and check. I glanced back to the group to confirm, and then down at Maxi full-out on the table.

Could I have imagined what I just thought I had seen?

I turned back. My hand, as it propelled the marker across the silicon surface not just as steady as before.

What was happening behind my back?

Could that have been an open zipper?

What do I do?

Keep writing. Keep thinking. You need another glance to be certain.

A swift turnabout. An eye-sweep of the table. A covert glance in the direction of Maxie's jeans. No. My eyes had not deceived me.

I turned back.

Is this a set up? He is so far forward perhaps no one else sees. If they do, what do I do? Got to be certain before I act.

A determined flourish of the wrist. Underscore that last point. Turn. Direct a question at Charlie Conlon.

Charlie responded without hesitation.

Pablo twitched his nose behind Maxie's back, indicating his irritation that something was *coming between him and his teacher* – which I took as evidence, nobody else in the room had any idea what was taking place in front of their noses.

The moment Maxie's hand moved towards the abyss, I knew I had to act. It was that precise moment, the fellows later complimented, I earned my stripes. Using a standard put-down-line my sister, a nurse, passed on, and seeing the looks on those bloke's faces when I swung the marker towards Maxie's unzipped fly, was reward in itself. What did the trick for Josephine, did the same for me. Her ploy was to offer her patient an enema. "*Only checking, pet. Thought I saw a wee worm crawl out of the jammies*".

An adaptation of Josephine's line, I am pleased to report, worked just as effectively in a prison classroom as I assume it still does in a hospital ward.

Maxie leapt from the table like Jumping Jack Flash. 'Fucking jumpin Jaysus, my fucking fork's busted!' he shrieked, as hand shielding his shame he fled the classroom, leaving behind multiple sets of dilated eyes.

Wiping his brow, Pablo called for coffee. 'Black for the lady. Six sugars,' he shouted after Joe. Someone else handed me a roll-up. I was on my third puff when I realised I hadn't supervised the content, but at that very moment I trusted everybody around me.

'You're a *cracker,* mate,' complimented Eugene McQuillan, raising his two feet on to the yellow Formica-topped table where they properly belonged. And raising a mug of tea to me, he reckoned, 'No charges will be brought for handling *swollen* goods.'

10

'**B**unch of bloody skivers, if you want my opinion.'

I had not asked for anyone's opinion.

'Strutting around the place wielding biros like bloody billiard cues. Phwaa ...' They were not fooling him.

'I'm surprised they have the energy to lift the bloody books. One of them boys, let me tell you, wouldn't understand what a day's work was if it hit them in the face.'

'Will we bring back capital punishment Chris?' I kidded the officer from the comfort of his soft chair, where I sat smoking one of his cigarettes while waiting for the kettle to boil.

'By God, but some of them boys have the wool rightly pulled over the teacher's eyes. You mark my word, if you think you are going to reform any of them boys, let me tell you ...'

Sometimes a class did dissolve into absolute farce. But for every skiver, there were those who harboured a genuine desire to use their time constructively. Someone like Charlie.

'How would someone from my background, with this broad Belfast accent, ever fit into a university?' he asked.

'It's *what* you say, Charlie, not *how* you say something that really matters.'

'Depends who's listening. Know what I mean?'

'One change you could make: stop attaching "know what I mean" as an add-on to every statement.'

He took note, admonishing himself for the gaffe.

As time passed, Charlie grew in confidence. Attitudes softened. 'You see Conlon there. On the wings he associates with the worst possible elements, but you see the same boyo with Winston, and it's like you had a reptile that shed its skin,' the officer remarked.

Despite what anyone else thought, Charlie walked with his head high. When I remarked on his proud demeanour, he said, 'It must be the Native American blood in me.'

'We can expect you to take out your pipe of peace any moment, can we?'

'My paternal great-grandmother was a full-blooded Cherokee Indian.'

'Seriously, Charlie?'

'Seriously.'

'So peace has a chance then?'

If only!

The mass exodus of Protestants from the classroom was a conundrum.

'Notice anything strange about your class?' Susan had her head round the door, and I couldn't say I had.

"Hatchet' Anderson,' she said, 'just this minute told me he's away.'

'Released?'

'No. Back to the wings. Said, "I'm f'ing out of here Susan fast as my two f'ing legs can carry me. This class of yours is full of f'ing Fenians." Fenian, of course, synonymous with Catholic, Nationalist, Republican, terrorist. Hatchet claimed to be a brigadier in the outlawed Ulster Defence Association (UDA), a paramilitary organisation dedicated to the defence of Ulster. Although not in my classes, I made a special point of being *extra charming* to Hatchet whenever our paths crossed. 'Have you looked at your own class, Patricia?' Susan pressed. 'Check who you have? When Hatchet skedaddled I realised there wasn't another Prod left.'

'Good God, Susan,' I looked around. No Winston. No Billy ...'

A Brigadier in the UDA? Scared? Running for his life? We looked at each other.

'Some brigadier, our Hatchet! The last man to cop on the army had left the battleground?'

'He's your baby, Susan.'

Instinctively we both knew where to look for answers. Not with the governor. Not with the officers. Not with administration. But with Pablo, who confessed.

He thought he was doing the teachers a favour.

In an unguarded comment, one of our colleagues had alluded to the possibility of classes being axed due to falling numbers; possibly a tactic to encourage attendance. Pablo's ears picked up and he panicked. He liked his trips across to education. He liked that link with the outside world, and resolving to keep it so mounted a recruitment drive back on the block. Calling in some old favours, he concentrated specifically on Catholics – his own – particularly those who *owed him one*. First he asked.

Then he demanded. And finally, he exercised the whip, selecting only the brightest and the best.

As the posse of Catholics advanced on education, alarm bells sounded. Protestants retrenched. Until such time as they could gather sufficient intelligence to muster the troops and mount a counter-attack on education, Pablo's men held the day.

Nigel arrived with the returning Protestants. Upfront, he placed his cards on the table.

'Nigel Blackman: Portadown Protestant.'

'Here to make a stand?' scoffed one of our wits.

Nigel did not like the sound of social studies. He liked the sound of socialism less. Marx, Lenin, Mao Zedong were not his Supermen. He wanted to make his position perfectly clear right away

'Port-*e*-down!' tittered the resident wit, to the general amusement of the pack.

Moscow! COMMUNISM. In Nigel's book herein lay the enemy.

Not accusing me outright, but, Nigel knew all about *Reds*. He was well fit for the left. If anyone thought over here they were going to …

'Sit down Nigel,' I said to the tall, good-looking young man, with the earnest blue eyes.

Had I read George Orwell's *Animal Farm?* Reading that book told Nigel all he needed to know about communists. There had been talk about this social studies class back on his wing – casting me, I suspect, as a Fenian, a Free-stater, a Pope-ridden Republican, indoctrinating the masses with Socialist ideas.

'Do you know the book I'm talking about?' he asked.

'I read *Animal Farm* many moons ago, Nigel,' I admitted, 'so will you refresh my memory.'

'It's all about a farm where some of the animals seize power and run everything to suit themselves. It shows what can happen when communism takes hold.'

'And you think that the same thing is about to happen in Ulster?'

I was aware that issues raised in class generated some discussion back on the wings. Nigel did not like the sound of what he was hearing, so he decided to brave the lion's den and put me straight. He was here to uphold the twin principles of Protestantism and Democracy, as opposed to

Catholicism and Communism.

'In what way do you believe your Protestant ethos is threatened by anything said in this class?' I queried. 'Say, for example, the fictional farm Orwell constructs to symbolize the communist system were a reality, are you not heartened that he depicts the new order, though initially otherwise intentioned, as eventually adopting the principles of the former capitalist regime?'

Nigel had no intention of hanging around awaiting long-term outcomes. It was the here-and-now was his concern. '*1984.*' Had I heard of that book? He had heard of it, but hadn't read it. *Animal Farm* was enough.

'Look,' he offered, 'if you provide a sheet of paper I'll draw where I see you coming from.' We placed a blank sheet of paper before him, and watched Nigel draw a straight line. He indicated the two extremes, left and right. He placed a large X – himself – to the extreme right-of-right. Then his hand hovered. Perhaps on balance, I was not quite so far left-of-left as he was right-of-right, but my X also went pretty close to the edge.

Nigel's reservations might well have some basis in fact. The class attracted a steady attendance, and stimulated heated discussion – not always politically correct discussion. Lessons were structured around core issues: law and order, religion, education, politics, criminality, sexual deviancy, inequalities in society. Some topics more popular than others.

Cultural and class divisions in society really got Provo Joe going. He had difficulty accepting that the RUC merited any rank order on the social scale. 'No way,' he said, after I slotted police into the same category as teachers.

'Joe, just write the stuff into your copybook,' I pleaded.

'No way, Patricia. No fucking way am I for putting them bastards into the same box as any of yous teachers. It's not on. I don't care what. It's just not on, so it's not. And another thing,' he added, 'if them bastards up in the NIO think they are going to slip a trick question like that into the examination, I'll be for ripping up the paper, so I will.'

Since Joe could barely read or write, I reckoned police and teachers could rest happily in the same box for the foreseeable future.

Nigel took heart when I told him, that, for the life of me, I could not visualise Joe's United Ireland coming about for generations. Eventually

Nigel talked about what led him to prison.

'Crippled a young police officer. Put the bloke in a wheelchair for life.' His blue eyes powered by intensity, he described those critical few seconds between good and evil; those seconds when he still had a choice. When he could have stayed on his own side of the street. Not crossed over.

A group of friends had been partying. High on magic mushrooms, and without a thought for the damage they were causing, they had been jumping on beds in the rented house of some girlfriends, until the beds went through the ceilings below. Perhaps neighbours complained. The cops arrived. Across the street his mates had isolated an officer from his colleagues. They were beckoning Nigel to join in. He knew it was wrong. Knew the moment he stepped off the pavement to cross the street. Still, he kept going, and the madness took over. The young police officer going down and down and down. Boots going in, and in, and in. Looking down at his Doc Martens. The officer groaning. Him running away. Running with the pack. It was all over in a few seconds. They were Protestant young men, attacking a Protestant police force in a Protestant town. He was ashamed. His family was ashamed of what he had done. A close relative had been severely wounded in an IRA attack. His family had suffered throughout the Troubles. Nigel was confused. '*Animal Farm?* It would make you think!'

And then, clean out of the blue, love was in the air. Pablo going AWOL, I believe, set the ball rolling. We were not to panic, word filtered in, he would return after he smelled the roses.

Escorted by his *friends*, the RUC, he arrived back. But what a flitter he was in. He had met this gorgeous girl on his last night of freedom. She was in love with him!

'Great,' we all chorused. 'This girl could be the makings of you.'

No way was he ready for marriage. He was disappointed in the lot of us. We were no better than his ma.

A week later, and he was in an even greater tizzy. The girl had written. She was definitely in love with him.

Another week and it was outright panic stations. His ma and the girl were in cahoots. On their way to Magilligan.

'See me in six months' time when I get out of here,' he sobbed.

'Shackled. Chained to the leg of the kitchen table? My life finished before I ever had a chance to have one.'

Next to fall foul of romance, was Nigel.

'Write to a Prisoner', the ad in the magazine said, and a lady from upstate New York wrote.

Nigel sent her his photograph.

And why did it not surprise me to hear that the lady was on the next plane into Shannon Airport, planning to travel North in a hired car? Because! Had I been thirty years younger myself, and received a photograph of the handsome Nigel Blackman through the post, I believe I might well have taken to the air. So I did not blame Miss Colleen O'Shaughnessy one little bit.

Her visit to Magilligan was scheduled for 11pm Thursday. Nigel attended class as usual. An officer would signal when his visitor arrived. Nigel would not be alone. Four mates had arranged visits to coincide.

A rattle of keys. The officer put his head round the door: '8921 Blackman. Visit.'

With good wishes ringing in his ears, we waved him off. Our fingers were crossed. Our hopes high.

Half an hour, and a stricken faced Nigel was back. His escorting officer saw him safely seated, glancing back protectively towards his charge as he withdrew.

The lesson stopped and we all looked at Nigel, his clear blue eyes blue as blue.

'Well. Did she show up?'

Those blue eyes spun in his head.

'Well?'

He accepted the spliff Joe handed him. His power of speech returned eventually. Ten minutes, Nigel spent in Miss O'Shaughnessy's presence before his urinary tract gave way. 'The officers saw it coming,' he explained, 'and came running. They were wetting themselves as well.' He described how, face turned to the wall, he made it past his four mates sitting in Visits, and into the toilet.

Officers unlocked a side door and got him out, leaving the lady from upstate New York sitting placidly in Visits, chewing her cud, waiting for Romeo to return from the toilet.

Later that day, I discounted all rumours about two prison officers seen struggling in the visitor car park, attempting to roll a Michelin tyre into a car with a Southern registration.

But never let it be said by anyone that prison officers do not have hearts.

'Any love interest in your life?' I asked Charlie.

With pending exams, he and Winston had much better things on their plates than to entertain such frivolity. His reply indicated that maybe *I* should be concentrating on better things myself.

I had to be joking, Eugene McQuillan corrected me, when I mistakenly assumed he had worked as a lorry driver in London. I'd taken my credit card out of my purse in class and Eugene had just fallen for it.

'Ran a twenty-four-seven business there. Articulated lorries, HGVs, juggernauts ... bumper to bumper up and down the M1. Took the eye off the ball and everything went wallop. Massive leasing scam.' He claimed to have spent time in Wormwood Scrubs where he rubbed shoulders with Ronnie Kray. The women in London, he swore – married, single, divorcees – were up for it twenty-four-seven, swiping gold credit cards and flashing Anne Summers knickers all over the place.

Terry and Brendan were taking note. There was a strong possibility Kuwait might be off the cards in favour of the English metropolis.

Eugene hinted he was 'well got' with a few big names round Westminster. 'Pulled some strings for the transfer back home.' He contributed across the board to political parties. He name-dropped.

Next time I met a recipient of Eugene's largesse, I asked, 'Does the name McQuillan mean anything to you? Says he's a friend of yours. Dined with you at Westminster.'

'McQuillan? McQuillan? Doesn't ring any bells.'

'Would Maghabery Prison ring a bell?'

'Maghaberry Prison?'

'Fermanagh, then?'

'For frig sake! That buck-eejit!'

'Big haulage contractor, I believe. Big contributor to the Party.'

'Where was it you said you met McQuillan?'

'In prison.'

'Doing what in prison?'

'Teaching him business studies.'

'Are you as big an eejit as him?'

Goms, he called them. A group of Irish fellows spotted by the police speeding up the M1 in a London borough council van, heading home to Fermanagh for the weekend to attend a crucial Gaelic game. McQuillan had borrowed the van from the depot where he worked in *refuse disposal*.

Finding the van packed with wheelie-bins, the police thought they were on to a terrorist cell. The bins, they believed were destined to be filled with explosives for a massive IRA bombing blitz throughout Britain that holiday weekend.

The families back home contacted politicians. Politicians were on phones to the London Metropolitan Police, the Home Office …

'Anyone with a bit of common sense between their two lugs should have known that those bunch of clouts were too buck-stupid for any organisation to touch them.'

Despite the shenanigans around us, there was always room for optimism. Three years was the maximum stay for any prisoner in Magilligan. Some would leave it all behind and be absorbed back into family life when released. Hughie might look forward to seeing Irene and the kids waiting at the prison gates. Myrtle would surely be there for Billy. Pablo's ma, and the girl would not be avoided. Winston had his career plan. McQuillan would head straight to the pub … And some would be back.

Until now, those waiting at the gates to greet Charlie Conlon ensured he never left anything behind.

11

The Elbow was relatively empty when I walked through the door. 'All right love,' the barman polishing glasses, lifted his head.

Two cherry-lipped ladies sat at a table by the window. The man with them had a lopsided jaw. A half-finished pint sat in front of him. The women were drinking shorts. They watched the street, nodding knowingly to each other, their eyes following passers-by. He watched the racing on the TV.

I chose a table close to the bar. A hollow-cheeked young man in a tight-fitting tweed jacket and white Converse plimsolls sat close by. He kept flicking sugar granules at his cup with a rolled-up fiver.

I draped my coat over the back of an adjacent chair, sat down and picked up the menu.

'There's no hurry at all. Just take your time,' said the smiling young girl in a short black skirt at my elbow. Her long hair kept falling over one eye and she kept pushing it away. She was happy when she saw I had located the menu.

'I'll have a glass of white wine,' I said, taking my glasses from my handbag. 'And I'll have a look at this menu, and maybe it will inspire me.'

'No problem.' She departed to fetch the wine. The barman was still polishing glasses behind the bar.

'A toasted sandwich; perhaps ham and cheese. What do you think?'

'You might as well,' she encouraged, pencil poised to record my order. 'What about tea, or coffee with your toastie?'

'The wine is fine,' I said, and casting a furtive glance towards the bar while replacing the menu between pepper and salt, I asked, 'by the way, is Sean Conlon on duty this afternoon?'

'I saw Sean in the back a few minutes ago.' Her eyes turned towards the bar. 'Do you want me to say someone's looking to see him?'

'Do please,' I said, and she departed for the back, pushing her hair behind her ear and checking my order on the docket in her hand.

The hollow-cheeked young man continued to flick sugar at his cup; the women by the window lit up two Benson & Hedges.

A tea towel draped over her arm, her black hair pulled back severely, a wholesome looking lady emerged from the back and came through into the lounge, picking up glasses and carrying them to the barman for rinsing. She surveyed the lounge from behind the bar; came out again and pushed a chair into place with a sturdy black shoe at the table where the young man sat. He skedaddled out the door with his rolled fiver in his hand. She wiped sugar from the table and moved towards me, concern in her voice. 'I'm afraid love,' she said, pointing to my coat trailing the ground.

I adjusted the coat, and thanked her.

'You were asking about Sean Conlon?' Her hands were balanced on the back of the chair beside me.

'Yes. Yes, I was,' I said, smiling up at her.

She scratched an ankle with the toecap of a sturdy shoe, eying me critically. 'You know Sean, love?'

'Sean? Yes, well … well actually it's not Sean. It's his brother Charlie I know.'

Her foot dropped to the floor like a dumbbell.

'Look,' I said, seeing her glance anxiously towards the bar. 'I'm a teacher, and have Charlie in class. I promised I would drop in to see Sean next time I was in Belfast. I just want to tell Sean that things are going fine for Charlie.

'Oh. A teacher.' Her relief was obvious.

'I'm down from Portstewart,' I added.

'Oh, Portstewart. Oh, I see. Portstewart's a lovely spot in the summer, isn't it? And you're looking to have a wee word with Sean, are you?'

Soon we were the best of buddies, Maureen and me.

'You never know,' Maureen confided, 'who comes in … Sean is in the back, but when young Emma came in and told me there was a woman in a black leather coat outside looking for him, I thought I'd have a wee dander out. In case …'

'I know, Maureen.'

Maureen suggested I move to another area of the bar, over by the window where Sean and I might have our 'wee chat'. She offered to carry my coat; said she'd have young Emma bring my 'wee toastie' across.

I said I could manage, but she helped me anyway, the tea towel tucked under her arm. She settled me down by the window with my coat and my bag and my bits and pieces all tucked in around me, and the glass of wine set before me.

There was a pillar between me and the racing on TV, so I looked out the window at the passers-by; idling my time, sipping wine, waiting for my toasted sandwich to arrive, waiting for Sean Conlon to appear. And when it happened, I truly believed I was having a biblical experience. For, walking towards me, through the lounge of the Elbow pub on Belfast's golden mile, came the eyes, the sandaled feet, the shoulder length tresses of John the Baptist in a white linen shirt. Maybe a taller, slimmer, much darker version of his brother, but undoubtedly, Sean Conlon.

'Hello,' he said, two dead-on brown eyes meeting mine. Any scruples I might have harboured about the propriety of my visit vanished.

Sean seemed sincerely glad I'd called. 'I'm kept fairly up to date,' he explained, pulling in a chair and indicating with a nod towards the glass of wine that I have another on him. Recently a mate of Charlie's, out on parole, had dropped by the pub.

It became obvious the family had taken a deliberate decision to let Charlie *stew*. The implication being that they were fed up waiting for him to *wise up*. Sean sounded genuinely chuffed when I told him of Charlie's exam ambitions.

'Good for Charlie,' he said. 'Sitting two A Levels, and a stage three RSA. Now I am impressed. That's something I'd love to do myself. You know Paul Gupta? – referring to a mutual acquaintance – Paul ran round with me and Charlie when we were kids, and Paul's back at university now. Maybe Charlie will make it to someplace like that one of these days.'

Eventually we got around to the real purpose of my visit: Charlie's application for a university place. 'I have encouraged him to apply,' I explained. 'An application in itself does no harm. But, to be honest, my real concern is the degree of family support he might expect were he to go down that road? I can nudge Charlie in certain directions, and good exam results can bolster his confidence, but without external support?'

'There was a period when Charlie went straight,' Sean said. 'We were beginning to think he had finally *wised up*. He got a job with a community development project that appeared the makings of him. But then, as far as I know, the project folded and Charlie was out of work, and something from his past caught up with him, and he was back to square one again. He falls back so easily.'

I shared the belief with Sean that if Charlie could be kept focused, made to play to his intellectual strengths rather than his physical ones, there was the possibility that he could break away from his past.

'The thing about Charlie and crime,' Sean was convinced, 'is that he never has an agenda of his own. You would think someone of his mind would have some sense. But he's led. Or he's provoked. Or he's doing favours for wee fellows that were with him in jail. Fellows he feels sorry for. He has them after him like flies. Charlie has to feel wanted. That's his problem. Then he runs when the police come on the scene; or he ends up taking them ones on as well. Most of the arrests happen over things that could have got sorted out on the spot if he wasn't so hot headed.'

'How much of this do you think stems from childhood? Charlie believes he's *owed*.'

'Something happened at school involving a teacher, but I was too young to know the extent of it. Charlie just went away, and I was at home with the house to myself. He was let home some weekends. I remember that as a nightmare time. He was hanging round with fellows a lot older.'

'About Fallowfield? I gather that he believes there was no justification for him going there.'

'I don't remember much being said at the time, except years later them saying, how Uncle Bill, driving Aunt Margaret and my mother and Charlie to Fallowfield in Bill's car, turned to my mother on the way in, and said, "don't leave him, Maura". It wasn't until years later any of us realised he went there 'voluntarily'.'

'You mean he wasn't sent through the courts?'

'His was a voluntary placement. As far as I know, most others, if not all of them, were there on court orders. I believe he was the youngest. You had this kid of eight mixing with lads of up to sixteen; most with criminal records of one kind or another. Charlie knew no better. At Fallowfield he was just exposed to the wrong sort – older boys who were basically criminals, and they became his peer group. They taught him all the tricks. Inside, it was an environment of eat or be eaten. If you had a fight with someone, basically you were stuck with them for the next week, so he learned that the only thing to do was to fight back to stop being bullied. That became the pattern for his life.'

At Sean's insistence I succumbed to a second glass. The alternative was a pot of Maureen's tea, who hovered in the background keeping a motherly eye on Sean.'

'Working away. Smoking like a chimney.' He said when I enquired after his mother. About the tiff you mentioned, between her and Charlie? You were saying Charlie told you he wanted no more contact. Well, basically, Patricia, that's up to Charlie.'

I promised to convey as much.

'About Charlie's transition from borstal to training school?' Sean was happy to fill in the details.

'He was twelve or thirteen at the time. Out of Fallowfield, when this day he was spotted by a patrol as he was walking down the Carnmoney Road. It was the middle of the day and Charlie had just burgled two or three houses. How they knew something was up, he was wearing a man's leather jacket, the jacket down to his knees. A kid this height ...' Sean's hand, level with his chest, indicated Charlie's height. 'Watches, jewellery, money, stuffed into the pockets. The cops drove by, one saying to the other, "Hey, what's going on here?"'

Recalling a related event, Sean chuckled. 'All of us were brought in by the social services for a family conference following that burglary. So they could compile this pre-court assessment. It was when me and Charlie found out my mother was never married. There was a psychologist and a social worker and what have you: them talking about family interaction, and values, and basically all that psychology stuff. My mother was asked beforehand if she minded that there was a two-way mirror in the room. Charlie and me, we were more interested in it than anything being said. You knew there were people behind the glass watching you, and we wanted to see if we could spot the eyes. The whole session was being videoed. The next thing we knew, we're hearing my mother in her best Sunday voice going: *"Oh, yes I told my kids that me and their father was never married"*.

'Here's me and Charlie, one looking to the other, expressions going, *"well, this is news to us"* kind'a thing.

'I'll tell you this much Patricia,' Sean chuckled again. 'If someone could lay their hands on that video, it would be worth anything for training purposes these days. *A classic for how not to tell your kids their parents were never married!*'

I knew Charlie had spent time in the Maze. He'd told me about hiding out in the showers rather than join other inmates on manoeuvres. He was scathing in his comments about the IRA's military style drill imposed by the COs, believing such manoeuvres to be the height of stupidity.

'If he didn't espouse Republican ideals, what got him involved in the mêlée in the chapel in Crumlin Road?' I asked. 'Surely it was engineered by Republicans?'

'I was in the Crum at the time,' said Sean, 'serving thirty days for non-payment of a fine, so I had a ringside seat. I've always believed the prison officers had wind of trouble brewing. They were pretending segregation wasn't happening inside Crumlin Road when the dogs on the street knew it was. Loyalist and Republicans had reached a gentleman's agreement over not sharing recreational facilities. A blind eye was turned by the officers until questions were asked in Parliament. What they done was, they selected a few fall guys from the Catholic side, and put them out for recreation with the Loyalists so they could prove the point that no segregation was going on.

'That particular day, myself and another fellow had our names down for Mass, but neither one got called. I'm not pretending I'm a Mass-goer, but you know what it's like when you're inside. It's a way to meet up. About the only privilege guaranteed. So I couldn't understand why we weren't called. I believe they let only who they wanted into the chapel, and if they wanted they could have kept Charlie away. He wasn't part of any paramilitary organisation, and they knew what he was like. I think they wanted him in the middle of it for their own ends.'

Sean explained his presence in Crumlin Road. 'I was working in Germany for nine months, and had just come home. My mother, and – I suppose you'd have to call him her partner – Tommy, met me at Aldergrove; Tommy with his face bashed in. *Just what have I come back to?* I thought, feeling like getting back on the plane.

'Tommy, a Catholic, and basically a *rocket*, was ex-UDR. The man was a headcase all his life. I moved out when he moved in. He was a chronic alcoholic. Joined the UDR to impress his father. Claimed his father, who was an ex-British soldier, didn't love him enough. If it was to prove a point, Tommy took a peculiar way of going about it. Besides, half Tommy's family were out-and-out Republicans. A Catholic, joining the UDR! You'd be taken out by your own and shot for less. It appeared that the week before I arrived home Tommy had been drinking with a few of his Republican friends in a Republican bar. They started slagging off the

UDR. Saying, there wasn't enough of them being shot. Tommy took offence on behalf of the UDR. Can you imagine? Sitting with a group of IRA men in a Republican bar, and taking offence on behalf of the UDR? When the bar closed they headed to someone's house to continue drinking, and the row continued, so off Tommy went and got Charlie to come and defend him and his UDR colleagues.

'Charlie arrived and got things calmed down, and went back to whatever he was doing. Tommy went back in and continued drinking. Another argument broke out, and Tommy got hit.

'Back he went for Charlie. When they returned the fellows inside had Tommy locked out. Tommy kicked the door and it flew open. Out burst a fellow, wielding a sledgehammer. Three others behind.

'A fight started, and Charlie ended up decking all four.

'The following week I arrived home. Saw Tommy beaten up, and Charlie back in prison. What really incensed me when I attended Charlie's trial was watching those involved – people who knew our family – sitting up in the court laughing their heads off when the judge read out a sentence of three and a half years on Charlie.'

Sean, young and hot-headed, acted impetuously. 'When I witnessed what had happened to Charlie I was furious. That night I went up to the guy's house and put his windows in. Then I nicked his car. I ended up getting a restitutional order from the courts. Twelve hundred pounds compensation to the fellow for the damage I'd caused. No way, I said, am I giving this fellow money. No way, after what they done to Charlie.'

Two years later the warrant was served and Sean joined Charlie in Crumlin Road.

I glanced at my watch. The bar was getting busy. 'There's no rush. I'm here till the place closes,' he assured me, saying he appreciated my dropping in, and was grateful that somebody was taking an interest in Charlie.

'He's pretty hot at the moment.' I told Sean about the geyser incident, and promised I'd look out for him while the family let him cool.

'That's Charlie all over,' he laughed.

'Has he anything to show for his life of crime? A stash of dough hidden away?'

'His guitar is about the only thing he possesses.' Sean was beckoning to someone at the bar to come and say hello. The fellow knew Charlie and some of his mates.

'What's the story on this girl chasing after Pablo?' I asked.

'Delaney? He should be so lucky. That wee girl is some dazzler.'

'And Joe McCoy? Can anyone tell me the story there?'

'Everyone knows Provo Joe. A few Provies took him up an alleyway a while back, shot him in the knees. Antisocial behaviour, but Joe can't seem to get the message. Joe's nothing but a big *eejit*.'

12

Those two guys are sitting far too close for comfort: Charlie Conlon and Kieran O'Brien virtually billing and cooing into each other's eyes as they sat side by side in the classroom.

Then I noticed Kieran had a black eye, so I asked how he got it.

Both looked at me as if I had two heads.

'A black eye?' Kieran fluttered his lashes at Charlie. What was she on about? He had no idea. Neither had Charlie. And neither did anyone else sitting in the room. Nobody saw anything irregular about anyone's eyes.

I took a mirror from my bag, and handed it to Kieran. 'Look for yourself.'

Kieran fluttered his eyelashes in the mirror. 'A black eye?' Charlie beamed lovingly on while Kieran continued to gaze admiringly at himself in the mirror. The compact was handed back. There was no black eye.

Break time, and Joe delivered a mug of tea to Charlie and one to Kieran. Charlie's arm remained slung over the back of Kieran's chair for the duration.

I couldn't figure it out. I knew they were friends, but not this close. Kieran O'Brien, a Dubliner from a middleclass professional background, had landed-up in jail in the North when he detoured on a return flight from Amsterdam. 'Let's just put it this way,' said the officer, 'a sniffer dog took a fancy to him at Belfast International.'

Educated in one of Dublin's most prestigious private schools, Kieran charmed us all, officers included. He had formed a friendship with Charlie, but I never suspected anything intimate involved.

The class came to an end; me no closer to solving the mystery of the black eye.

So I thought I would take a rise out of Margo, a teacher colleague in whom Kieran was known to have confided.

'Margo,' I said, finding her in the staff room rinsing a cup at the sink, 'you may not like to hear this about your boyfriend, but from what I've witnessed this morning, I think you have competition. I hate to be the bearer of bad news, but I think Kieran O'Brien is gay. And moreover, I think he and Charlie Conlon might well be lovers.'

'What's got into your head, girl?' Margo spun round with the wet cup in her hand.

'They were ogling each other all morning,' I explained. 'Unfortunately I think poor Charlie might be the one most smitten. He's making all the running.'

'Why? Are you jealous?' quipped Margo.

'No, indeed,' I bantered, 'you're the one who's always expounding Kieran's charms. I'd hate to see you taken for a ride.'

'Who? What? Where's the charmer?' It was young Maeve from Admin wanting the gen on the charmer in our midst. Margo bottled out, leaving it to me to portray Kieran's attractions. I decided the best way was to walk Maeve through a classroom experience with Kieran. I placed my elbow on the table, resting my chin in my palm to support the long lingering gaze I was bestowing on Maeve. Her eyes across from me were sucked into mine.

'I love the colour of your lipstick, Maeve.' I said. It was Kieran talking. I moistened my lips with the tip of my tongue.

She moistened hers.

I believe my charm had completely captivated Maeve, when Margo broke the pair of us up.

'Your imagination's running riot,' she scoffed, 'Charlie Conlon and Kieran O'Brien lovers? You're around Magilligan far too long for your own good, Patricia.'

Back in the classroom after lunch, I got no closer to solving the mystery of the two lovebirds. Kieran was not in my afternoon class. Charlie linked up with Winston. There were no outward signs of anyone pining for anyone.

I tried to wheedle information out of Pablo, but the mystery of the lovers and the black eye remained.

It was Eugene McQuillan who finally spilled the beans. I suspect, with an eye to a flash of my credit card.

'Conlon landed a wallop on O'Brien. Did nobody tell you?'

My surprise was obvious. 'Why on earth did he hit him?'

'Threw a punch. Caught him in the eye.'

'But I thought they were friends.'

'You can be friends with Conlon,' said McQuillan, 'but you don't know Conlon.'

'Did Kieran provoke him, or what?'

'Provoke Charlie Conlon!'

'Well, did they have an argument? A dispute?' Eugene could not explain. Maybe he did not understand himself.

Kieran forgave Charlie, or so the story went, and they concocted a cover story for staff to account for Kieran's injury. But I was another matter. Charlie knew that on Tuesday morning I would be asking questions. So the cosy charade of brotherly affection in the classroom was arranged to throw me off the scent. Nobody had broken ranks, until "Big Mouth" McQuillan had to go and open his trap.

Margo was right, of course. Those guys were not gay. Margo was right about most things. A woman of clear principles, whose sense of humour matched her sense of justice, she worked diligently on behalf of the prisoners and was a great sounding block for other teachers.

When she realised Kieran was due for release before the date of examinations, she arranged that he sit his paper in an examination centre in Dublin, and had everything sorted before he left prison.

When I eventually told Charlie about my visit to the Elbow he smiled. Especially, when I described his brother as a fine upstanding young man. Days later he was first through the classroom door, anxious to show me a letter he had written. The letter was to his mother, his first communication in eighteen months, and he wanted me to read it before posting. Sean had written following my visit, promising to come and visit. Charlie was so relieved that the family had made the first move.

'Charlie,' I said, 'the letter is to your mother. Let her eyes be first to read.'

Provo Joe rolled up the leg of his jeans to show me his knee-capped knee.

'Good God, Joe,' I exclaimed watching his finger trace a ridge from knee to ankle, 'did the Provos do that to you? The pain you must have endured.'

'*Tiocfaidh ár Lá,*' said Joe, chanting the Irish Republican Army mantra, 'Our Day Will Come', while he rolled up the other leg to reveal another bullet hole.

'You're an *eejit*, Joe.'

'*Tiocfaidh ár Lá.*'

End of term, and a planned family holiday to France, with a promise to send postcards. Last day of class, I brought some family photographs in. My three girls were greatly admired, and offers of marriage declined on their behalf.

Charlie reached for one of Ronan, enquiring how his studies were progressing? What exams he was sitting? His football ambitions? Terry and Brendan focused on a Christmas-Day shot of the family around the tree. The furniture in the background was minutely examined. The telly and video recorder noted, and as quickly rejected as well past their shelf-life.

The computer? 'What room was it in?'

'It's in the ...' I stopped.

'Go on your holiday without a worry, the house'll be as you left it,' I was told, and I didn't know whether to be pleased or disappointed that my home didn't merit a break-in.

After the girls, my husband's picture came in for its share of approval.

'Looks like a *mon* who could *hould* his drink,' I was told.

And so life jogged on. End of July, the family went on holidays as planned. As promised I sent postcards, choosing each card carefully so as not to provoke the censor's wrath. I resisted one mischievous impulse, imagining Pablo's glee at receiving a saucy postcard from his teacher of a comic French couple romping *en décolleté*. Instead I chose picturesque views, saying I was looking forward to seeing them all in September.

Home again, I telephoned the prison for exam results and had every reason to be pleased. They were excellent. I bought some books, revamped my lesson plans, and looked forward to the coming term.

Until, out of the blue, the letter arrived.

The children and I were enjoying the last few leisurely mornings before school started, when I picked up the post and carried it through to the kitchen.

The brown envelope was stamped: On Her Majesty's Service. It was from the prison, and read:

Dear Patricia,

I am writing to inform you that we will not be requiring your services at Her Majesty's Prison, Magilligan, when term starts in September. A survey has been conducted amongst the prisoners, which shows a lack of uptake for the subjects you offer for the coming term. Should the situation change at a later date we will be in touch with you."

The letter was signed, "*Yours sincerely . . .*"

I turned the page over; I turned it back again. I read the contents again. To say I was gobsmacked would be an understatement. 'I don't believe this,' I said to the children, 'they've stopped my classes at the prison.'

'But they can't have, Mum,' their disbelieving looks mirroring my own incredulity.

I read the letter to them. 'But what does it mean?' they wanted to know.

'I don't know what it means other than what it says.'

'But, Mum, you loved working there,' pleaded my daughter, her little face crumpled with concern for her mother.

'I know, darling,' I consoled the troubled child.

'What's Pablo going to do without you?' was Ronan's concern.

'Pablo?' For a second I had problems remembering who Pablo was.

'What's Charlie going to do?' asked Niamh. Then a thought struck her. 'Maybe he'll really kill some of them now?' Did I detect a hint of optimism there?

'What am *I* going to do, is more to the point?'

I was genuinely baffled by the letter. It made no sense. A survey conducted on prisoners? No uptake for my subjects? Fellows half-ways through courses jacking it in? It occurred to me: were there threats?

I knew intimidation would be investigated and teachers duly warned. This had not happened.

As the morning progressed disappointment turned to hurt. And then hurt turned to anger. I had no contract of employment. Part-timers hadn't. Had I known sooner that my subjects were being phased out I could have sought other employment. Now it was late August, and how was I expected to find work?

I telephoned Susan. Then Louise rang me. I rang Margaret and she rang someone else. There was no reply from Margo. 'Not back from holidays,' Margaret believed. All had received letters confirming the date when term would commence.

So, what had *I* done wrong? I racked my brain for clues.

Then I remembered the hankie Charlie had presented to me that last day. Decorated with a hand-painted pink rose, and inscribed *Thank you Patricia*. He had commissioned another prisoner to do the art work. No big deal. Teachers frequently received this form of token from prisoners. Believing it wise to err on the side of caution, I handed it over when passing through security on my way out.

No matter how I racked my brain I could come up with no *hanging* offence. And neither could any of my colleagues.

Until Margo rang.

13

'So you got it then. I knew the letter was on its way before I left for holidays but couldn't alert you because you were away yourself. I'm just in the door.'

'How did the holiday go, Margo?'

'Great, great. And yours?'

'The same. Fantastic. But tell me. How did you know about the letter?'

'I can read upside down.'

'Amongst your many talents,' I quipped.

'So, what's your interpretation?'

'I'm mystified,' I said, 'we're all mystified, hoping you can shed some light.'

'And well you might be,' she replied, 'because I saw the survey circulated to the prisoners, and your subjects were not included. Everyone else's were; but not yours. I talked to some of the fellows when I realised what was happening, and they just assumed your classes were going ahead automatically.'

'So tell me? How can they say … ?' I was searching for words. 'How can they put it down in black and white that there was no uptake for my subjects when the subjects were never offered in the first place … ?'

'Pre-cisely,' said Margo, with deadly diction.

The think-tank, formed to agree a course of action, was of diverse view.

'It's a pity we're not in a union.'

'Ring up Labour Relations and find out where you stand.'

'You're the only Roman Catholic part-timer. Go to Fair Employment on grounds of religious discrimination.'

'Go to the top?'

'Definitely the top.'

And so it was decided, I would go no lower than the very top.

As an opening gambit, I would write a letter to The Director of Education for Prisons in Northern Ireland asking for a copy of the survey referred to in their letter to me of such-and-such a date. You have a right to see it,' Margo advised.

The letter was drafted, stamped and posted, and with fingers crossed that Jeremy in the bank would be lenient about the overdraft that financed the sojourn in France, I delayed making another trip to the Job Centre.

Meantime, Charlie and his bid for a university place were on my mind. He was disappointed, I learned, about his sociology result. So I wrote to him, saying his mocks had sent warning signals, and this was not the be all or end all of anything.

Charlie wrote back.

My girls, when they read the letter thought it "sweet". And a far cry from what they expected from some brutish thug determined on murder and mayhem.

To me the letter spoke of the distance Charlie had travelled since we first met little more than a year before.

The letter was dated August 31 1993, and came from C wing, H block 3, HMP Magilligan. It read:

Dear Patricia

Thank you for your lovely letter and card, it was good to hear from you. I gave the lads your messages and, I have to say, we were all sad to hear you won't be coming back this term, you will be missed.

I am sorry about the delay in replying to your letter, this past week or so has been a bit hectic for me. I was up in court – nothing happened – and I had my interview for university amongst other things. I gave a really bad interview, so I don't think I will be going anywhere this year. However, I will try again next year. In the meantime, I intend re-sitting the A Level Sociology, doing an A Level in English and a GCSE in Computer Studies. I'm also going to dabble a bit with French and Spanish, so hopefully all that will keep me busy until I get out. My GCSE Mathematics result is in, I got a B. I suppose I'm happy enough with that, but I was hoping for an A.

There will be no full-time education this year, so I've had to compromise my principles to get what I want, i.e, an education, and work with the system for a change, not against it. I took a job as the Library Orderly, which means I will be helping to maintain the prison, and that really galls me, especially since I've spent half my life trying to wreck it. But if I learned anything from you it's that you have to compromise sometimes. But still, ones like [John Shepard] and [Norman Wilson] better not ask me to make them tea though, because I know they won't appreciate the answer they will get!

In your letter you wrote of being proud to have been associated with my work – to date I have got three GCSEs and one A level, all grade B, not bad for one year's work – well, I am proud of myself too, but I know that without the encouragement, support and guidance you gave me none of it would have been possible. So, thank you very much for everything, Of course I understand that your association may not continue, but you have helped a great deal in pointing me in the right direction and starting me off, and that will continue. [Margo] has been brilliant, and I know I can count on her help when I need it, so everything should stay on course – I won't mind making her tea!

Ronan's results were brilliant, you weren't being a bit biased when you said he is a very bright lad. Give him my congratulations and tell him I said let's see a repeat performance with his A Levels. Thank Niamh for the card and the help she gave me letting me have her Sociology notes. I still have them, and more to the point, I'm still using them. I hope all the rest of your family are doing well.

Well, Patricia, it was a pleasure for me to have had the opportunity to get to know you and I hope the future holds nothing but happiness for you, it's what you deserve.

Fondest regards.
Charlie.

I put the letter to one side, but not without a tinge of nostalgia for the prison and the prisoners, and for the work I had so enjoyed, and found so fulfilling.

My ex-colleagues kept in contact. Messages were conveyed that, when word filtered through to Pablo that my classes had been axed he decided to get on my case: take some direct action to highlight the injustice. He did not quite know what form such action would take. A rooftop protest was on the cards. Then again, he might just "burn the whole shagging joint to the ground". It was still up in the air, but Margaret was to assure me his head was working on it. Meantime, he would embark on a letter-writing campaign. And, like me, he chose 'the top'. His top being The Secretary of State for Northern Ireland, The

Right Honourable Sir Patrick Mayhew MP.

On learning the contents of his letter, I could but pray to God the communiqué met the same fate as Charlie's crutch-request to his MP.

Fading memory allows for the dimmest recollection, yet some lines will stay with me to my grave.

"A Testimonial to her Greatness."

... this modern-day Atilla the Hun, leading her army of men out of the dark tunnels of ignorance into the bright corridors of learning and enlightenment, deserves to be put back in her job, given a rise in her pay, and better conditions of work, forthwith. THIS IS A JUST DEMAND.

The telephone call inviting me to a face-to-face in Dundonald House came within days of my letter landing on their desk.

The bureaucrat was extremely pleasant on the phone.

I was equally convivial.

She invited me to meet her.

I accepted.

She preferred Dundonald House.

I consulted a blank diary, finding a vacant slot for three on Thursday of the following week.

I put down the phone, picked it up again and reported developments, receiving further valued guidance.

'Let them do the talking, and make sure you document everything.'

'Have your own list of grievances.'

'Ask why you weren't offered professional counselling following Maxie's exposure.'

'Come on Margo.'

'Seriously Patricia. Keep it as a fallback position.'

The tipoff from the insider came on the eve of the appointment. Would I rack my brain? Think of anything I had done with a prisoner which might compromise me? In recent days, it emerged, my detractors had moved from a position of relative weakness to becoming cock-a'-hoop.

I screwed my brain. Fraternising with criminals outside work would be frowned upon. I recalled a chat with the bartender, an ex-prisoner, in a pub in Coleraine. The postcards from France: "Having a lovely time. See you in all September". I had handed over my pink hankie. I had not attempted to bring a bomb into the prison. I had phoned an MP, but they didn't know that. The afternoon in the Elbow? Sitting under the watchful eye of Maureen, washing down a cheese-and-ham toastie with tea and white wine? Sean was no criminal.

Well, whatever their game? I would use my own ammunition.

Why not mention the memo from management to part-time teachers, warning us we had a "shelf life"? That could make for an interesting exchange!

I had no reason to expect other than that the meeting would be conducted in a friendly and proper manner. We had met previously. In my opinion The Lady would be fair.

Coffee and biscuits were at hand.

'No, the traffic wasn't bad at all,' I was declining another custard cream. She liked what I was wearing. Black and white, she said, suited me. I was on the verge of returning the compliment when she chose that moment to reveal that no survey of my subjects had been conducted amongst the prisoners.

'You knew?' she said.

'Yes. I knew.'

'I suspected as much.'

Digging in a blue manila file, her lips pursed, she extracted the survey, and smiled wryly.

This upfront admission put the ball firmly in her court. I raised my briefcase on to the desk and slid out some papers, arranging them in order.

She picked us her coffee cup and cradled it in the palm of her hand.

A problem shared, is a problem halved. I read it in her eyes as she pressed the warm cup to her bosom.

So what? I felt. *A lie has been told about a survey. And a lie is a lie.* The message in my eyes was equally clear.

'There are problems, as you may well know,' she conceded.

Yes, we both knew there were problems, and what those problems were. I said my bit, she said hers. But why me? What had I done wrong?

Maybe I had been critical of administration. If I had, it had been in relation to paperwork. Making phone calls to the Department from my own home to ensure exam registration. That could not be construed as a sacking offence. Or could it?

'No.'

She searched for a tissue. Took her glasses off. Polished them. Rummaged in the file for another printout. Consulted it. 'You were pushing very much on the qualifications front,' she remarked.

'I thought that was the idea,' I replied.

Her next remark surprised me; thankfully Margo had prepared me. 'You have a significant number of Roman Catholics in your classes. A lot more than in the classes of other teachers.'

'Is anyone monitoring numbers of Protestants attending Protestant teacher classes?' I responded, which put an end to that line of questioning.

'Charlie Conlon gave you a handkerchief. I see you handed it in.'

Phew . . . Big Brother really is watching.

Charlie Conlon's Open University application? She could not see why Charlie was denied funding.

If *she* could not see, who could? I asked myself.

We moved to issues on *my* list.

At this juncture she realised she should have been taking notes, and with my indulgence set about righting the oversight. In support of the record she consulted her blue file to ensure she had covered all points. These notes would be typed up and sent to me for approval.

Indications were that the formal business of the meeting was drawing to a close. Save for the apology.

She checked her notes one last time, adding comments here and there.

She looked at me. And I looked at her. She pulled forward the manila file.

'Patricia ...' she said, her hand hovering over the blue dossier.

'Yes,' I said expectantly.

'There is something I should ask you.' Her eyes were focused on the file, her voice less certain than before.

'Ask me?' I asked, waiting to be asked.

She cleared her throat; then obviously backing down, 'No, I shouldn't.'

Was it my place to say, 'Oh, come on?' I thought not.

She appeared to have second thoughts. Fished a document from the file, and laid it on the desk between us. Unlike Margo, I was not proficient at the upside-down reading.

As our eyes met, a weird sensation was starting to creep up my spine. 'Patricia,' she said, finally taking the plunge, 'it is reported here that you kissed a prisoner.'

And that, let me confess, fairly knocked the snot off me.

I repeated the charge in stunned disbelief. 'I kissed a prisoner! You say I kissed a prisoner?'

'That is what is reported here.'

'Who reported that I kissed a prisoner?'

'It came from the prison.'

'It came from the prison,' I repeated, parrot style.

'Yes. It came from the prison.'

I should have asked, did the prisoner complain?

Instead. I felt I was having one of your near-death-experiences, with my life flashing before my eyes. Charlie appeared, sitting with his scalded foot on a chair beside me. In quick succession came Pablo serenading his lady-love round the room. Philip rushed past with a master-key to a bedroom. Billy's trousers lay at my feet, while Maxie Mitchell struggled with a faulty zipper. McQuillan was in the act of raising a pint to me when blip, blip, blip ... Kieran O'Brien appeared on the scene.

'Can I guess where you may be coming from?' I regained my composure, having decided that cross-examination was not the woman's forte. Any guess, I reckoned, would be welcome. 'I wonder are we talking about Kieran O'Brien? That last day prior to his release? In the library?'

I was getting warm.

'You'll see his name on the list as one of my exam entrants.' She lowered her eyes to the file, grateful for the diversion. 'Kieran was released before the exam date, but Margo arranged that he sit it at an outside centre. All those arrangements were in place beforehand.'

I played up Kieran as the model prisoner, omitting, of course, any reference to sniffer dogs, or to his other *charms*. I painted this picture of a frightened youth from the Republic in custody in the North, surrounded by Loyalists. How terrified he was of his environment. How respectful he was towards officers. How they, in turn, reciprocated, and the good example this set for others. And, I was telling no lie. 'I'm prepared to put my hands in the air,' I continued, 'perhaps Kieran felt an affinity with me, a fellow Southerner. And that was why he gave me a farewell peck on the cheek in the library his last day. Maybe he did the same with other teachers? I don't know.'

She was listening. Still she was waiting.

'I suppose what happened next could have been avoided, and again I'm prepared to put my two hands up. Paul Delaney – everyone calls him Pablo – was present for the farewell, and, him being Pablo, wanted in on the act. He turned to me with this hung-dog expression saying, "You'd kiss him, but you wouldn't kiss a *nigger*".'

'Perhaps I felt there was a sting in the barb. Perhaps I didn't think at all. Maybe it was the puss on the fellow's face made me bend down, tousle his hair, and give him a peck, telling him to keep taking the pills. It's the way we all handle Pablo. Except, he probably went back to the wings boasting his teacher had kissed him.'

'And that was all that happened?'

'That was it.'

'In that case, Patricia, you didn't have to explain a thing.'

She was back fishing in her manila file. 'A letter arrived from an admirer of yours some days ago,' she said. 'Where are we? Yes. Here we are. Paul Martin Delaney. Will I read it to you?' She was already picking out a few choice phrases.

'Please, please, Marianne, spare me,' I begged.

Although I left Dundonald House that afternoon in the sure knowledge that I was to be reinstated and compensated for loss of earnings, still the victory felt hollow. On the drive home I felt a resurfacing of the first feelings I had when I received that letter. I had figured out what my sin was before I even set foot in Dundonald House. I had pushed on the qualifications front. Rocked a boat that was getting along nicely just treading water. I was not the main force behind the drive for excellence in education – my limited contract ensured as much – but I was a supporter of those who were, and I was the softer target. *Kissing a prisoner? My foot!* Using that tactic was nothing more than a cheap manoeuvre, employed at the eleventh hour to prop up a shabby excuse to justify getting rid of a niggling annoyance.

"You go with the flow in here," the prisoner had advised. Maybe life would have been easier had I taken his advice.

14

Following my trip to Dundonald, we shook hands on the past and life continued as before.

It would be gratifying to report that my return was greeted with jubilation by the prisoners. Such was not the case. My reappearance coincided with one of Pablo's *happy days*.

'All right, sweetheart?' he greeted me, Joe in a semi-stupor lolling in the chair beside him.

I glanced at the faces around the table. Couldn't care less whether or not I had the jar of coffee. Couldn't care less if I had that moment landed from Mars. If I told them the prison gates were lying wide open, I doubt they'd have had the inclination to drag themselves through. A spliff was doing the rounds. Eugene McQuillan, his two eyes out like a croaking frog, having his turn.

'I thought you were supposed to be out of here by the time I got back?' I said.

'Out?' The fellow had no idea where "out" was.

The heady atmosphere eventually drove me from the room. The pungent aroma followed me to the kettle, where Charlie Conlon sat chatting with the librarian. He had been offered a university place, deferred until the following year. Winston had already taken up his offer. Charlie's co-accused, Rab McConville, was still AWOL, the case going ahead without him.

The reason Charlie hadn't come into the classroom involved another prisoner. Mickey "Money Bags" Mooney, the godfather of drug dealers in the North. The pair were at daggers drawn.

Later, reading of Mooney's untimely death, I saw that Charlie was credited as the only person who had ever taken Mooney on physically, and won. At age 34 Mooney was later shot dead in the centre of Belfast, the first murder claimed by the IRA using the cover name, Direct Action Against Drugs.

Re-establishing my teaching programme took some time. Meanwhile, selected prisoners were allowed one-to-one tutorials. First day Charlie arrived for his special class I thought the fellow had gone bonkers. He was distracted, nervous, edgy, perspiring profusely, no longer projecting the hard-man image. I was curious about him and Mooney and asked about the hostility between the two.

Charlie bristled. Nobody scared him!

I ventured further, asking if he was very disappointed about not being at liberty to take up his university place, seeing as how he'd worked so hard.

Achieving good grades had given him an enormous boost, but his new found confidence was slipping away. When the university offer came through he'd hoped for early release. Why Winston, who had defrauded a vast amount of money compared with his paltry gains, why was he let out early? Why not him? The sociology result had been disappointing, and that was very much on his mind. Some officers had made sneering remarks. "Thinking he was better than others. Thinking he was heading to university". Mooney's crowd had sneered as well.

He missed working with Winston. At the end of the day he was just one of the lads, and prison was the only place where he had any control. You needed a hard attitude, he stated.

'Maybe you should talk more about these feelings,' I suggested. 'Find a way to ignore taunts.'

'You're on your own, Patricia.'

'You're not, Charlie. Look how the teachers have helped you.'

'And look what they done to your classes for you helping me.'

'You have a goal now and should hold your head high. Leave the past behind. Move on. Mooney doesn't matter.'

Gradually the tough veneer began to crumble, and little by little he talked about his early years. He was eight years old when he went to Fallowfield. When he witnessed his first debauched act. His introduction to sexual depravity. He was concerned he might be upsetting me as he struggled to describe a scene, using gestures rather than language to communicate; taking me to a place it was painful for him to revisit, and to a sight it was equally painful for me to see.

'No. No, it's fine, I can listen,' I assured him, thinking if this grown man has no language to communicate such an awful experience, how might an eight-year-old child look for help?

'But there is no shame for you in what you tell me. And, no, Charlie. I promise, I will never talk about what you are telling me.' One promise I am certain to keep, because like Charlie back then, I do not have the words now, and even if I had, they would be too painful and too impossible for me to use. Save to say, it was his strength saw him through, physically unscathed. Teeth, head, fists, feet. 'You fought back,' he explained. 'You acquired a reputation, and others started relying on you.' Eventually wee lads came to depend on him. He 'minded' them all. He feared nobody.

But I had only to look into those startled eyes to know that that past had coloured his world forever more. He had left nothing behind. Being kicked around like a dog because of his colour would never break him; just made him more determined.

'Have you talked with anybody before about any of this?'

He handled things his own way.

Everything about Fallowfield was not bleak. There were some decent people on the staff; people who genuinely tried. He was made a prefect early on. Put in charge of his dorm. Some boys wet their beds. That kind of thing went on all the time. It was his responsibility to get boys up at night. One of his charges was mentally retarded. Everybody stole. Everybody bullied someone else. You could run away but they knew where to find you. His face brightened as he remembered something else. A Queen's University psychology student coming in to conduct an experiment for his thesis. One of the questions: "If you could take another boy home with you for the weekend, who would it be?" And they all wanted to bring *me* home with them. *Me!'*

Other boys had visitors. He never had. His mother came once, but only when she was sent for. Money had gone missing and he got blamed, but he had not stolen the money. 'You'd expect your own mother to be on your side, wouldn't you? You'd be on Ronan's side if someone down at his school accused him of something he never done? If someone in authority told my mother something, whether it was right or wrong, she'd never challenge. She went along with everything other people said. I might as well have taken that money.'

He was not trying to cover things up. He did nick stuff. He was ashamed, especially taking his brother's Action Man and selling it on the street. He was sure Sean must have hated his guts by times.

'All right,' he conceded, 'I may have said hard things blaming my mother, but then again she was just compliant, and they used her. She was a good, decent person.' All his people, he repeated, were upright, hardworking people, and again the question was, so why was he any different?

'Maybe,' I suggested, noticing his spirits lift, 'it would do no harm to talk to a professional.'

'Talk to a professional? It's too late for any of that stuff. I'm like an electric cable with the outer coating stripped away. Anybody touches the exposed wires and they are in for one severe shock.'

'But Charlie,' I made a last plea.

'Patricia,' he said, 'nobody re-moulds damaged cable.'

Charlie's trial went ahead without Rab. (I understand the two cases: Conlon *v* the NIO and the NIO *v* Conlon, entered a plea-bargain arrangement.) Charlie would be out in time to take up his university place the following year. He reckoned he still had a margin to play around with: twenty-eight days loss of remission and he would still make the deadline for university registration.

Was it my sixth sense? Before asking, I already knew the answer.

'Why is Charlie not across with the rest of you this morning?' Pablo could no longer avoid meeting my eyes.

'He's in solitary.'

I was incredulous. 'Is somebody having me on? It's the first of December, not All Fool's day.'

'On a charge of injuring a screw. The whole thing's crazy, I know, but you know Charlie yourself.'

'How could he be so stupid?' I was genuinely disbelieving.

'You go and talk to him,' Pablo's coaxed.

'He'll listen to you,' others tried to convince me.

'But I can't just barge up to the punishment block and announce that I want in.'

They were not convinced. 'Look, ask one of the screws up at the desk to ring down and tell the screws down below to let you in.'

'And you think the officers will jump to my demands?'

Nothing would convince them otherwise. I had *clout*, they said. If only I would go up to the desk and ask, I would be let in to see Charlie in lockup.

Their version of weekend events aroused my curiosity. I would like to hear Charlie's excuse, if excuse there could be. Maybe I would approach the officer after all. Maybe I could hand in some education material.

'I'll ring down for you ma'am,' the officer unlocked the door to the cubby hole and lifted the phone.

I did not hold my breath.

'The SO says, twelve-thirty is lockdown, and you're to get yourself down well before.'

'Where do I go? Or what must I do to get in?'

With instructions clear, I returned to the class, and reported progress.

Instantly they were on Charlie's case. 'Bring him this,' somebody was pushing a pouch of tobacco across the table towards me; others set to rolling joints. I overheard someone say, 'they'll not search *her*.'

'No way,' I warned. 'I hear what you're up to.'

'It's only a wee bit of auld backie.' Joe tried to persuade me.

I agreed to have a packet of regular cigarettes in my handbag, but only if I could see where they came from. Billy handed over his pack of Silk Cut.

A pen. Paper. Books. 'Bring two or three pens,' the call went out. They scurried around and loaded me up.

I rattled the gate before noticing the buzzer. I buzzed, and waited. An Alsatian in a pen stretched its neck and growled. I did not dare buzz again. Eventually an officer came and opened the gate. I showed my pass, and followed him inside.

'Conlon's in ablutions,' Senior Officer Wilks informed while checking my bag. 'Wait in there.' In there was a small kitchen.

I recognise the orderly. 'Is this where you're hiding yourself these days, Fred?' I asked.

An officer standing at the sink was sorting out his lunchbox. Conlon should be out of the showers any minute,' he said.

'How are the ribs, Fred?' I asked, passing him a Silk Cut when the officer left us alone. Fred's present circumstances were a far cry from the days he taught classes of young boys.

'Oh, fine, fine. No problem.' He put the Silk Cut behind his ear.

The officer was back, another with him; Conlon was back in his cell. Follow them. 'I'll check if he's respectable,' the officer said, lifting a flap on the cell door and calling in: 'Conlon. Teacher to see you.'

Charlie was sitting on an iron-frame bed. The radio was on. A blue bakelite mug sat on the floor beside the bed. I marveled at the Cardinal Red floor; hadn't seen a shine like it in years. There was a chamber pot sitting in the corner.

'I've brought you some work, Charlie,' I greeted him.

He removed some items of clothing from a chair. 'Hold on a minute,' he instructed, lifting the radio off the windowsill. He turned up the volume before planting it in the open doorway. The sound would drown out conversation. A glance sent a message to the two officers, backs to the wall outside: *I'm king of this castle.*

I had a general idea what I was about to hear. He had been in the canteen with other inmates, all complaining about the quality of the food, which, in their opinion, was crap; wouldn't feed it to pigs much less humans. To emphasise just how rotten the food was, Charlie lifted a lid off a food-container and slammed it down, clipping the side of an officer's face. He sat down with his mates, thought about what he'd just done, got up and apologised to the officer. The officer accepted the apology; there was no great harm done to anybody.

However, the incident was reported, and some time later Charlie was told to ready himself, he was being removed to the PSU, charged with assaulting an officer on duty.

Judging by other incidents, Charlie believed his misdeed did not merit such severe punishment. Perceiving another injustice, he 'lost the head. Picked up the TV in the recreation room and flung it at the wall.'

Under prison rules the Board of Visitors had sanctioned his detention in the PSU for a period of one month.

'So this is serious then if the BOV are involved,' I said. 'How long will it take to arrange the adjudication? And does it mean you will be spending Christmas in solitary confinement?'

'Christmas?' said Charlie. 'What's Christmas?'

'Charlie … have you no thought for yourself, or for others who believe in you?'

He cast his eyes to the floor. He pinched the corners, but not hard enough.

'I'm very, very sorry Patricia.' he said. 'I've let you down.'

'I didn't deliberately hit the man,' he endeavoured to explain. 'The lid scratched him. Yes, I admit. But it was accidental. I was angry, and wasn't watching.'

'Angry about what?'

'About the slop they're serving us for food.'

'But you've eaten the same "slop" most of your life.'

'And I've felt no different about it all my life.'

'But why, at this of all times, start making stands and hitting out?'

'You can only take so much.'

'They told me outside, your first night over you went on hunger strike.'

'I refused food at the start. But I went back eating when I saw it only gave them satisfaction to see me hungry.'

'What were you trying to prove by going on hunger strike?'

'I didn't go on hunger strike. When they brought me over I lay on the bed, just wanting to be left alone. I didn't want to eat. That was all. I knew I'd let myself down. Then that so-called SO above at the desk, when he seen me not eating he came to the door and sneered in: "*I see you're enjoying your hunger strike, Conlon", and* I jumped up and flung that piss-pot at him. I'm not proud of it, but they know how to wind me up.'

I enquired about charging procedures; worried what might yet be added to the list before he got the length of any adjudication.

'I've done my three days loss of privileges, and I've got the radio back. But I'm not having anything to do with the BOV because they'll have their minds already set.'

The officers outside were becoming restless. One put his head in the door. 'It's feeding time in five minutes, ma'am.'

'I'll do my best to come back on Thursday,' I promised Charlie, omitting to pick up the packet of Silk Cut off the bed.

15

In recent months I had been appointed to the Board of Visitors at Maghaberry prison, a sister body to the one adjudicating on Charlie at Magilligan. Although I had yet to visit the segregated unit, or serve on an adjudication panel, it was the Members' Guidelines I consulted for information on how to advise Charlie.

Those guidelines did not make for encouraging reading. If the governor felt that "the prisoner's presence on the wings was a threat to security, or interfered in any way with the maintenance of good order and discipline throughout the prison, a case would be made to the BOV to continue sanctioning solitary confinement." Even more worrying: Charlie's infringement of rules – assaulting an officer on duty – ranked amongst "serious incidents". In which case, it was within the remit of the BOV to grant three months' loss of remission. Charlie, with twenty-eight days leeway before registration, might well be bidding goodbye to university.

'Project a positive image to the panel at your adjudication,' I was advising Charlie on my next visit to the PSU. 'Show the better side of your character.'

'No, Patricia.' He was not going to participate in the adjudication. He would not be party to any charade.

'Anything is worth a try,' I encouraged. The members of that panel will be ordinary citizens like myself.' (The prisoners, aware of my appointment, were not overly impressed that I was helping to maintain the system.)

'Patricia . . .' Searching to find words so as not to offend me, he explained. 'I don't deny these people are decent people, but at the end of the day they will do what the system put them there to do. It's all-the-one in the end. They have a tariff, and they'll not move from that tariff.'

'Charlie? Would I give up my time to come in here to be used as a rubber stamp? What, with your history, I don't deny they might have no compunction throwing the book at you, but at least give them the opportunity to hear both sides. Others have a duty to see justice done as well as yourself, you know. So, please Charlie ...'

Still, I had one last trick up my sleeve. Prison Rules state that a prisoner could request a McKenzie friend at adjudication. This McKenzie friend might not participate or intervene, but could prompt, remind; just be there to offer moral support. The request might not be granted, but it was worth exploring. It could be another prisoner, a probation officer, a Chaplain … It was the prisoner's call.

'Or me, Charlie?'

Charlie thought about what I said. And we were in business.

Charlie's request was granted and the date for the adjudication set for two weeks hence. Provision was made for the prisoner to consult with his McKenzie friend. His McKenzie friend had just one piece of advice. 'Throw yourself at their mercy.'

Meanwhile, my trips to the PSU continued.

Reading about a problem might not cure, but it might help. The SO leafed through a psychology tome – searching, I assume, for contraband – I through might interest Charlie.

'I wish you luck,' he said, handing the book back.

If only I could set Charlie thinking. Tentatively, I suggested there was something wrong; asking why he lashed out on the least provocation, where the blind rages came from? 'These acts,' I told him, 'have all the hallmarks of some uncouth thug bent on mayhem. That is not the person I see in you Charlie. But I have never been subjected to your fury like some of those officers outside have, and the truth is, Charlie, they are afraid of you.'

'Yes, Patricia, and that's how it's going to stay, let me tell you.' He was leafing through the book.

'Won't you let the experts in?'

'Experts here!' he looked at me in horror. 'I learned everything I know from the likes of them ones. They're experts here at using any information they can unearth to your detriment. I cooperated in the past when they done up a psychologist's report on me. Instead of help, you had ordinary-rank screws, who couldn't even read their own names much less a psychologist's report, predicting I'd kill someone. '*One day that fellow'll kill someone. We saw it in his file. A psychologist wrote it. We know''. Bla bla bla …*'

'Does such a report exist?' I asked those I thought should know.

Nobody knew anyone who knew anything about anything. But, following a presentation by an in-house psychologist to the BOV at Maghaberry, I stayed behind for a word. I learned that by today's rules, a psychologist's report would form part of medical records. Other than the medical profession nobody else had access to those records.

Could Charlie be persuaded to trust a second time?

Charlie and his McKenzie friend were allowed last-minute consultation before his adjudication. We had a smoke to steady our nerves. (I had taken up serious smoking again.)

Word came through. Our BOV panel awaited us.

A large table dominated the tiny Portakabin. We squeezed in opposite the panel: chairman, two panellists, and one observer. An officer sat either side of Charlie and me – in case the prisoner made a lunge for someone, I suppose.

Like every good story, things got off to a flying start. Charlie answered to his name and number. The charges were read: Injuring an officer and destroying prison property. The TV was specified, but not the chamber pot.

I had been led to believe, by both Charlie and his mates, that the officer had only sustained a scratch. Here, the facts, as presented, had the injured party leaving his duty-station with blood pouring down his face and uniform.

Whispering was out of the question because of the nearness of the panel.

'Send for Officer Jacks,' the chairman called.

As a consequence of the assault, Officer Jacks was on sick leave, and therefore not available to give evidence.

'Were there witnesses to the incident?' asked the chairman.

There was one witness. Officer Jones. Officer Jones was available to give evidence. Officer Jones came in. He read a prepared statement. It agreed with the charging officer's statement, with one exception. There was no mention of the spilling of blood.

'Was the cut on Officer Jacks' face bleeding?' asked the chairman. 'Did you see any blood?'

'No,' Officer Jones replied. 'Nobody was bleeding.'

'You saw no blood on Officer Jacks' face?'

'No. There was no blood. I saw no blood.'

Officer Jones glanced to the officers either side of Charlie and I. *Help me out here.*

'Do you want to question the witness?' the chairman asked the prisoner.

Charlie asked his first question. 'You saw no blood?'

'No,' the officer grudgingly agreed, hesitant to answer to the bidding of a prisoner.

'You saw me go up and apologise afterwards?' Charlie explained how he got up from his seat, walked up to Officer Jacks and offered an apology.

'I saw you go up and say something. I didn't hear what you said.' Officer Jones's self assurance was returning. 'It could have been anything you said. How was I to know?'

The chairman turned his eyes towards the prisoner, inviting more questions to the witness.

'No,' Charlie did not wish to question the witness any further. Nor did he wish to call any witnesses on his own behalf. Instead he reiterated the facts as he saw them. He was unequivocal. The accident happened. There was no blood. He expressed regret. He did not grovel. It was a dignified performance, as I later told him. Formal proceedings were at an end, except for consideration of the guilty or innocent verdict.

The McKenzie friend might remain in the room during deliberations. The prisoner was led out and an officer brought in a file: a record of similar breaches of discipline going back in time. We were then joined by a governor who presented a character profile of the prisoner. It was my turn to be surprised.

'Problems? Yes. Problems? Plenty.' But in the main the governor spoke of a civil, courteous, well-mannered prisoner, although qualified by 'in my dealings with him.' Reports from the wings, he added, showed Charlie getting along quietly with his studies.

Taking everything into consideration, the panel decreed there was no getting around the facts. The prisoner had lost his temper, injured a prison officer, and caused damage to prison property. They consulted their tariff. Charlie was escorted back into the room. The "loss of remission award", brought his adjusted release date to within two days of university registration.

Following proceedings, Charlie was allowed a few minutes for debriefing with his McKenzie friend.

We had time for another smoke, before he was called away for feeding.

Charlie agreed to a meeting with the psychologist, conditional on consultations being conducted in private. No humiliation. No one else to know. 'It will be the end,' he warned, 'if any officer throws this in my face.'

Sessions went well. He was given material about techniques to control reflex action. He applied these techniques and monitored his own progress, pleased with the outcome. There was nothing grievously wrong with him, he was told, nothing that could not be fixed. Encouragement for someone so paranoid, and so very, very mistrustful.

This did not mean he was not still in control, he cautioned. Anyone who showed a lack of respect would be met with an equal lack of respect by him. I was surprised when, after a few sessions, he reported that was it. So, how was it so simple? And how come something similar had not been tried before? Reservations remained, leaving lingering doubts that a person so stuck in the traumatic memories of his childhood could progress before deeper issues were addressed. But, like Charlie said, the techniques seemed to work.

I asked questions at board level regarding the provision of psychology facilities throughout the prison service, and was told that existing services were stretched to the absolute limit. The needs of staff took precedence; the suggestion being that the psychological effect of working in the prison service during the Troubles produced such a high level of emotional stress, the subsequent drain on resources to cater for staff needs meant access to psychological therapies for prisoners was severely limited.

Before the summer recess, and the end of my teaching days at Magilligan, Pablo made one final effort to improve the lot of the teachers. On his way back from the gym, he spotted a Tin God from Dundonald House walking between blocks.

'Hey dude!' he hollered into the prevailing wind, his hand cupped to amplify the call. 'Why are yous fat cats up in the NIO cutting down on the teachers' pay?' quoting verbatim some recent development affecting teachers, and telling the guy to get on his bike and do something about it, pronto. Get it sorted, or else!

Tin God from Dundonald House was not about to allow a cat-burglar to accost him in the course of his duty. This much was related to me in the staff room. Also, that a tribunal of enquiry had been established with the remit to investigate teacher misconduct: "Alleged collusion between part-time teachers and inmates on pay and conditions of service". A directive had been circulated compelling all teachers to appear.

Despite what anyone said, I knew I was prime suspect.

The hearing was in the Portakabin where Charlie's adjudication took place.

'I'm the prime suspect,' I said, squeezing in before my inquisitors.

At least the governor had the good grace to smile.

'There are no suspects here, Mrs Farren,' he said, glancing towards the blue manila file on the table.

Only the condemned! I hardly needed remind him.

When he left, Pablo asked that no tears be shed. He would keep in touch. And true to his word, late one night:

'Mum, are you awake?' I struggled to consciousness. 'Did you not hear the phone ringing downstairs? Some cowboy looking for you. The guy kept calling me his mate, and his friend. Saying what a great ma I had. He told me not to wake you. Said you needed your beauty sleep. Then he told me to go back to bed myself and dream some happy dreams. He kept repeating, "Happy days my friend".

'Is he some friend of yours Mum, or is he just mad, or what?'

It was time served for others. Some I never heard of again, but I managed to keep tabs on a few. I met a man from Portadown whom I recognised from Nigel Blackman's description of a relative injured in an IRA attack. Nigel, I learned, had 'married a wee girl from the Free State,' and had two or three children.

Miss O'Shaughnessy's fate remains unknown. No other prisoner, to my knowledge, especially from within the group who attended the *viewing* in Visits, sought out an American penfriend.

Eugene McQuillan was released just in time to attend a crunch Gaelic game, predicting: 'Ballyferrit minors are about to bate the shite out'a Mullaghhoran in a friendly this coming Sunday'.

'We'll keep our fingers crossed, Eugene,' I promised.

A guy with raven black hair, called 'Black & Decker', appeared on the scene to occupy Eugene's vacant seat. 'Took a chainsaw to the wife,' the explanation given for the alias.

Pablo phoned again. This time he was on honeymoon.

'Hold on,' he said, 'and I'll put Julie on.'

So pleased with life was Julie, she could hardly speak from giggling. She handed the phone back to Pablo. 'Happy days,' he giggled, and I could but speculate that whatever was delighting one, was delighting the other equally.

PART TWO

MAGHABERRY

16

It was in 1993 I received a call from the Anglo-Irish Secretariat asking if I would consider an appointment to the Board of Visitors (BOV) of Maghaberry prison. My name had been selected from a panel drawn up to redress persistent imbalances in public appointments in Northern Ireland.

I understood the Board to be a totally independent watchdog, charged with safeguarding the rights and well-being of all prisoners. There were no specific qualifications required. The commitment called for energy, dedication and considerable free time. I knew the insides of one prison. I had first-hand knowledge of the various components that kept the place in gear. Getting involved at BOV level might afford me the opportunity to help people from diverse backgrounds during difficult times in their lives. Apart from which, the opportunity could only develop my understanding of the marginalised and the misunderstood.

Beyond reimbursement of travelling expenses and a meagre subsistence allowance there was no other monetary compensation. The appointment was for a period of three years, which might be renewed for three further periods of equal length. It came at a time in the troubled history of Northern Ireland when any name going forward from the Secretariat raised eyebrows as to the *agenda*.

I said yes.

A vast, sprawling establishment, Maghaberry opened its doors in 1986. The complex held male and female prisoners, men occupying four blocks, or houses: Bann, Erne, Foyle and Lagan. Females were housed in Mourne House.

My appointment allowed for access to all areas of the prison, day and night. Wherever interest brought me I was free to go. Conversations with prisoners might be conducted out of the hearing of officers. And, I was assured, the governor's door was always open.

Historically Maghaberry operated an "integrated" regime, where inmates from all persuasions and none were expected to conform and share common facilities, as distinct from the situation in the Maze prison where inmates from the North's different communities with their mutually hostile political sympathies were housed apart. Forced to live cheek-to-jowl in Maghaberry, some awaiting transfer to the Maze, Republicans and Loyalists did not make for cosy bedfellows.

Mourne House accommodated the North's entire female offender population: remand, sentenced, and young offenders. Mourne also acted as a mini-Maze for female paramilitaries granted their right to be housed separately from ordinary prisoners, or "social prisoners", as the Republicans branded the ODCs

There were tensions and pressures everywhere, which made for interesting visiting.

Had my move from teaching in one prison to active membership on the BOV of another developed into a case of out of the frying pan into the fire? During my teaching days in Magilligan I formed many new friendship so, when I moved on, it was no great surprise to find some familiar faces moving with me. From time to time a head would pop out in Erne or Bush, Bann or Lagan and shout, 'How's about ya, Tricia!'

On one visit, it took a moment to figure out the face of Terry Maguire grinning at me from a cell doorway.

'I expected yourself and the boys would to be in Kuwait by now,' I said, accepting the invite into his cell. Have you brought your mates in with you Terry?'

'Ouch, for fuck's sake, Tricia.'

I was offered a chair. 'Tea? Coffee? But hold it till I get you a decent cup from the screw on the landing.' He came back shaking water from the cup, 'I fuckin' screwed it up. But sure what the fuck. You don't want to know the half.'

His mates were not involved. Last time it was joyriding. Now it was bald tyres, faulty brakes, no tax, insurance or driver's licence. 'You have to make a fuckin' living at the end of the day, don't ya?' Needing transport for work, Terry could afford the banger, but not the extras.

My notebook was an open invitation to make a complaint. 'And I'm going to tell you another thing, Tricia. Things have deteriorated in here since the last time I was in, so they have. If things doesn't start to happen soon, this whole fuckin' place is going to fuckin' explode one of these days. So it is.'

Board meetings were conducted under the watchful gaze of the Monarch.

Sixteen of her loyal subjects gathered in the boardroom, in the presence of her gilded portrait, unselfishly committing their time and energy to her service.

Teddy and I bonded right off. Teddy had a good strong voice, one that carried right up to HM's feet, but when Teddy heard my Southern brogue, he decided that this was a voice he could put to some effect.

'Don't forget to ask the governor' he prompted, 'about the allocation of jobs in kitchens.'

'But, I thought you were going to raise …'

He stopped me. 'No. It's far better coming from the likes of you. Question why there are disproportionate numbers of Roman Catholics in sought-after work areas? Raise what Mooney reported the other day: twelve prisoners allocated work in kitchens. Of those twelve, only two Roman Catholics?'

Teddy and I had bumped into Robbie Mooney on a rota visit. He told us he had been monitoring allocation of work, and claimed that all the popular jobs were being allocated to Protestants. 'Catholics are being discriminated against,' he stated. 'So what's the BOV going to do about it?'

We checked with Job Allocations. 'When prisoners get into the kitchen they tend to stick,' said the officer. 'Our policy is to replace like with like. The two Roman Catholics there are lifers. I'm afraid Mooney's chances are slim.'

The governor glanced over his half-moon specs to identify the speaker. The situation with job allocations was not simple, he told me, giving a convoluted explanation of the complexities of the problem.

I had no follow-on question, so I elbowed Teddy, who said, 'This is a very serious issue Patricia has just raised, governor. Should we not be looking into it in greater depth?'

The governor made a note while Teddy shoved a print-off of the prison population and their religious affiliations, alongside work assignment, across to me, whispering, 'Good for you, you've rattled them. I've been banging on about the same thing for ages, but they don't take a blind bit of notice because I'm a Prod. But coming from the likes of you!'

The chairperson was anxious to move to the next item, but Teddy interjected. One more point. What you say is all very well, Governor, but what do you make of the figures Patricia dug out?'

'It appears to me,' I was quoting from the areas Terry had highlighted in yellow on the print-out, 'yes statistically Catholics have their share of work, but not in *popular* locations. Kitchen is twelve work places, two allocated to RCs. Visits, even worse: eight places, one RC. Working-out teams: nil RC. Your figures take a holistic view, and relate to the religious divide of the North. Whereas mine, relate to the population of this prison, which is currently fifty-fifty.'

The point I was missing, I was informed, was security. Only reliable prisoners could be allocated to *sensitive* work locations. 'Not every prisoner is suitable for kitchen work: proximity to knives.'

'Are Loyalists safer around knives than Republicans?' I asked.

Strip-searching of female prisoners was another sticking point. I was still on that learning curve and regularly put my foot in it. Naively I raised an incident that occurred before my appointment.

A child, on a weekend visit to its mother in the Republican wing of Mourne, was overheard by an officer remarking to a friend, "My mammy's got a gun". Forty-eight hours elapsed before the matter was reported and a blanket strip-search of all female prisoners ordered, with the BOV invited to send in observers.

The remands, sentenced and young offenders couldn't care less and readily complied. But all hell broke loose when the searchers moved on to the Republican wing. Refusing to comply, the women barricaded themselves in, and fought the searchers tooth and nail. They were wrestled to the ground, and their clothing forcibly removed. The chain of events that followed made it into the media.

Guidelines for BOV observers recommend maintaining a distance. Their role: to observe, not to intervene. One observer left the scene after a short period, her obvious distress noted by the prisoners. That snippet of information was later conveyed to the media. The media in turn contacted the observer.

What the Republicans expected was the BOV to say that they condemned outright the practice of strip-searching women in prison. This did not happen. Rather, the comments made to the media were interpreted as the BOV justifying the search insofar as it conformed to strict regulations. Consequently the Republican wing of Mourne became a no-go area for the BOV.

Except that a few stalwarts would accept no such *diktat*. Their stance was unequivocal. They would allow no *'band of harpies'* tell them where they could, or could not, visit in *their own* establishment! A long serving member of the board, Pearl, outlined the position for my benefit. Each month two members would walk those landings, sending our message home to Republicans, no prisoner would deny the BOV access.

The situation simmered on. Then an article appeared in a Church publication attacking the practice of strip-searching women in prison. A copy was tabled at our meeting, the item was introduced with an attack on the publishers of the *Gazette*. Believing the article was penned by Monsignor Denis Faul – the veteran civil rights campaigner – my ears pricked up. But, no! It was a Protestant Church publication arguing its case on humanitarian grounds. Protestants critical of Protestants! 'This from our own?'

Naively, I asked, had anyone on the board ever attempted explaining to the women that some of us were just as uncomfortable with the practice of mandatory strip-searching as the voices in the article were?

Pearl just about went ballistic. *Who is this woman amongst us?*

'But I'm only saying . . .' I attempted.

'One final point, governor,' said Teddy. 'For all intents and purposes you had a prisoner with a gun in your prison, and forty-eight hours after getting the information the prison officer thinks fit to report it. What might have happened in those intervening hours had there actually been a gun on the wing? Has disciplinary action been taken against that officer for not reporting immediately?'

The chairperson moved the meeting to the next item, while the governor made a note.

Slowly, I was finding my feet, joining forces with other members to highlight issues of mutual concern. The jobs issue had not gone away. While Mooney pursued that elusive post in kitchens, another prisoner was encountering similar problems in Visits. Sonny Devine was a Catholic, and like Mooney, was firmly of the belief that religious discrimination was 'rampant' in Maghaberry.

Daphne, a fellow BOV member, and I took up Sonny's complaint. Since he was a life-sentence prisoner we were mindful of the warning that not everyone was suitable for work in certain locations, so our first point of enquiry was a character reference from the SO on the lifer's landing.

'Apart from the fact that he killed a man,' said the SO, 'he's a lovely fellow. Just like the rest of the lovely fellows I have on this landing.'

We checked periodically with Job Allocations, feeling justified when we learned Sonny had got the coveted job. When we dropped by his cell for a progress report we expected to be greeted with a huge grin of satisfaction.

The grin was there, but not for the reasons expected.

'Oh, I got the job fair enough,' said Sonny, inviting us to be seated. 'I lasted two weeks before I was sacked.'

'You never, Sonny!' Daphne sank down on his bed in disbelief.

Forty-six pounds had gone missing: proceeds from sales of snacks and drinks to visitors. And Sonny was prime suspect.

'They can't pin a thing on me,' he assured us.

'But Sonny . . .?' Daphne's expression was one of despair.

'Because there is no *prime facie* evidence, Daphne.'

'Maybe it's time we tackled these Republican women,' suggested Teddy, encouraged, he said, by my spirited performance at our recent board meeting.

'I'm on,' I said, 'if you are. Why not present ourselves as new brooms. Apologise for what went before. Say we are coming to listen … hear their side.'

We planned our visit for the following week. But the omens were against us from the outset.

We met up at the entrance to Mourne and moved towards screening. I placed my handbag on the moving belt. The bag had a gilt chain-link strap. 'Be careful with that gold,' I joked to the officer monitoring the screen. Suddenly, *wham, bang,* the belt came to an abrupt halt as an eagle-eyed officer rushed forward. 'Is that gold?' he demanded.

'Don't be ridiculous,' I scoffed, and found I was the only one laughing.

Teddy rescued the situation before I was charged with attempting to smuggle bullion into the prison.

'The Republicans will be a walkover after that carryon,' I attempted to reassure Teddy, when, tail between my legs, I was allowed proceed.

Mourne sat in lawns of flowering shrubs and leafy trees, in stark contrast to the austerity of the men's quarters the other side of the wall. The illusion was short-lived. Exercise cages, barred windows and fortified black doors loomed ahead.

We buzzed but got no response. We tried again. Finally an officer signalled from a watchtower to try another door. Inside, we asked to be taken to the Republican wing. 'Tell their commanding officer that two members of the BOV are here to see her.'

Our request was met with stony silence. Teddy rephrased: 'Who's in charge at the minute? Would you tell her that we'd like a word?'

The officer consulted another officer. We knew who the CO was, and so did they. The pretence continued until eventually the officer walked towards a grill. We followed and were directed into the recreation room.

'Be-times they can make you feel very welcome in this place,' said Teddy.

'Can't they just,' said I.

We glanced about us, remarking on the homely atmosphere the women had created: gingham tablecloth, floral curtains, patchwork cushions, bowl of fruit in the centre of the table.

Someone was approaching. A slim female dressed in black coming down the corridor. Her footsteps stopped in the doorway. Eyes focused on some needlework she carried, her fingers working a tricky detail.

Introducing ourselves, Teddy, invited her to come and join us. She did not advance, but continued her stitching, narrowing her eyes when inserting her needle. Making certain that needle emerged exactly where she intended. 'No!' She would certainly not join us.

'Why?' I asked.

Her weasel-green eyes moved from her needlework to bore through me.

WHY! Was I stupid, or what? We were nothing but lackeys, the two of us. Pathetic tools of a corrupt establishment; the last bastion of the British Empire yet to be toppled.

Her every word was emphasised with sleight of hand. Time in prison might have robbed her of her lustre, but certainly not of her tongue. I was a traitor to the Republican cause. We were rubberstamps, while she, and let her make herself absolutely clear on this, *She* was a PRISONER

OF WAR, as were the other twenty-something women on the landing behind her.

It would have been the mercy of God had the ground opened up and swallowed me when she started chanting *Tiocfaidh ár Lá* in front of Teddy.

And finally, with a tongue sharp enough to cut thread, she ran the pair of us.

'*Crowd of harpies,*' I muttered to Teddy, passing screening on our way out.

17

Ayear had now passed since I left Magilligan, and from time to time it crossed my mind how Charlie Conlon was coping with university. The previous November he had called from a coin-box on campus, and we talked until his money ran out. He said he was surviving. I had no number to call back, but talking to his brother later I heard that Charlie had left campus accommodation and moved back in with his mother, and things were going fine.

In the New Year I had checked with an acquaintance at the university who confirmed that Charlie had sat his Christmas exams and would be proceeding to the next semester.

It was June when I bumped into Paul Gupta – that childhood companion of the Conlon boys.

It was news to Paul that Charlie was at university. He was surprised and pleased. 'Good for Charlie,' Paul said, 'Charlie and Sean grew up in the same area we did. We played football together as kids. We had it tough, but I can tell you, they got it a hell of a lot tougher.' I asked about contacting Charlie, and Paul said he would drop in on Charlie's mother, and ask her to tell Charlie to give me a bell.

That same evening the phone rang. It was Paul; he had been in contact with Charlie, and had arranged that we all meet in the foyer of the Europa Hotel in Belfast a week later.

When the two young men walked through the revolving doors into the marbled hotel lobby – Charlie, cutting a dash in a black leather jacket and pink open-necked shirt, flanked by Paul in blue.

'Love the leather jacket, Charlie,' I jested, shaking hands.

'You're looking good yourself, Patricia.' It was said with such candour he made me feel I was.

Gone was the fellow I had last seen in a faded anorak. Gone was the tracksuit. Gone were the down-at-heel trainers. Even his teeth looked brighter.

The strands of grey in his hair were no more prominent than before; not multiplying as profusely as those in my own.

'What's the story on this bomber jacket?' I joked. 'Fall off a lorry?'

It was a year since we had last met. Meantime the IRA ceasefire of August 1994 had contributed to a renewed buzz around Belfast. Even the weather smiled down on the city that summer. How was life treating him? I enquired, and how was living back with his mother working out?

He hoped it would not be for much longer. He had not seen his brother recently, nor had he heard anything of Pablo, who he believed was *on the run*. I told him, Pablo was married, and we agreed to differ. 'You've made it, Charlie,' I applauded when we finally got around to what was on my mind. 'Made it through your first year.'

'Just about,' he said.

'Just about beats not at all,' I encouraged. Paul was equally supporting, relating from his own experience as a mature student.

'I'm not going back to that place in September.' Charlie surprised us both with his outburst.

Paul talked of experiencing similar doubts. I spoke of being down the same road with the children, yet everything worked out fine. But there was a resolve in Charlie. He meant what he was saying. From the start, his college experience was not as anticipated.

On his second day out of prison he arrived on campus, totally committed, determined to keep out of trouble. He bought the books and moved into student halls; away from all his old pals, away from occasions of trouble. He knew nobody on campus. He went to all his lectures, read his books, but there was nobody of his own age group to socialise with in halls. 'They were kids. If they hadn't gone to school together, they came from the same town. They all stuck together, behaving like a batch of school kids. Silly. They fell dumb when I went into the kitchen to boil a kettle. It was not like anything I had expected.'

Still, he wanted to fit in.

'The whole place cleared out at weekends and I was left on my own with nowhere to go.'

He didn't want to go back home. He wanted to stand on his own feet, make a go of things. People drifted off in separate groups after lectures. He ate his meals alone, didn't go near the bar and spent most of his time in the library. He felt very strange, totally out of things.

'You hinted as much when you phoned, Charlie,' I said. 'But why didn't you call back? Did you get the money I sent you, care of the university?'

'I appreciated that, Patricia,' he said, 'but I was afraid you'd think I was looking for money if I rang back, and I knew you had enough on your plate with your own family. I should have rung you, I know, but … well, things started to pick up after that phone call.'

And, he put it was all down to one girl.

'She started talking to me after a lecture. It was just about the course work to start, and then she asked if I wanted to go for coffee with her and her friends. It was such a good feeling, to feel you were being accepted, and sit around and talk about the course and the lecturers and things that were going on.'

He hastened to add that the girl was a nice jolly type, the kind of girl who is genuine no matter whom she is talking to. 'You could see she was sincere. She was very mature although she was young; the type of person gets on with people. There was nothing more to it than that. We just chatted and went for coffee with the others.'

Charlie talked about the good feeling it was, getting to know people, and feeling part. 'One day I was walking out the main door and I bumped into her. She was going home for the weekend, and was on her way to get the bus into town. I was doing nothing so I said I'd walk with her to the stop, and we chatted there until her bus turned up. Do you see anything wrong with that?' he asked Paul and I.

He explained what happened next.

'One day soon after, this fellow who had been for coffee with us one of the days, caught up with me when I was walking back from the library. I thought when I met him first that maybe the fellow was the girl's boyfriend. But afterwards I figured they went to the same school; came from the same place. I don't know whether he was interested in her or what. Any road, he came up to me, and said he knew who I was. Knew I had been in prison. He was warning me to keep away from the girl. He said he knew her family and was looking out for her.'

After which, Charlie stopped attending lectures. 'I felt I didn't fit in with them sort of ones. I just read in my room, like I was used to in the cell.'

His next remark spoke volumes. However far Charlie Conlon might have moved in terms of replacing a prison yard for a university campus, it revealed how little he had moved in other respects. 'Although the fellow looked bigger than me,' he said, 'I knew in a straight fight I would have downed him first. I don't know how many friends the bloke had to back him up, or if he had any, I didn't hang around to find out.'

He did OK in his Christmas tests, but his money was running low, so he decided to move in with his mother. He didn't go to lectures any more. But he still read the books. The university contacted him and told him he had better sit end of term exams even if he failed, otherwise there would be financial consequences. 'Yes, I got them,' he said, 'but I probably only scraped through.'

He had no money to tide him over the summer. As a registered university student he could not draw unemployment benefits, so he de-registered with the university. He would have to re-apply if he wished to continue in the autumn.

That was no big deal he said, 'because if I do ever go back I want to study what I want to do myself, not what everyone else tells me I have to do.'

He was unimpressed with his course content. He hadn't the aptitude for arts subjects. They led nowhere. Paul had studied history and tried to encourage him to keep on with his studies. Charlie had questions for Paul. 'What help is some obscure nineteenth-century writer when I'm writing a letter to some government official complaining about the dire living conditions my mother lives in? Is knowing about the Wars of the Roses a lot of use when the RUC is kicking your door in? Know what I mean?'

His plan now was to set up in business. Retail business. Sell men's clothing. Leather jackets.

'But Charlie. Hold on a minute here,' I begged. '*You?* Running your own business! Where will the venture capital come from?'

Charlie just smiled.

'Have you considered who your friends are? How long do you think your leather jackets will last on the rails when friends drop in for a browse?'

Charlie made reference to a backer. 'Are you being serious?' I asked. 'Are you sure it's not a *laundry* this backer is interested in?'

He wanted to make money. Run a car. Wear decent clothes. Get his mother out of Bawnmore and into a decent house. 'I'm not like your middle-class kids up at that university. I can't afford the luxury of being an undergraduate for the rest of my life. When you ask some of them ones what they're studying for, they tell you, "until such time as I find out what I want to do with my life".'

He knew what he was good at. If he was to stay at university he wanted to do maths or business studies, and he wanted to make money fast.

I had two suggestions. I would investigate possibilities for a transfer to a more appropriate course. And I would look into the possibility of extra funding support. I knew of one charitable organisation committed to giving limited grant aid to help ex-offenders through college.

Since I was going on holidays within days, and Charlie's mother had no telephone, we arranged I would phone Paul if I made any progress in the short term.

But before any of that might happen, there was another phone call I needed to make. I needed to phone Margo.

18

'Guess who I met yesterday?'

'Take me out of my misery.'

'Charlie Conlon.'

'Well, haven't some of us all the luck.'

'He sends his regards, Margo.'

'You know, that fellow often crosses my mind, but since I left Magilligan I haven't had a minute to catch up with anybody.'

'He just about scraped through,' I told her when she enquired about his progress. 'Problems with both university and course.'

'He's not living a hundred miles from me,' she commented. 'Wouldn't you think he'd have had the wit to contact some of us?'

We agreed the first major hurdle had been crossed. Charlie had stayed out of trouble for a year, and that in itself was progress. Not wanting to continue his studies did not surprise Margo, but it did get her going.

'It really does scale the heights of incredulity. A fellow they predict will kill someone, and what happens: they let him walk out the prison gates and straight on to a university campus without any preparation for the world he's entering. Sheer, downright lunacy! Unbelievable!'

I agreed that it beggared belief.

'Let me ask you something,' she was back on her hobby horse. 'Did anybody from the prison pick up the phone to you over the past year? We all know these fellows are no angels, but how many of them achieve anything like Charlie achieved, apart of course from the paramilitaries? What is rehabilitation supposed to be about?'

She paused, knowing she alone had the answer.

'Charlie might well have been a model student with us, but anyone with half a brain should know he needed support on the outside. It's about time someone took up this whole issue, Patricia. Look at our own kids. Friends of ours, their daughter decides halfway through first year that she was in the wrong faculty. Didn't sit a single end-of-year exam. Parents furious. Girl had excellent A Level results in science, but left to her own devices, what does Lizzie decide? Decides science is not for her. Leaves it to February to announce that history and politics is where her real interest lies. Now Jack and Mary have to turn round and find five thousand pounds for a repeat year. But getting back to Charlie Conlon. How did he ever end up in an arts faculty when it was maths he wanted?'

'He was interviewed by the university, Margo, and was offered foundation arts. He felt he had no bargaining power.'

'Oh, just don't get me started about prison education. But tell you what. I'll do a scout around and see if there is any more suitable course at any of the other colleges. You know Patricia, some of these so-called new universities are no better than factories. Conveyor-belt education'.

It was mid August and late in the evening when we returned from holiday.

Lazy habits die hard, and next morning we all slept late. I wandered out to the garden to inspect the pot plants and decided the watering could wait. Went back inside, poured a bowl of cornflakes and picked up the newspaper from the kitchen table; dragged the sun lounger from the garden shed and set myself up in a sunny corner to breakfast *al fresco*.

Winnie, next door's cat, strolled by on the wall and decided to keep me company.

I lifted the newspaper. Scanning the headlines, one caught my eye. "MAN BARES ALL IN COURT".

Ever so gingerly, I lowered my bowl of cornflakes to the ground. Using both hands to steady the newspaper on my lap, I read from the top again:

In the Crown Court in Belfast today, twenty-nine year-old Mr Charles John Conlon, with an address at Bawnmore Avenue in the North of the city, appeared naked before [Lord Justice Black] as two prison officers struggled to shield Mr Conlon's loins with a towel. Representing Conlon, his barrister, [Mr Spring], acting for [Spring & Dodge Solicitors], told the court that his client was forced into taking this stand due to the inhuman and degrading treatment he had received at the hands of his jailers in Crumlin Road Prison. Conlon had been held in solitary confinement since his arrest ten days ago and was being subjected to harassment and deprivation which went against natural justice, Mr Spring said. The charges before the court arose as a result of an affray outside a bar in the north of the city. The case was put back for hearing.

I read the report a second time. I had to believe my own eyes.

In his buff. Charlie standing stark naked in the dock.

What in the world was he trying to achieve?

Just three weeks before, Charlie in his snazzy black leather jacket, the heavy gold chain at his neck, the colourful pink shirt opened a few buttons down. What led such a polished young man to make such an exhibition of himself? As Margo might say, it beggared belief.

I did not need a newspaper article to tell me Charlie Conlon was a loose cannon. But how had I convinced myself that he would not revert to form at the first hurdle?

Back when violence was at its most intense, Charlie had alluded to an offer of work he had received: a bouncer in a Belfast city club. How could anyone of right mind, I thought at that time, consider Charlie for such work?

"An affray", the newspaper reported, "outside a bar in the north of the city". Had he taken up the offer recently?

I wondered how far Margo's enquiries had progressed. I needed to call her and Sean. And there was one other disappointment. I had contacted the Lawlor Foundation, a charity offering study bursaries to ex-offenders. A requirement of the foundation asked for evidence of commitment to study on the part of the ex-offender. Up until ten minutes ago I believed Charlie's undergraduate year was proof positive.

Later, when the family sat down to lunch, talk was of the report in the newspaper. Although my children had never met him, all felt they knew Charlie. Niamh, studying for a social science degree, was particularly interested in his criminal career since she planned to work in the field of criminology.

I firmly believed, and I said so again, that Charlie Conlon was not a devious or calculating individual. Most times he ended up charged with offences unrelated to the main deed. As his brother said, had he kept a cool head, he might have 'walked'. But Charlie could not keep a cool head. For a seemingly intelligent man to go along with so many no-win schemes when he must have known the rewards could not possibly justify the risks, raised question over his judgement.

'Yes Niamh,' I said, 'you do have to ask yourself, is there something wrong in his head?'

'Charlie's performance in court yesterday, those are not actions one associates with either the petty criminal or the drug dealer.' She was testing her theories on me.

'Well, Charlie's answer is always the same. "If they leave me alone, I'll leave them alone".'

'But, sure who was doing anything to him in the courtroom?'

Niamh might as well have looked to Winnie the cat, sitting outside on the wall, for an answer.

Charlie was unable, or just unwilling, to move beyond his childhood experiences. He had faith in nobody other than himself; it never crossing his mind that he was his own worst failure? 'Has this chip on his shoulder,' officers said. 'Has this persecution complex, this thing about uniforms.'

'Did people never try to find out why?' Niamh probed.

'Niamh,' I said, 'Charlie differs little from others in prison. Fellows with short tempers, easily provoked, acting on impulse, their own wilfulness their greatest enemy. Not many though,' I had to admit, 'are as trapped as Charlie.'

'From what you tell me, Mum,' she persisted, 'a child from a perfectly good home, a close knit family, his mother a loving parent, could one "bite" really be the catalyst for all that followed?'

Or was there something else missing? Perhaps Charlie craved a father figure.

Yes, I thought, Charlie might well crave a father.

The image I had formed of Charlie's parents was a figment of my imagination. Romance and adventure in a foreign land, ending with the fallen hero on the battlefield. For the storybook ending I needed a fuller embodiment of my two main characters, and being nosey, I had earlier asked Charlie if he had any family photographs to show me.

He bristled. 'In here?' He would not sully the family image by taking a photograph into prison.

'Your father? Is there one of him anywhere?'

It had disappeared with his mother's other bits and pieces when they were intimidated out of their first home. But he recalled one of his father in military uniform.

As for any further information on the man, he was categorical, 'You have no idea how vague my mother can be when she wants.'

When I first met Sean, it had crossed my mind they did not look like brothers. 'Certainly, you both have Africa in your genes,' I later remarked to Charlie, 'but Sean looks like he's got the lion's share.'

Charlie was not one bit pleased. He wanted to be the black man in the family.

'Well, Charlie, I'm afraid in your case the Celt or the Cherokee got the upper hand.' He had invested in his African roots, and was unwilling to concede an inch, even to his brother.

Plans hatched in Magilligan were that one day I would meet his mother. He would take me to Bawnmore to see at first hand the appalling conditions in that estate. After that eye-opener, I would go back and tell my friends in the SDLP where the needs of the people lay. I reckoned a visit to Bawnmore was now off the cards.

'Mum. There was a call for you while you were out.' Niamh met me in the hall when I returned from shopping. Her tone was sombre. 'I think it was Charlie's mother. Said her name was Maura, and it was about Charlie, and that she would ring back.'

'Is that Patricia Farren?' said the voice on the line, 'this is Charlie Conlon's mother.'

'Maura,' I said, 'I'm so glad you called back.'

'Sean was trying your number after Charlie went back to prison, but he wasn't getting any answer. I hope it's all right for me to ring you. Me and Sean have just come out from the Crumlin Road and I told Sean I'd try ringing this time because I'm very worried about what's happening to Charlie. Sean said that maybe you being on the visitors could find out what was going on. I don't have the phone myself. I'm in my neighbour's house at the minute. Will I give you her number?'

I explained how I had only, that morning, read the piece in the newspaper, and that I had phoned Sean at work but was told he would not be in until later. 'But first,' I said, 'poor Charlie, tell me what happened?'

'I just don't know what is going on.' She explained in dejected tones, 'When Sean and me went up to the Crumlin Road today they wouldn't let us see him (most likely because Charlie was refusing to put his clothes on). My heart is torn,' Maura continued, 'with everything that is going on up there at the Crumlin Road, I just don't know anything. Charlie was living with me. He was working to that fellow on the building, but then that stopped and there was the other fellow, but Charlie didn't talk much about what he was doing. He wasn't in any trouble since he got out last year and I thought things might be going right. Until this happened. Since Christmas me and Charlie had got very close, and we talked about a lot of things, and he talked about you, and the way you helped him, and believed in him. I don't know, but he wasn't interested in going out in the evenings, and we used to just sit down together and just read and talk. I was never happier. We had gone over a lot of things about his past, and I want to thank you for helping him in Magilligan. Charlie told me you were brilliant, and that there was other teachers there the same. He said yous give him a lot of help and he appreciated that.'

'All any of us did Maura,' I said, 'was to show a bit of confidence in him.'

Referring to his striptease performance in court, her tone was resigned. 'That's just my Charlie. He is no angel but he doesn't deserve what is happening.' She would have Sean phone, and fill in details.

Sean, when he called, was not sure what Charlie had been up to since he hadn't been allowed see him. What he did know was that someone had been injured in a pub, and that Charlie left before the police arrived.

'What was Charlie doing in the Rainbow?' I enquired, knowing it was Belfast's premier gay bar?'

We guessed at answers. Delivering? Collecting? Maybe himself and the guy with him were thirsty and needed a drink? Maybe anything, but for sure a knife was drawn, which Charlie knocked from a hand. The falling knife injured a patron of the pub. Charlie was arrested at a taxi rank across the street.

I guessed he did not go quietly.

Sean was very concerned. Neither he nor his mother had forgotten the riot back in 1991, after which Charlie had been hospitalised. Nor, according to Sean, had the prison officers forgotten.

I had been asked, and so I wanted to help.

At a previous board meeting one of our members, a local government councillor had asked for permission to visit a constituent, then on remand in Crumlin Road prison.

'By all means,' came the reply, 'go through the chairperson of the BOV there.'

Since the precedent was established, I went ahead and telephoned the chairperson.

'By all means,' said the chairperson. 'Tell you what I'll do meantime: while the formalities for an inter-prison visit are being processed I'll pop in myself and see what the score is, and I'll get back to you.'

A short time later he returned my call, having been in to see Charlie. Matters had settled. The prisoner was calm, and raised no complaints. When my visit was sanctioned I would be met at the prison gates and taken directly to the prisoner's cell. I was promised a tour of the prison as an extra bonus.

A week passed and no phone call. When the chairperson did phone the embarrassment in his voice could not be masked. My request to visit Charlie Conlon had been vetoed at a senior level.

Questions had been raised. "Who is she, this woman requesting a visit to Conlon? Conlon! of all prisoners?" It was pretty obvious Charlie's reputation was low, and by association mine had also plummeted.

So, who better to turn to for advice than my friend, Teddy.

Neither one of us was that dumb. We both knew there was a simple solution. Nothing prevented me arranging a visit through normal prison visits, but such a solution would satisfy neither of us. We had a bone of contention and were not prepared to let go. Teddy reminded me how I was a serving member of the system just as the good councillor was. 'You can only see this as a personal snub.'

Which, I reassured him, I did.

While Teddy and I planned our offensive, Charlie wrote me from prison.

The letter was dated, September 24 1995.

Dear Patricia,

I hope you are well. I am as fine as can be expected under the circumstances. I just wanted to write a few lines to thank you for the reference you wrote me and everything else you have done for me. I truly appreciate it, and I am very sorry for letting you down. I don't know what else to say. I am also sorry for not getting in touch sooner, but I was too ashamed.

This place has changed since I was last here, '91–'92. The paramilitaries have gone and there is a more relaxed regime in operation, so there is less pressure. However, I did encounter some victimization when I first came in, but I protested against this by stripping in court (it was that or explode) and that seems to have stopped it. I guess they don't want a naked man in court every week. They are actually being quite nice to me now.

[Gerry "Bugsy," Doyle] is here too, [Josey Reynolds] has just finished a six month sentence, and I hear [Pablo Delaney] is on the run. Same old faces in the same old places!

I see in the news that they are opening American-style "boot camps" for young offenders next year. Not a good idea. All that does is create tougher, more bitter criminals, and win a few votes. Pablo, Joe and myself are all products of the last round of "short, sharp shocks." It was misguided and unintelligent then, and I believe that holds true today. But if it helps to improve the Conservatives' opinion poll rating I suppose it must be a good idea.

Ronan must have the results of his A Levels by now. I hope he did well. It doesn't seem that long ago that he got …

I hope the rest of your family are doing well too.

Kindest regards

Charlie.

The "reference" referred to was a character reference I had provided through his solicitor, following my Crumlin Road barring. In it I had asked the courts to consider the possibility of allowing the accused undergo psychological assessment and counselling outside prison. Having long abandoned any earlier belief that Charlie could be released straight back on to the streets of Belfast without special support, I was clutching at straws, but maybe I still nursed the hope that with professional help there was the possibility that he could be guided on a path of rehabilitation. Otherwise, I feared a return to prison would serve only to further damage an already fragile psyche. More and more I was accepting that Charlie needed support of a kind beyond anything either his family or his friends could provide.

Sean phoned to tell me Charlie would be joining me in Maghaberry. Conditionally released under licence back in 1993, he was being recalled to serve out his sentence.

At the first opportunity I went along to the wing.

'Conlon, BOV to see you,' the officer poked his head into a darkened cell. A curtain, half off its runner, allowed a glimmer of light fall on the man lying on the bed.

The officer called in again. This time Charlie stirred. Like a grizzly bear surfacing from hibernation, he lifted himself off the bed, and woozy with sleep, glanced our way.

'Can I come in, Charlie?' I asked, while the officer stepped aside to allow me pass.

Groggy and bleary-eyed, he put his two bare feet to the floor and ran his fingers through his hair.

'Would you mind,' I asked, sitting down and turning round to tug at the curtain, 'if I let more light in?'

I looked around the sparsely furnished cell. No posters adorned the walls. No photographs were pinned on the display board. No carton of milk was keeping cool in the cross breeze. Nor was fruit arranged on the windowsill. An open book lay on the bed, with more stacked on the small desk. I examined titles: history and history again, a biography. On the floor, beneath the desk, a bulging file.

'So, how are things going?' I asked.

'They've kept their distance this far,' he was up and pulling on a white T-shirt before shaking hands with me. Needless to say, I didn't have to ask who "they" were.

'Well, so far so good, Charlie.'

'It won't be too long, let me tell you, till they're up to their old tricks.'

'Is this it?' I nodded towards the file on the floor.

He lifted the bulging file and spread the contents across the bed. His solicitor was visiting later that day.

'I could be looking here at three to five years,' he said, handing me the list of charges:

WOUNDING WITH INTENT
AFFRAY (COMMON LAW)
ASSAULT ON POLICE
ASSAULT ON POLICE
ASSAULT ON POLICE

He envisaged delays with the case coming to trial, followed by adjournments.

Back on my old hobby horse, I suggested, he might consider studying law, given his hands-on experience. An Open University course might be an option, particularly if he was anticipating a long stretch.

In reality, the OU was a non-starter; in all probability Charlie would serve most of this sentence on remand, and as such would not be eligible for OU funding. Yet, a case might well be made to the NIO justifying funding on the grounds that Charlie was surely his own best guarantee that he would complete any course he embarked on while in prison. But I doubted if the NIO would trade-forward on those terms. And so I abandoned ideas about making a lawyer out of Charlie.

On subsequent visits I talked with the officers on the wing.

'He sleeps his life away,' one said. 'Just you wait,' said another. 'He must be on drugs,' commented someone else.

'What has you sleeping so much?' I asked Charlie. 'Every time I come here you are in bed. Why are you sleeping your life away?'

'It's only for a while during the daytime I sleep,' he said, 'I don't sleep nights.' He complained of his head. 'I lie on the bed all night with my head going round and around, thump, thump, all night long.' He felt his head would explode.

19

While Charlie slept things off, and his solicitor negotiated bail, I looked over the fence again to the women in Mourne.

Life there followed a similar routine to the regime on the male side regardless that females presented lower security risks, and were involved in far fewer serious incidents than their male counterparts.

Occasionally the young offenders created their own fireworks. High jinks meant trashing the recreation room. Friday evenings a flash-point; letting fling when the realisation hit them that instead of putting on make-up, meeting up with friends and heading out to the disco, they were fenced in.

Such was the scene when I arrived on the YO (youth offenders) wing that morning. From the doorway it was obvious the recreation room had taken the brunt of the weekend blitz – slashed cushions, splattered walls … It was about ten o'clock, the TV on, a young girl watching. She turned when she heard someone approach. Her smile died when she saw the stranger, and she averted her dark hazel eyes.

'Am I intruding?' I asked.

'No. No,' she flicked her wrist towards the screen, 'you can turn it off if you like.' She then proceeded to turn it off herself, and found she had nowhere to look. Her back to me, hair tied back in a ponytail, she sat dainty as a doll concentrating on the darkened screen.

I established she was from Belfast, and told her I was from Portstewart, but Portstewart might well have been on another planet. We talked only of Belfast, where she had her own flat, which puzzled me because she seemed too young to live away from home.

'Kerry,' she said her name was.

Kerry was relieved when we talked about her flat. '*Fantastic*,' it was. 'Really, really great.' The living room she had done out with cushions and throws and rugs, and everything. Scented candles all over. She loved scented candles. Just loved everything about that flat. She had moved in from *the* flats. Her mother was keeping up the rent while she was inside. She just could not wait to get out and back into her own wee place again.

'Your name again?' I asked.

'Kerry-Marie.'

'Yes, but Kerry-Marie what?'

'Delaney.'

'Do you have an uncle, Paul? Pablo?'

'Oh aye, Pablo,' she beamed, and then the beam faded. 'How do you know Pablo?'

'Magilligan. I taught him.'

'Oh,' she said, and averted her eyes again.

'Pablo and me, we were great buddies when he was in Magilligan. He told me all about you, and your trip to America.'

'Oh,' again, and to avoid further questioning asked if I would like a coffee. She was relieved when I said I would, and she fled to the kitchen.

I followed, and while she filled the kettle I mentioned some of Pablo's pranks. Setting up a cup and spoon, removing milk from the fridge, asking if I took sugar, engaged her while I enquired more about her flat.

There was a lot of outlay at the start. She wanted things nice from the beginning. That was where the money difficulties arose. Claiming 'the social' on the double was her big mistake, but then, all her friends were doing the same. Everyone claimed. So she thought she could get away with what everyone else was doing. But she had learned her lesson and she would never do the same thing again. 'Never, ever. No way!' She had only one more week left before release, and she just could not wait. When I asked where Pablo was living, she shook her head. She had no idea.

'He sent me a Christmas card,' I said, 'but didn't give an address, and I have no way of sending one back.'

'Will I give you the address?' she asked, without a second thought.

Around this time Crumlin Road prison was closing down, with remand prisoners transferring up the road to Maghaberry. In future, if Charlie re-offended he would be committed here.

The logistics of the inter-prison move were occupying staff at both locations, the atmosphere highly charged. Anything could go wrong on the day. And indeed it did.

James McDonald, (Jimbo to his friends, and a particular friend of Charlie's) and his younger brother were in Crumlin Road awaiting transfer when they received the sad tidings that their father had died. Sensitive to their distress, staff allowed the brothers private time together. Had circumstances been different their request for compassionate parole would have been activated immediately. Instead, they were assured that arrangements would be handled after the transfer operation. Whether rightly or wrongly, the brothers believed that when they reached Maghaberry they would be allowed share a cell while the machinery was set in motion.

The atmosphere in Foyle, the designated remand house, was notably tense that morning. Processing so many new committals was by no means an everyday occurrence. Nobody had time for special cases, and the brothers were dispatched to separate cells. This was not as they had expected, and so added to their general distress. James became emotional, then angry, and hit out at an officer for not honouring the commitment given.

My understanding of ensuing events was that James was summarily C&R-ed (control and restraint) and placed in solitary confinement. Staff in the PSU saw to his immediate needs. While exercising in the yard another inmate spoke through the cell window to James, and later reported him complaining of chest pain. He would be the last person to speak to the prisoner. Within the hour a prison officer discovered that James had collapsed. His heart had stopped. Resuscitation efforts failed to revive him. He died, 37 years of age.

The autopsy revealed a number of broken ribs, concluding that they were broken as a consequence of pump-action pounding of the chest during resuscitation attempts.

'Not so,' said the prisoners, '*Jimbo McDonald was murdered in Maghaberry jail.*'

Politicians and commentators were called upon to give their views. BOV members asked questions at meetings. It was a tragic event calling for sensitivity: a family losing a father and a brother on the same day. Surely the prison could have been more responsive to the family's distress?

The McDonald story was still running when a prison officer was viciously attacked in another house.

'The two incidents are linked,' said the governor reporting to our meeting, 'belief is the attack on the officer was in reprisal for McDonald.'

'That attack had nothing to do with my brother's death,' said James McDonald's brother when I called to his cell on his return from compassionate parole for the double family funeral. 'My brother was murdered, and what are the BOV going to do about it?'

To an extent, the depth of emotion generated by Jimbo McDonald's death might be connected to the place where he died. The PSU. The subject of rumours and rumblings within the prisoner community, the unit had been a focal point for BOV attention for some time. A strict Christian ethos prevailed. An open bible, passages underscored, lay on the desk. Wow betide those who did not subscribe to the rules of this military style operation.

The names, with religious affiliation, of prisoners held there were displayed on a board behind the desk. It did not escape BOV notice that the prisoners in solitary confinement were predominantly Catholic. If nothing else, the disproportionate numbers in the PSU sat uneasily with the disproportionate numbers in sought-after job locations.

And now a young Catholic man from west Belfast had died there.

James and his brother were remand prisoners, not convicted criminals. They had cooperated with officers in Crumlin Road, and the transfer had gone smoothly. So, why did nobody show a modicum of compassion when a phone call might have smoothed matters on arrival?

To look for answers, look to the staff – a predominantly Protestant labourforce. Had the brothers hailed from east or north of the city – a recruitment pool for officers – someone on the staff would surely have heard reports of the father's death, and consequently made it their business *to keep an eye out for the two boys*, the majority of prison officers being as compassionate as the next person. Unfortunately, that was not the case. And so, the notion of "murder in the PSU" took wings.

It was into this atmosphere Charlie would soon return.

The block where the alleged retaliatory assault on an officer occurred housed a number of prisoners with links to the paramilitary Irish National Liberation Army (INLA). The officer's assailant, allegedly came from within this grouping. The attackers were hooded. Balaclavas had been found on the stairwell of the landing below. All evidence had been collated and dispatched to the police in Lisburn for forensic examination, including all items of clothing belonging to the four main suspects, all of them INLA. We could expect developments in ten to fourteen days. Management were certain they had their men. I had already met the prime suspect. He was Christopher "Crip" McWilliams.

Curious as to why McWilliams would revenge James McDonald's

death, I took up his request when he asked to see the BOV. Daphne accompanied me.

McWilliams, acting as spokesman for the group, said all four suspects were totally confident forensics would reveal nothing. They were innocent men. He asked if we were aware that every last stitch of their clothing had been removed, virtually off their backs? We said we were. Were we aware no self-respecting Republican would be seen dead in prison clothing? Yes, we guessed as much. Were we aware that the replacements provided from stores were deliberately wrong-sized so as to demean the men?

Chris summoned his three compatriots into the cell, ordering them to dress up so we could see for ourselves.

We couldn't but agree with Chris, there was room for a second man inside one fellow's jeans. We also agreed that a grown man's T shirt should not touch his knees, nor his shorts skirt his ankles.

The men were demanding their own clothing back.

We took a note and set out to follow the trail.

While our investigations were underway, Charlie returned, and went directly to the PSU.

'Too hot to handle anywhere else,' said the officer. 'Good men may never work again.' A reference to injuries sustained by RUC officers escorting the prisoner back to prison.

Charlie was sitting on his bed reading through some documents when I arrived at the cell. He stood up and we shook hands.

'Are you OK?' I asked.

He glared towards the half-open door. The officers outside closed it a fraction. Charlie continued to glare until they closed it to his satisfaction.

'What happened?' I asked.

He searched through the mound of papers on the bed, extracting the charge sheet. I counted seventeen separate counts, ranging from common assault on a child, to common assault on an adult; resisting police, assault on police, obstructing police, occasioning actual bodily harm, disorderly behaviour, criminal damage …

'Added to the current five?' I lifted my head from the charge sheet.

'Yep.'

There was no chair so I sat down on his bed.

'But hold on till you read what they've done to me.' He handed me a doctor's report documenting abrasions on various parts of the body. It was accompanied by diagrams of a man's torso, front and back. The diagrams were notated with Xs, depicting injury points. On paper, the scale of injuries looked horrific.

I asked him to stand up and take off his T shirt so I could match the Xs with the abrasions on his body. There was heavy bruising and discoloration on the chest and shoulders. He had taken some thumping. 'Look at your eye!' I exclaimed, insisting his eye was crooked. I asked him to look in a mirror.

'You're in a jail, Patricia, not in a beauty parlour,' he reminded me.

'Have they done a brain scan?' I was still concerned about the position of his eye.

There was nothing the matter with his brain. Why should I think there was anything wrong with his head?

'But Charlie,' I tried another approach, 'there's no loss of face in the doctor suggesting a scan, particularly amongst a battery of other tests.'

Within earshot of officers was no place to discuss brain scans with Charlie Conlon.

Despite all the bruising, he looked fit as a fiddle. I asked if his family had been in contact, but when he looked a little uncomfortable, I suggested I would phone Sean later on.

The officers outside the door were getting restless. I turned back to Charlie, wanting to ask about the work placement I had arranged for him some weeks before, but reckoned the answer could wait. And with not a notion what best to do for him any more, I left the cell.

A phone call to Sean that evening told me everything I needed to know.

Following his release on bail Charlie had behaved admirably. He lived with Sean's family for a period. They had talked a lot. Feelings were revealed, regrets expressed. Sean said he believed that the greatest obstacle Charlie had to overcome was, 'for Charlie to get it into his head that life could hold possibilities beyond a life in prison. It's like he's an alcoholic who can go on the dry for a period of time, but always knows that the next drink is waiting for him round the corner. Charlie's addicted to jail. The family are convinced Charlie likes it inside; it's what he knows. Charlie knows how to deal with his demons in jail, but not on the outside.'

I asked Sean about the work placement.

Charlie had never been happier. 'It felt good', he told his brother, 'to be working alongside mature and caring people, sharing the workload, feeling you were one of a team, sitting behind a desk, your views listened to. Particularly those on juvenile delinquency'.

'Some woman up there was very good to Charlie,' Sean continued. 'Took an interest in him, and helped him get a flat. But then he got on the phone to me, and he sounded worried. Said there was talk of sending him out to speak to young people about his experience in prison. Charlie is convinced that it is only a matter of time until he is back in jail, and I think he baulked at the notion of talking to others about keeping out. Basically, he sounded scared he would let everyone down again, but I think he was more scared about not being sincere about what he might have to say to others. There was some talk about a trip to America, and Charlie just got more frightened that these people didn't know everything they should know, he was going to let everyone down again. He just ran scared.'

Next, the RUC enter the scene.

Because he was in receipt of remuneration while on placement meant Charlie was not signing on. It was time to call in an old debt – money from his university grant loaned to a mate almost two years before. He went round to the fellow's house. Guessing why he had come, they locked him out. Charlie tried to kick in the door. They rang the police, and Charlie ran.

'Headed into a housing estate,' Sean continued, 'knocking down a child on the footpath. Some auld boy, out in his garden mowing the grass, saw it happen and phoned the police. When Charlie ran out the other end of the estate they were waiting to corner him, and then he decided to take them ones on as well. And that's basically it, Patricia.'

If it was 'basically it' for Charlie, I feared it might be a similar story for Daphne and I if we failed to report on the whereabouts of the INLA men's clothing. A check with stores revealed that Chris McWilliams' suspicions could well be true. All sizes were in stock.

'Don't worry Chris, we are still on the case,' we assured him.

'And, when might the prisoners expect to have their clothing returned?' we asked at our next meeting.

'Anytime.' Anytime normally meaning a few weeks.

Week after week, one or other of us raised the question of the return of the men's garments.

'Nothing to do with the prison service.' It was down to the RUC.

'Would somebody ring the police, and find out why it is taking so long?'

Back to McWilliams, saying we were hopeful of developments pretty soon.

'Those fellows are pretty darn certain they are in the clear,' I remarked coming away from the cell.

'It does make one wonder sometimes,' said Daphne.

With the INLA men on our backs, we raised the matter again. This time we were advised to see security.

Progress at last! 'Let's go this minute and tackle Trevor Shacks. See what he has to say for himself.' Teddy was to accompany me since Daphne had to leave after the meeting.

Trevor Shacks was standing at a filing cabinet, top drawer open, flicking through files. 'First I heard of it,' he said, glancing our way. 'Didn't even know the stuff was still with Lisburn. Leave it with me.' The bang of the drawer closing indicated we should exit.

Time passed. Still the clothes had not been returned; neither had anybody been charged with the assault.

Back we went to McWilliams. 'Not to worry, Chris. We are still on the warpath.'

Back we went to security.

'Oh, did nothing come back on that yet? Leave it with us.'

I decided to take matters into my own hands. I rang Lisburn police station explaining my association with the prison. The officer I spoke to went off to investigate. 'Forensics,' he returned to tell me, 'have long been completed. Nothing found. It's up to the prison to collect the stuff. They left it in.'

'So why has nobody collected?' we asked, again to no avail.

Eventually we decided on another tack: ask the governor for access to McWilliams' security file.

'You want to see McWilliams' *security* file!'

'According to Rule 126(3),' I quoted directly from the rules, '"The governor shall allow the board reasonable access to any of the records of the prison".'

'Can I, or can I not, see McWilliams' file?' I pressed.

'I have no problem with you seeing the file. See security.'

'We had better not just barge in on Trevor, don't you think,' said Daphne. 'Shall we just ring upstairs first?

'Make sure he's in no doubt what we want,' I prompted while she was speaking to upstairs. 'Don't let him think he'll pawn us off as he did Teddy and me.'

'No problem. Come right up.' Daphne was paraphrasing Trevor Shacks at the other end of the line. 'Good.'

We had already asked Chris if there were skeletons in his cupboard, something that might account for the attitude towards returning his belongings. 'If I find there is something in that file that you are not honest with us about, Chris,' I told him, 'you're going to hear from me.'

He'd like that, he said.

'Daphne! Patricia!' Surrounded by filing cabinets, Trevor Shacks leaned back in his swivel chair. 'And what may I do for you ladies today?'

'Well Trevor,' said Daphne. 'You see, really, it's this question of Christopher McWilliams' clothing? Patricia and I … well Patricia and I believe …'

'McWilliams? McWilliams? Let me see?' Using his foot he propelled his chair closer to a filing cabinet, and opened a lowdown drawer. 'Where have we got McWilliams? Dum de dum de dum … here we go. McWilliams!' He rolled himself back to the desk, and leaning back in his black leather chair crossed his legs. 'How may we help?'

Daphne, at some pains, explained, 'We've spoken with a number of officers and we've spoken with governors, but we're having little success understanding why the prison has not collected the men's clothing from the police station. We were wondering if there is, perhaps, something on McWilliams' file that would indicate …'

'We feel like we're being passed from pillar to post,' I rowed in. 'The police tell us one thing today; the prison service another story tomorrow. Is it out of the question for us to have a look at McWilliams' file?'

'I have no problem with the BOV asking for access to a prisoner's file,' said Trevor. 'Any prisoner-file you ladies want to see, just come along to me!'

'Security,' Trevor, loquacious to a fault, explained at some considerable length, 'underscores this whole regime …'

The file! Ten minutes into the homily I woke up.

'Yes,' said Trevor: 'The file! And removing the file from the desk he brought it to rest in his lap.

He thumbed through some documents, re-sorted half the file, extracted a page, glanced at it. 'Mmm …' It was handed to me. While I read, Daphne was handed another. When I'd finished, Trevor nodded towards Daphne, a signal that I should wait until she had finished reading. Next prompt: exchange documents.

Yet another was handed across to us, and then another, and another; us exchanging with each other until we were blue in the face.

'Well, there's nothing of grave importance here, it's just … well routine stuff really,' Daphne looked my way.

More of the same, we said, exchanging papers.

'Are you aware what McWilliams is in for?'

We said we were.

'Double murder.' Trevor couldn't resist repeating the charges.

We told him again we already knew. That Chris had confided all about his case. Talked with us about his pending appeal.

Passing us another page from the file, Trevor Shacks purred a satisfied hum. And that was how he wore us down. Handing us stuff of no consequence, and distracting us, and telling us things we already knew, while all this time, fifty percent of the contents of Christopher McWilliams' file remained securely balanced between his thighs.

Nobody was ever charged with the assault on the officer.

On the very last day – if not the very last hour – that the prison authorities could lawfully retain evidence without filing charges, their clothing was returned to the men.

20

Was I free to come in that afternoon? Carmel, secretary to the BOV, was in a panic. A Rule 32 – the order committing a prisoner to solitary confinement for a period of one month – needed signing.

'You've saved my life,' she said. 'I've exhausted the list. The only other member I can get hold of is Maurice. He can't make it until four.

Then I remembered to ask who was being Rule 32'd.

'Charlie Conlon,' she said. At which point excuses were out of the question. Carmel was desperate. I had committed. I was being called upon to do my duty.

Normally, the case for restricting association resulted from threatening behaviour towards staff or other prisoners, fights, bullying, wrecking up. Occasionally a case was made 'for the prisoner's own protection'. A chat with staff. A chat with the prisoner. And the picture easily formed itself.

Members of the board had a policy of acting in pairs, and exercised extreme caution when endorsing the rule. In theory we could refuse, but in reality someone else could always be prevailed upon to sign. Even if every member of the board walked away, management still had recourse to the NIO. A designated official would sign the order on behalf of the Secretary of State, thus overriding any authority the BOV felt it had vested in it.

Refusing to sign was the exception.

Since his arrival, bruised and battered, four months previously, I had spoken to Charlie on a few occasions. After a short period in the PSU he was transferred to the wings. There he remained until November, when he had an altercation with a governor. Back in solitary, the last two members of the BOV to validate Rule 32 had stipulated a two-week segregation period rather than the customary month. Those two weeks had expired, and now Maurice and I were being called upon to review circumstances.

A call came through to the PSU to say Maurice was cutting it fine. Lockdown was four-thirty. Would I like to go ahead and speak to the prisoner in advance?

Because of my association with Charlie, I decided, it was better to have a second opinion, and wait for Maurice. Meantime I would speak with officers.

Principal Officer Prendergast straightened his back and capped his fountain pen. Since transfer to *his unit,* the prisoner's conduct had met standard criteria. The prisoner obeyed orders, was respectful to staff, spent his time reading. In his considered view, and that of *his men*, he had no hesitation recommending Conlon return to normal association – a cue for an officer at another desk to butt in. Officer Wallace agreed with *the boss.* 'He's out of harm's way when he's over here. There are no disputes in this unit for him to involve himself with. As a matter of fact, I think Conlon's happier here than on the wings.'

Maurice arrived minutes after lockdown. PO Prendergast had retired behind his desk to read his bible. Charlie's file lay open on the PO's desk for inspection. Maurice read reports and the comments left by the two previous signatories, recommending the prisoner return to normal association on or before two weeks. At which point we were pretty certain what our decision would be, and since that decision meant return to the wings, there was hardly any need to speak to Charlie.

Maurice looked at me, and I looked at him.

'I'm happy to go along with what I've read in these reports,' he said, 'taking into account what the PO has said to you …'

We agreed. We didn't need to see the prisoner, but just to be on the safe side we looked over the report sheets once more. 'I'd like to know why they even bothered putting the journey on us,' Maurice commented. Apart from anything else, Christmas was looming, and neither one of us wanted to see someone spend Christmas in solitary confinement.

We closed the file, certain we were making the right decision. We would not be signing. We turned to the PO to indicate our decision.

PO Prendergast raised one hand. He laid his bible on the desk and dialed an extension.

'It's your decision. Purely your decision,' he said, waiting for someone to pick up at the other end. 'It's entirely for the BOV to make up your own minds. But I'd like you to hold until the house governor has a word.'

The phone was picked up.

'Governor McGonnagle will be here in a minute,' we were told.

Maurice and I sat down to await his arrival. I lit a cigarette.

PO Prendergast went apoplectic. Did I not see the sign? He directed me to a NO SMOKING sign on the wall above our heads. 'Step outside this office, please.' I was fouling *his air.*

Maurice exited with me, and while hanging around in the passageway, we decided, since the house governor had something to say to us about the prisoner, that maybe it would be a good idea to have a word with Charlie first.

I put my head in the door and asked if the PO would have an officer show us to Conlon's cell.

The PO raised his eyes to the clock on the wall. Lockdown time! I must be incapable of reading the hands on a clock, as well as a no smoking sign.

'No joy,' I turned to Maurice, 'better try some gentle persuasion if we want to get out of here before midnight.'

Gentle persuasion did not work. No cell doors would open during lockdown period *in this unit*. We could come back in an hour if we wished to see the prisoner.

I tried the only ploy left me. I raised my voice. 'I have driven seventy miles to get here, PO Prendergast. My colleague got held up in traffic, otherwise we would have accommodated your opening hours. All we require is five minutes of officer time.' I glanced at the officer at the other desk, his jacket off, his feet up, his head in the *Sun*. It might be lockdown, but, officially, officers were still on duty.

The PO was as unmoved by my pique as he was by my appeal.

Maybe it was high time I reminded this man of our statutory rights, and I decided to do just that.

'PO Prendergast,' I said, walking up to his desk, 'are you aware that under the powers vested in us by the Secretary of State, the BOV have right of access to all parts, and to every prisoner in this prison, day or night? All we require from you, or any of your men, is to open a cell door and ask the prisoner if he is willing to meet us.'

The bible hit the deck. The PO was round the desk. *He's no bigger than me,* I thought, *if he does square up to me.*

Governor William McGonnagle chose that moment to walk through the door, two long arms hanging by his sides. PO Prendergast backed off, as did I.

Maurice cleared his throat. In answer to an unspoken question, he said, 'I think, Willy, it would only be right for us to speak to Conlon before talking with yourself. Patricia is just explaining the situation to the PO. But there seems to be a problem with getting the prisoner out during lockdown.'

The governor looked to the PO. The PO was again buried in his bible.

'Surely someone can open a door?' I said.

The governor turned to the officer at the other desk. The *boss* had not spoken so he kept his eyes hidden in his newspaper.

'I take the blame for not making it in before lockdown,' apologised Maurice, 'but the traffic …'

'Maybe we could phone across, Sammy,' the governor was looking to the PO. 'Get two men over from the house to unlock Conlon.'

Glancing towards the telephone the PO indicated that the governor was free to help himself. *Ring any house you wish; ring the Secretary of State. Ring Downing Street. This is lockdown time in my unit.*

The clanking of keys heralded the arrival of the men from the house. 'Do you want to see the prisoner in his cell, or do you want him brought to the interview room?' we were asked.

We opted for the cell, and followed the two officers down the corridor. The cell door was unlocked. 'BOV to see you, Conlon,' called in.

The presence of the BOV at a cell door on the eve of a Rule 32 expiry normally boded badly for the prisoner. It signalled the governor's intention to press for renewal rather than automatic return to the wings. Charlie would have guessed our mission.

He was sitting on the bed eating his last meal of the day: burger, chips and turnip. He stood up and we shook hands. Despite our protestations to finish his meal he insisted on laying it aside. They would heat it up for him later on. 'So, relations are good between you and *them*, Charlie,' I said, 'if *they* are heating up meals for you?'

The regime in the unit was even-handed, and in Charlie's book, he could live with that.

The row of Christmas cards on the windowsill caught my eye. 'All from girlfriends?' I joked, turning round to pick one up.

'All from friends, Patricia,' Charlie corrected, not displeased I had noticed the number of cards on display. I thanked him for the one he had sent me.

It came time to get down to the purpose of our visit.

'Look,' said Charlie, 'I gave lip to McGonnagle. I admit it. I don't like the man. Call himself a governor? He was one of the ones overseeing things when I was set upon in the chapel in the Crum.'

Maurice focused on the more recent incident.

It began in the refectory weeks before. Charlie filled in the details. 'There was a protest. I was involved no more or no less than anyone else. These kinds of things happen all the time. The whole thing was over when McGonnagle showed his face. I don't know what brought him, other than he knew I was there. I admit, when I saw him I started mouthing off.'

Charlie explained how a few of his mates, realising he was getting wound up, formed a mini cordon around him and quietly inched him out of harm's way. But, later that same evening the governor ordered his transfer to the PSU, where he had been ever since.

'These threatening remarks you made to Governor McGonnagle? What exactly did you say?' I asked.

'I called him a dickhead, amongst other things, and for doing that I got loss of privileges. With any other prisoner that would have been the end of it, except when it comes to me.'

Maurice then moved to enquire into his present frame of mind. Was he penitent? The query was not put in so many words.

'Do you mean would I do the same again? The answer to that is, if they leave me alone I'll leave them alone. I slobbered at McGonnagle, and I've paid for it since. I would rather be back on the wings with the lads instead of holed up here. If that means someone is sorry, then that applies to me as well as to anyone else.'

The reason given on the form for his detention under Rule 32, was: "for the general maintenance of good order and discipline of the prison". Now, having heard his side, it was up to us to decide if the prisoner was still a threat to that good order and discipline.

'How can we be sure you won't flare up again at the least provocation, or at the first sighting of Governor McGonnagle?' I asked.

He fixed me with a steady gaze.

'OK,' I said, 'I know. Nobody can be certain about anything in this world.'

Paying the price for his hot temper had become second nature to Charlie. The odds on him returning to the PSU at a future date were pretty high. Asking him to change the habits of a lifetime was pointless. Nobody was going to break him! Charlie had grown impervious to pain. Every punishment compounded his determination never to kowtow to anyone.

I had glimpsed Charlie's emotional frailty back in that classroom in Magilligan. Could Governor McGonnagle, waiting in the office, be persuaded to see Charlie in the same light? And, more immediate, what was Maurice's impression?

We stood in the passageway weighing up what we had heard. While we could not measure exactly the depth of the prisoner's remorse, we judged there was no malice intended. We had read the daily reports, listened to the PO and his men. We knew the views of the previous signatories. We agreed to recommend his return to the wings and tell the governor we could not justify signing Rule 32.

The governor's eyes were riveted on us as we walked through the door. Hands in deep pockets, his dark double-breasted overcoat buttoned for the walk back to the house, there was an awful lot of white in the eyes that bore into me.

'Well, we've talked to Conlon,' Maurice opened, 'and we are happy to go along with what the PO said earlier.'

The governor cleared his throat.

'We've heard all sides,' I added, 'and our view is that he should go back to the wings.'

Maurice took up the cudgel again. 'Since the two other members talked with him two weeks ago nothing has changed. Margaret and Seamus were of the same mind then as we are now. He is ready to go back. We're surprised they bothered bringing us in, Willy.'

The governor took his hands out of his pockets.

'I have known Charlie for a number of years,' I said, 'and I know that there can be problems. I got to know him quite well when I was teaching at Magilligan, and I think that a lot of the trouble he gets himself into is …'

'That may be well and truly so,' the governor stopped me. 'But I have to tell the both of you, that Conlon must remain where he is for the present time. Conlon can not be returned to the wings if this prison is to function over Christmas.'

'But what grounds do you have you for your decision? What more can the fellow do to convince you that he has taken his punishment?'

'Grounds! The justification for Conlon being where he is today is that Conlon is a violent and destructive man, unpredictable, and a force onto himself. Conlon on the wings is a danger not just to the staff but to the other prisoners. If you know anything of Conlon's history from

Magilligan you will know that Conlon left an officer up there who'll never work again. Are *you* prepared to answer for Conlon when he kills someone if he's allowed back on the wings?'

The word "kill" just about put the kybosh on it for Maurice. His resolve, I suspected, was weakening.

'Isn't he the same danger however long you hold him in solitary?' I ventured.

'I am operating the house on reduced staff levels over the ten day Christmas period. If Conlon returns, I cannot guarantee the other prisoners' safety, let alone my men's safety.'

'Leaving him to fester in solitary confinement? How can that help? What about psychiatric help?'

'That could certainly be looked into, if that is how the BOV feel.'

'Is there any other house that would take him? What about Bann or Erne?'

'I will ask no other house governor to put men's lives at risk.'

Nor, in the end, could we.

'But Christmas?' I made one last plea. 'You plan to leave the poor fellow here on Christmas Day?'

Laying down his newspaper, the officer at the other desk chipped in: 'If you ask my opinion I think Conlon finds life less bother over here. He's away from the hassle of the wings. I think it's the pressure gets to him there. It's a different pace in this unit; here he knows where he stands. I often hear himself and Billy Wright chatting away. [Billy Wright, the paramilitary leader of the Loyalist Volunteer Force (LVF), and a small band of associates, were being held in the PSU at the time.] If you want my opinion I think Conlon's better off here, getting his time done quietly.'

'If the BOV are prepared to take responsibility for Conlon on the wings when we are short-staffed that is fine by me,' said the governor, as if relinquishing responsibility.

'And, if we don't sign, Willy? What happens?' asked Maurice.

'Have you spoken to your chairman?'

'You mean, if we don't sign, you will try someone else?' I knew he also had the NIO option.

'I have no other alternative. I cannot run the risk of Conlon on the wings while I am short-staffed. I cannot put men's lives in peril.'

Could we dictate to a governor in a high security prison where he should house a dangerous prisoner?

Charlie Conlon was just a name to Maurice, another amongst six hundred other names and numbers. He knew nothing of Charlie's history other than what he heard since coming into the prison a short time before. And prisoners can be very plausible. They can spin you a convincing line. 'I think we should listen to what the governor is saying, Patricia.' Maurice had his mind made up.

By signing we could record misgivings. If we did not sign, and the NIO signed instead, it was unlikely they would have any such misgivings. It gave us some control. The prisoner could consult his solicitor if he felt there was an injustice. He could seek judicial review, have disclosure of comments.

Or, I could just walk away and sign nothing.

21

Hearing that Billy Wright – founder and commander in chief of the extreme paramilitary organisation, the LVF – and Charlie Conlon were having cosy chats, surprised me.

Nicknamed "King Rat", Billy Wright was under threat of execution from the Ulster Volunteer Force (UVF), the organisation from which he had broken from to form the LVF. Wright was under threat from Republicans and Loyalists alike, especially INLA man, Christopher "Crip" McWilliams, which is why he was in the segregated unit for his own protection.

I had never met Wright, but other members had

'*The Protestant people of Ulster will remember what you have done this day.*' Wright told the two members who went to see him before authorising his first Rule 32. That function was duly relinquished to the Secretary of State's representatives in the NIO, there being no volunteers on our board for martyrdom by Rule 32.

From Charlie's cell window, some weeks before, I had observed Wright and another inmate shelter under an awning in the exercise yard. On a wall, across from where we stood, a six-foot high poppy had been chalked on the wall. 'The handiwork of Loyalists commemorating Remembrance Day', claimed Charlie. 'Done under the eyes of officers and cameras, and not a hand lifted to stop such an arrogant display of strength, defiance and superiority. One rule for Loyalists. Another for everyone else.'

When I enquired why an emblem, immortalising what his own father had given his life on the battlefield for, should upset him, he assured me that was not the point. He quoted Equality Commission guidelines on the display of emblems in the workplace, drawing my attention to a host of other rule infringements the Loyalists were supposedly getting away with.

'Yes. I do see your point Charlie, and I will investigate your complaint about violating prison property. And I'll ask if anybody has been charged with rule infringement, and why nobody had put a stop to the activity in the exercise yard.'

'Give me a minute and I'll get you a bucket and mop,' said the officer when I brought the matter to his attention. 'You can go out there yourself and tell Wright to wash his writing off the wall.'

Since nobody wanted to be immortalised by the Protestant people of Ulster for washing a poppy off a wall, the poppy stayed put until such time as a firm of outside contract cleaners was hired to wash the chalk away.

The letter arrived around New Year. I recognised the handwriting on the envelope. Inside it was stamped "CENSORED".

Dear Patricia,

I hope this finds you and your family keeping well as it leaves me not doing too badly. Oops! I shouldn't have said that. It might be construed as me preferring to be isolated and locked in a 9'X6' cell in the punishment unit, without a television or radio, for 23 out of 24 hours, with the other hour spent alone in a bare exercise yard for months, rather than on the wings with the boys for the crack.

Please, forgive me for not providing you with any good reason for extending my period on Rule 32, such as being threatening, abusive, violent, disruptive, etc., since being put on Rule 32 over two months ago, and forcing you to say that keeping me in solitary confinement was for my own sake, and that I functioned best in this environment, away from the pressure on the wings, in order to justify signing me on Rule 32 for another month.

It is my considered view that the Board of Visitors is nothing more than a rubber stamp committee for the Governor, and about as useful as a chocolate fireguard.

I resent the reason you gave for extending my Rule 32. The boredom of captivity only fills me with mounting anger. So, how can you say it is for my own sake, especially as I would not be under any threat on the wings? When I'm on the wings I occupy my time by playing the guitar (and giving guitar lessons), physical training, chess, cards, reading, listening to music, watching TV, and generally socializing.

If I were sentenced (I have spent almost 2 years in prison since getting out of Magilligan in 1994, all of it except 5 days, on remand. Think about that, Patricia!). I would also be doing education and vocational training. At the risk of sounding immodest, I am a fairly popular guy because I can get on with most people. So how can you say that I function best in this environment, removed from the pressures of activity on the wings?

Oh yes, according to the Prison Service, I am probably one of the most dangerous and volatile prisoners contained in Maghaberry Prison. Never mind all the murderers and rapists. I have never murdered or raped anyone, and the biggest sentence I ever received in my entire life was four and a half years for a robbery (during which no one got a finger laid on them).

In the eighteen months or so that I have spent on remand in Maghaberry, I have only assaulted one person, another inmate, whom I hit one punch on the chin. He was a six footer, in his early twenties, and he had it coming.

That led to a chain of events which ended up with me being Rule 32ed on this occasion, on top of being punished at Adjudication.

I have threatened one officer in the past eighteen months, been charged twice for damaging prison property — a picture board a year ago, a toilet two months ago — and about half a dozen times for disobeying orders (THAT'S THE REBEL IN ME, AND IT'S STAYING IN ME). I am a 32-year-old mixed-race, working-class, Catholic who has spent more than half his life in one institution or another. I have been brutalized, degraded and humiliated — treated like an animal — by the system. You or no one else is going to convince me that the Orange-dominated system was doing it for my own sake.

Any other reports about my behaviour in Maghaberry are unsubstantiated allegations that I haven't been given the opportunity to defend myself against, and I dispute them. I am being persecuted because of things I am alleged to have done (some of them I did do, and was punished for years ago.) To be honest with you, Patricia, I am proud that I fought the system.

I've been thinking about Sociology. It really is just a load of bullshit that calls bastards love children instead of bastards. I've been thinking about the SDLP. It is the party of middle class Nationalists. Sinn Fein, Democratic Left, Workers Party, IRSP are the parties of working class Nationalists. Do you know Martin Morgan? [SDLP Councillor on Belfast City Council] He got his arm broken by the DMSU [Divisional Mobile Support Unit] out where I live. I've had my arm broken by them and my eardrum perforated, and a thousand other cuts and bruises. Oh yes. Then when I complained, because I wasn't a Belfast City Councillor,

I was charged with assaulting them to justify my injuries. Of course, because some of my injuries were severe, I had to be going completely mad, foaming at the mouth, bla bla bla, etc, and that was why I received so many injuries; being restrained. Something like the way Jimbo McDonald received eleven broken ribs when they tried to resuscitate him in here.

Anyway, I don't know what Morgan was doing there. Mark Langhammer, Independent Labour is Bawnmore's Councillor on Newtownabbey Borough Council. I think Morgan was concerned about the unrest on the Serpentine Road, because I've yet to see an SDLP (except [Connor Clarke] and he's Democratic Left now) do anything for the working-class Catholic people of Bawnmore. 200 families surrounded by tens of thousands of Orangemen. Twenty-six deaths we've suffered during the Troubles and many, many more injuries. Bawnmore is one of the most deprived areas in Belfast.

Since I'm waffling away here: I asked in the Crum years ago to do a GCSE in Sociology!

I was told I would be better off doing Anthropology!

I ended up doing GCSE Mathematics, which I wanted to do. I always felt I was good at Mathematics. Well, I didn't do the exam because I fell into your capable hands. I owe you my sanity because the Grade B I got in my A Level Accounting proved I wasn't stupid. The last time I was in here (in the PSU) I asked to do A Level Maths. I had A-level in Accounting and Business Studies – Grades B & C respectively. And, GCSE Maths – Grade B. The teacher put me off, so I asked for Philosophy instead and they got it for me.

Why would they let me do A Level Philosophy, but not A-level Maths?

I spent about three months studying the AS Level Phil. Course. The same length of time I spent on my Business Studies, and I still got a C at that, although, granted, I had Accounting which gave me a head start. Now I have lost the study bug altogether. Perhaps, if I was doing a sentence or something?

When I get out this time all I want to do is settle Accounts, and make money. And whatever happens to me happens to me. I don't care anymore. I think it best if there is no further contact between us. Liberalism doesn't appeal to me anymore. I need a strong attitude – no compromise! Your reasons for extending my Rule 32 is tantamount to saying that I can't do

my whack on the wings. That hurt my pride. Through everything, I have
never had to take medication to cope, although I like to relax with a bit of
pot. I don't see anything wrong with that. Ask The <u>Right Honourable</u>
Bob Marley.

    Good Bye
      Charlie

And there it was for all to see. Charlie's opinion of me, and everything I
stood for. During the season of good will, I had failed to put my neck on
the line for a friend. I felt pretty chastened when I finished reading.

'Well Mum, are you going to let us have a look?' chorused the family,
with outstretched hands.

A string of plaintive 'Aaahs,' and 'How-could-yous,' and, 'Why did
you have to go and sign that old, whatever-it-is, rule thing?' was followed
by 'I don't see why you couldn't have just let him back to spend Christmas
with his wee pals on the wing.'

'I don't care what anybody else thinks,' one said, obviously very
impressed by Charlie's arguments, '*I think Charlie is great.*'

'So do I,' her sister backed her up, 'I love the REBEL in him.'

'Just wait till Dad gets back, and we tell him what Charlie thinks of
the SDLP.'

Mending bridges was foremost in my thoughts as the officer led me to
the cell door. Manpower was back to normal levels, yet Charlie remained
in solitary confinement. Two other members had since extended the rule.
The pressure was mounting to keep him where he was.

In the intervening period I'd had a phone call asking if I felt there was
a vendetta against Charlie Conlon. 'He's not the worst by any means,'
Margaret, an earlier signatory shared her view. We talked at length, deciding
to make his continued detention an agenda item at our next meeting. I
had asked her if she would smooth the path for me with Charlie, and she
had promised him I would visit following our next board meeting.

Charlie was expecting the visit. We shook hands, wishing each other
Happy New Year.

I briefed him on family reaction to his letter, their conviction that *I*
was in the wrong. They wanted to meet him. He would have to come
and visit when he got out.

'You've done a good job bringing them up,' he told me.

How did you get through Christmas?' I asked.

'Christmas?' he looked puzzled, as if just reminded of a missed dentist appointment. 'I hadn't got it marked on the calendar if that's what you're on about. It passed, like every other day of the week passes. They unlocked us around eight and said if we wanted we could watch TV in the upstairs room. The Loyalists were in there all day playing cards. Billy Wright sent word down that I was welcome to join. He was all right about it. But I have nothing in common with them ones. So apart from talking to your wee fellow Saggart who was here as well, I talked to no one else.'

'Bobby Saggart? Still here?'

'They won't let him back to the wings because he's going for judicial review. I'm in the same boat. I've done the same.'

The outcome of the board meeting would bring little comfort to Charlie. Due to further infringement of rules over the holiday period, all argument for his repatriation fell on deaf ears. 'If the prisoner is not prepared to make the effort and cooperate with the system,' said the governor, 'he will be dealt with as every other prisoner is dealt with in this prison.'

'I had nothing to lose', said Charlie. 'If I was going to be punished, it might as well be for something I'd done.'

'But Charlie . . .?'

Charlie knew their tricks. 'You can only take so much, Patricia.'

And so I left the prison that day, knowing that for the foreseeable future, Charlie Conlon was going nowhere.

22

A Case Conference on Conlon was scheduled; date to be decided. If I wished to attend, I would be facilitated.

I decided to put some thoughts on paper and submit them in advance, setting out the position from my perspective:

> *... the prisoner believes that there is no valid justification for his detention in the PSU, and is seeking Judicial Review. I understand his case awaits the outcome of [Saggart] before progressing.*

Adding that I did not believe, as had been touted, that Charlie was "lawyer driven", rather that:

> *... regarding the incident which led to his removal to the PSU, he accepts that he bore some responsibility; that detention was in order, but that the degree to which this has now escalated is unfair, wrong and vindictive.*

On the issue of psychological help, and the way it had now emerged as a significant factor in the justification for his continued detention, I pointed out that I had suggested this remedy when I realised the full extent of the governor's determination not to uphold the prior recommendation of my two BOV colleagues Rule 32 signing, on grounds of Conlon's potential to "kill".

> *... He is willing to accept help by way of counselling, guidance and such. However, he is adamant that this willingness can be used as a means of vindicating his removal from association. Conlon has been offered and will refuse such help, unless he is first returned to a house.*

I asked that a more recent psychologist's report conducted at Magilligan in 1994 be brought into play. Saying that Charlie argues the prison is selective in their use of information, and that at the root is a vengeful campaign relating back to two incidents, one in Crumlin Road, and a previous incident in Magilligan, where prison officers sustained injuries and he himself was hospitalised. I added:

> *... The circumstances which led to Conlon being in the PSU today are not disputed by me. Nevertheless, I feel that an impasse has been reached, and that he is in for the long haul. There is such a torrent of unresolved conflict and anger in this intelligent, articulate and sensitive young man, that until this is fully addressed, he will never have the skills to hack it in the outside world. He holds that, until the Magilligan incident, his*

behaviour record in prison was reasonable, given the nature of the racist taunts he has endured all his life. Over a two-year period, he did make a valiant effort by gaining entry qualifications to university. My real concern is that the traditional method is producing a more hardened, more bitter and potentially more dangerous man.

This communication was sent in January 1997. While awaiting my summons to the case conference, a mate of Charlie's, stopped me on the wing. 'Charlie's looking for a word, so he is. I was talking to him in the chapel and he said to tell you.'

Charlie? In the chapel? The Charlie I knew had as much faith in God as he knew God had in him. No barrier, though, to demanding his right to attend Mass.

I found Charlie in his cell.

He was pensive. I mentioned that I planned to sit in on his case conference and promised I would bring him feedback.

A prisoner was exercising in the yard outside, moving past the cell window. Charlie stood up and beckoned me to join him at the window.

The man in the yard was Billy Wright.

I moved to Charlie's side and stood with eyes riveted on the lone figure circling the concrete enclosure. Next time round he broke step and came across to the window. Resting an elbow on the ledge, he leaned down and peered in. 'Allright Charlie?'

'Aye. You OK yourself Billy?' Charlie's tone was warm and friendly.

Seeing Charlie was not alone, Wright withdrew 'Talk to you later, Charlie.'

'Right you be, Billy, talk to you later,' Charlie called out.

'Oh, so we're on first-names with the LVF leadership now, are we?' I chided. 'Relations have improved since Armistice Day?'

'I have no quarrel with Billy Wright,' he said.

For a time I stood transfixed, my eyes following the lean martial figure parade past, yards from me. A second prisoner sauntered in beside Wright. (Rules had been relaxed since the arrival of the paramilitaries in the PSU allowing prisoners to exercise in pairs.) Deep in conversation, the two LVF men went past again and again, Wright's head high as a gander pacing a farmyard, keeping sentry on his flock. His ears sat out like satellite dishes.

'I could kill Billy Wright standing here.' Charlie's words came out of the blue.

'Oh, sure you could, Charlie. Tell me all about it. Tell me about all the things you could do standing where you are.' But something in his tone caused me to reflect on what a peculiar thing to say, "*I could kill Billy Wright standing here*".

Having seen enough of Billy Wright for one day I moved away from the window, saying, 'You're giving me the creeps, Charlie,'.

Charlie lingered, his mind seemingly occupied. 'If I had a gun I could do it easily from where I'm standing. Look Patricia,' he directed me with eyes focused on the back of the man outside the window.

'If you had a gun, Charlie! *If you had a gun?*' Omitting to mention others he might like to kill first *if* he had a gun, I asked, 'And how, in the name of God, would you get a gun?'

'Don't be too sure about that, Patricia. If I'd do it, don't you fear, they'd get a gun to me.'

'Too sure about what? About getting your hands on a gun inside Maghaberry prison? Or, that you'd kill somebody if you had one?'

'Billy Wright's never done anything against me.' Charlie had turned from the window and was looking me straight in the eye. 'I have no quarrel with Billy Wright, Patricia. He's supposed to be here for his own protection. Know what I mean?'

The visit came to an end, and it was only later I remembered, Charlie never told me why he had asked to see me. Yet, that bizarre conversation was one I would have cause to remember when Billy Wright was murdered later that same year.

I still awaited my call to the case conference.

'Until his judicial review is out of the way,' said the governor when I asked about progress, 'Conlon will remain where he is. My hands are tied.'

'And how long might that take.'

'How long is a piece of string?'

Although I had been preparing the ground for a meeting between Charlie and the prison psychologist, I knew it was a non-runner before his judicial review. To acknowledge any flaw in his character would be tantamount to handing the prison authorities his head on a plate. He was not about to hand ammunition to their legal team to wave before his barrister in court. They would twist anything for their own ends, he believed. He would have nothing to do with any psychologist before judgement was passed down from the courts. That would be showing weakness, and that was something Charlie Conlon would never show.

Time was moving on, and still no date fixed for the case conference.

The number one governor had retired; a new captain was at the helm. (During my tenure in Maghaberry there were six changes at the top, with constant changes at lower ranks.) Let the new man find his feet, I thought. Meantime, I would keep Conlon's continued detention in the PSU on the agenda.

The concept of an 'exit strategy' was first mooted by the new governor. No prisoner should be placed in solitary confinement without a plan in place to facilitate a return to the wings. This new Mission Statement impressed everyone. The board had become increasingly divided over Conlon. Most members had met Charlie. Most had signed a Rule 32 at one time or another. Some said they would not sign another. Some were beginning to show signs of *Conlon fatigue*. 'Talk to the staff about Conlon,' one member could not conceal his annoyance at so much board time devoted to this one issue.

'And when, might I ask, is this case conference ever going to happen?' I kept asking. 'I'll look into that for you,' they kept repeating.

I was walking through Red Square – surfaced in tinted pebble-mix and named it for its hue – the quadrangle that encloses Lagan and Foyle, the hospital, the PSU and Education, when I met Governor MacMahon.

'What's happening with Conlon,' I asked. 'I'm still waiting for a call to the case conference.'

'I was under the impression that case conference happened weeks back. Are you absolutely positive it hasn't?'

'I was supposed to be informed, Billy. I sent in a report, I assumed someone would phone me.'

'You sent a report? First I heard of it.'

'But I cc'd it to you.'

'Never saw any report.'

'So, who got it then?'

Search him!

'So what's the plan?'

'Plan?'

'Yes, exit strategy. How do you plan to get Conlon back to the wings?'

'You know he has taken a judicial review?'

'And tell me what's new about that? Don't they all.'

'Saggart's review is heard first.'

'And meantime?'

'Our hands are tied. We await the outcome of Saggart before there's any movement with Conlon.'

Regardless of the pace the court service was moving at, I needed to get a move on. I was on my way to the hospital to link up with Frances, another member. Charlie had accumulated a string of new charges over the past weeks. Baffled as to what to do for the best, we had arranged a meeting with the prison psychologist. Being a watchdog body, there was concern amongst some of our members that the prison segregation unit was becoming a dumping-ground for prisoners in need of full psychiatric care. Equally worrying was this notion that you could break somebody in that unit. Consequently, I carried this nagging fear at the back of my mind that one day Charlie might be *pushed* towards fulfilling that prophecy: "*One day that fellow will kill somebody*".

The suggestion that Charlie might have a personality disorder had been mooted more than once. From my limited knowledge of personality traits – the way we relate, perceive, and think about ourselves and our environment – I understood that disorders occur when traits become stiff and rigid. Those afflicted usually manifest symptoms by adolescence, the disorder becoming less apparent as the person grows older. If such were the case with Charlie, and he never got the help to enable him overcome his condition, then prison was simply aggravating the problem. The good news was that, depending on the degree to which the person was affected, many disorders could be alleviated, if not totally cured.

With more sinister undertones was the suggestion bandied around the prison that Charlie was evil. Some likening him to cold-blooded murderers, personified in names like Peter Sutcliffe, the Yorkshire Ripper, or Ted Bundy in the United States. Charlie, with his history of continuous antisocial activity fitted the picture perfectly for those who were not prepared to look beyond.

Just too many indicators of the sociopath did not fit easy with the man I knew. Charlie was no con-man. He had a high regard for the truth. And he was very capable of maintaining enduring attachments. Had he not said so in his Christmas letter: "at the risk of sounding immodest, I am a fairly popular guy because I can get on with most people. So how can you say that I function best in this environment, removed from the pressures of activity on the wings?" He had asked me to think about that.

And the *losing the head* theory, the plain *bonkers* theory? His brother's theory.

Again, if such were the case and he *was* mad, it might not be so bad. Insanity, or psychosis, I read, is relatively easy to diagnose, and with aggressive therapy most psychoses can be cured or alleviated. So if Charlie was simply *mad in the head*, there was some hope on the horizon.

Pride got no mention in any of the literature I consulted, and Charlie was a proud man.

Another concern was brain damage from all those bangs to his head.

But such investigation was the concern of the clinical psychologist, not the work of the BOV. All we sought was insight, anything to find a way out of an impasse. Even just the language to argue more forcibly that other avenues should be explored.

Had we expected to find a couch centre stage, we would have been disappointed. Instead, a young man sat in front of a computer. We had spoken on the telephone the previous week and it was at his suggestion this meeting was arranged. He knew all about Charlie Conlon.

I outlined my involvement, and talked about the prisoner's background and volatility. Of him opening up to me about his formative years.

The psychologist stopped me at that point. He explained his role in the prison service. It was clear he would not be barging into the PSU uninvited, offering his services to Charlie Conlon, or to any other prisoner for that matter. He queried the prisoner's own attitude to professional help.

That, I explained, was the nub of the problem. 'All he will agree to is this initial meeting between us. I have promised to get back to him afterwards, and we are to take it from there. I am here mainly to ascertain what therapy or counselling is available beyond anger management courses delivered by prison personnel. Charlie downright refuses to participate in anything involving prison officers. As to my second reason for coming to meet you, I suppose I'm checking you out. It may help that you haven't got two heads, or horns. At least it will be easier to plug the notion that an exploratory talk with you would involve no loss of face for Charlie.'

As we spoke I became more and more convinced that if Charlie got to sit on the chair I was sitting on, there was every possibility that further meetings would follow.

23

The case conference had not worked to plan, nor had I an opportunity to speak with Charlie after meeting the psychologist, before the summons to the Crown Solicitor's office came.

His judicial review application was listed in the courts that week. Therefore, BOV members who had signed Rule 32s since November were asked to appear before a barrister and provide sworn affidavits. The original forms outlining reasons for sanctioning solitary confinement were in evidence. And each person in the room was defending their reasons as stated.

As statements were recorded I realised this was nothing like what I had planned for. Faced with the question: Was there a valid and justifiable basis for signing? And, if there wasn't? Some of us were going to look rather foolish.

Where now were all those troubled voices I had heard vowing they would not sign Conlon on Rule 32 for one more day, much less one more month?

Yes, Margaret said her piece. Margaret was impassioned, and she was vocal. Something was not right. She would not go along with the prison on any further signing. Charlie Conlon was much maligned. He was a victim as much as anything else; a casualty of circumstances. She knew his area; his background. Her own working-class background shone through her passion.

Good for you Margaret, I thought. The barrister heard differently. *Yesterday* she had signed. What she would do *today* was immaterial.

Maurice, my co-signatory spoke next. His was a different approach. Measured. More focused. He concentrated on the salient point. To what extent had we satisfied ourselves that the prisoner presented a real threat to good order and discipline for the running of the prison?

He outlined the procedures he and I followed when coming to our decision. We had spoken with the prisoner, read reports. Spoke to the PO, to officers in the PSU; spoke with a governor. And the result! Two honest brokers, with no vested interest, had accepted, on balance, senior management's assessment that the prisoner did pose a threat. Otherwise, why else would we have signed?

The barrister's pen targeted the lady member sitting to the left of Maurice. Pearl talked about Charlie looking at her menacingly when she attempted to see him prior to a signing. He looked very sinister she said, and she shivered at the thought. Black. Dour. Threatening. She still wasn't the better of that ill look. The man sitting beside Pearl felt for her. None of us, he believed, should be subjected to ill looks from any prisoner. When his turn came, he easily justified why he signed Charlie Conlon on Rule 32.

And finally it was my turn to have my say. Could I disagree with Maurice? If I had signed under duress, then why had I not stated so on the form? I talked about the prisoner being in need of psychiatric help, not punishment. I talked about meeting with the psychologist. I tried as best I could to say that the PSU was not the right place to hold him. The barrister took note of what I said, but try as I might, the majority voice around the table was sending the message to the Crown Court that Charlie Conlon was where he was for very good reason.

Faces were sober while statements were wrapped up. Some members had travelled long distances to be there, and the roar of traffic was mounting outside the window. Everyone wanted to get on the road before the rush. Now it was up to the courts to decide whether or not Charlie Conlon was wrongfully detained in the PSU.

Before I even ventured near the prison again, I was in trouble. And this time big-time! The tip-off came in a telephone call.

'Crip McWilliams is baying for your blood.'

'What have I done now, Alexander?' I was not unduly worried since I was bound to be in favour with Chris following my efforts to have him reunited with his clothes.

'Circulated a rumour around the prison that McWilliams is a British spy.'

'Oh dear Jesus, Alexander,' I panicked. 'How am I going to talk my way out of this?'

'Why?' he asked. 'Is it true?'

The spy story was not of my creation, but I did play a minor role. Kevin McAlorum, a one-time associate of McWilliams, was serving a life sentence in Maghaberry. He came to BOV attention because he was housed in a ground floor cell, the window opening on to the exercise yard. He was scared for his life, fearing what might come through that window.

Both he and McWilliams had been INLA volunteers until a faction-fight caused a split, placing them on opposing sides. Such was the murderous power-struggle that over a period of one year, six people lay dead, including Chris McWilliams' best friend, Gino Gallagher, the leader of McWilliams' faction. McAlorum was blamed for Gallagher's death. (McAlorum's nine-year-old sister died after a gunman raked the family home with bullets in a reprisal attack. In 2004 McAlorum, himself, was shot dead in an ambush in Belfast.)

We negotiated a move to an upstairs cell for Kevin McAlorum and thus became acquainted. I now had an ear in both camps.

'Crip wouldn't waste a bullet in here on the likes of McAlorum, Missus,' John Kennaway another of the McWilliams faction made it clear when I touched on the issue of in-fighting. 'Crip? Serve time for the likes of McAlorum? You must be joking! But, let him fret.'

The McWilliams faction had the *frighteners* on their man, and that was good enough for the time being. 'But, don't you worry your head Missus,' added John, 'McAlorum will be done outside. He's putting it about that Crip's a British Agent.'

'So they tell me,' I replied, adding that it was outside the prison I first heard the rumour.

How was I to know that Kennaway would go hot-footed to Chris McWilliams. Patricia Farren, he reported, is spreading it around the prison that people in the know, on the outside, believe you're a spy.

Saturday morning, and instead of the family shop I was on the road to Maghaberry.

Chris's eyes flickered when I walked into his cell. We shook hands.

'You were talking to Alexander yesterday,' I said. 'He phoned me last night. I made it in as soon as I could.'

My first line of defence was to look worried. My second lay in the laps of the Gods. I did look worried. I was worried. Very worried. When on the mat before a man found guilty of murdering two men, with a bullet sharpened for a third, you get to feel what worry really feels like. I doubted if tears would work.

'I have some explaining to do, Chris.' I sat down without being asked.

'Being perfectly honest, I did agree with John that a rumour is doing the rounds, only because I thought the whole thing was a laugh. You? A spy? A British Agent? The very idea!'

'Enough said.' Chris was convinced. And together we agreed that the very idea was an insult to every Republican - dead or alive. And that the blame for the scurrilous rumour could be placed well and truly at the feet of Special Branch, linked to the forces of the Crown, the RUC, the NIO, the POA, the media … all in cahoots with the devil, I suppose.

Chris sounded most convincing.

While in the prison I used the opportunity to drop by Charlie's cell.

In recent days a ten-point exit-strategy plan had been drawn up. If he would guarantee good behaviour and sign up to the compact, he could return to normal association.

Charlie had refused point-blank to sign. From his standpoint the plan guaranteed nothing on the part of the prison. His contention that he was wrongfully detained in the PSU was steadfast as ever. He would not put his trust in deals with an establishment that would not guarantee equal rights to him. Since he had just been granted leave for judicial review he was suspicious, believing the NIO sought a way out – no prisoner in solitary confinement, meant no case to answer in court.

'Well Charlie, I wouldn't hold my breath waiting for support from those who signed affidavits,' I cautioned.

Charlie said he understood where the BOV were coming from. It was all part of our rubber-stamping role.

When I spoke of my meeting with the psychologist, he said I might forget about anything there until after his judicial review.

'When the time is right, Charlie,' I said, leaving.

The Crip McWilliams spy-gate might have put the frighteners on me a few weeks previous, but it was nothing compared to the tremor that ran down my spine as I arrived at Charlie's cell door some weeks later.

On our way down the corridor I had remarked to the officer how quiet things were. 'You should have been here the other morning. Then, you'd'a seen skin and hair flying. We had the psychologist bloke over. Said the BOV sent him over to Conlon. Conlon threw the head when I went to tell him.'

With sinking heart I stopped the officer in his tracks. 'Say that again.'

I was grabbing his arm to deter him, wishing I was standing anywhere other than outside that cell door. 'Did they meet?'

'Th'on' boy? See a doctor? If you want my opinion, it's a Vet the BOV should be bringing in here to Conlon.'

And, with the sure grace of his profession, he inserted the key in the lock and the cell door swung open.

Not waiting for an invitation, I entered the cell, sat down and said, 'I feel like crying, Charlie.'

He was standing by the window, talking to a prisoner in the yard. He glanced my way, surprised at the sudden intrusion. In one seamless motion he moved towards me, both hands dug deep in his pockets, fists clenched inside. His head darted between me and the door. First sound, I was certain, and he would land his first punch.

'I walked myself into it, Charlie.'

He didn't hit me.

I took heart.

'I shared my views with people I trusted, Charlie, and they let me down.'

A jerk of the head conveyed, he might well understand.

'How can I explain?' In my discomfort I was humble.

Charlie's eyes were on the cell door. 'They came in yesterday morning with the usual auld sneers on their faces. Taking delight in telling me: *"Oh, the psychologist is looking to see you, Conlon,"* bhla, bhla, bhla …'

He paced the cell like a caged animal, his brooding eyes focused menacingly on the back of that door. His fists ploughed deeper and deeper into his pockets. He looked ferocious.

'I'm causing you more trouble than it's worth, Charlie,' I said, laying my hand on his arm. 'I thought I was helping. That's all I was trying to do. I just wanted to help, and I got it all wrong.'

My spontaneous, artless gesture caught him unawares. 'What am I doing?' he said, taking his hands from his pockets, and raising them to his temples. 'What am I like?' He thumped the sides of his head with tightened fists. 'Here's me, getting angry with you, when I know you were only trying to do what *you* thought was right.'

He sat down on the bed. In seconds he was again the composed, collected Charlie I knew so well.

The psychologist's visit was yesterday's event. Today his barrister was

Leading Man. Pat Spring was not overly optimistic regarding the judicial review. Charlie had read transcripts of affidavits. The untimely arrival of a real psychologist in the PSU was helping nobody. Perhaps his barrister had had a word with Charlie on the back of those affidavits. God knows what Pat Spring said, but whatever it was, it did me no harm.

Opportunism was responsible for the crossed wires. Or so Teddy believed when I relayed how another member had taken up my suggestion of psychological help for Charlie, and ran with it themselves, going hot-foot to the psychologist – who mistakenly took it to mean that the prisoner wished to see him.

'She had no right to muscle in on my patch, Teddy.'

'Some folks want a hand in everything going,' agreed Teddy.

By March of 1997, a mass exodus from the PSU had occurred. Political status had been granted to Billy Wright and his LVF legion, and they had taken up residence in the Maze prison.

Saggart and Conlon also exited, both returning to normal association. It was never made clear whether the outcome of Saggart's judicial review had been determined by the courts or by legal opinion prior to hearing. As far as members of the BOV were concerned, we were content to hear that the prisoners were back in normal association.

April saw both of Charlie's cases come to trial. He was found guilty on all five counts for the incident in the Rainbow bar, and a three-year prison sentence imposed.

On the other seventeen counts – when he went looking for his money back – the sentence imposed was one year. Sentences ran concurrently, and since he had served almost all of it on remand, he was released before I had another chance to talk to him.

Against a backdrop of peace talks outside the prison, another saga was working its way on to the scene inside.

Breaking news of the event came on the radio. A prisoner in Maghaberry had produced a gun and taken a prison officer hostage. The incident had taken place in Red Square. The prisoner with the gun was Christopher "Crip" McWilliams. Following a visit to the hospital, McWilliams, with an accomplice John Kennaway, produced the gun and forced their way into one of the blocks. They then attempted to make it to an upstairs landing where Kevin McAlorum was housed.

The situation was contained, and the gun handed over.

The incident was reported at our board meeting, where it was claimed that killing McAlorum in such a daring manner would have impressed McWilliams' INLA compatriots in the Maze – from whose paramilitary wing he was exiled – thus paving the way for his repatriation back into the fold.

The interpretation made sense up to a point.

If McWilliams seriously intended killing McAlorum and failed, then why was he keen to leave the scene and locate to the Maze? Kennaway had told me that Crip, while inside, had no intention of taking out McAlorum. And Chris had never shown any desire to return to the Maze. Quite the contrary. It just did not add up, and I said so.

Recalling that weird conversation with Charlie in the PSU: *"How could anyone possibly get their hands on a gun in Maghaberry?"* And his reply: *"Don't be too sure about that. If I'd do it, don't fear they'd get a gun to me".* Was there a subliminal message in there?

I listened as the governor gave his report, and to the comments that followed, waiting an opportunity to suggest that McWilliams might have a target other than McAlorum. It was a wild card, and when nobody took up my point, I pressed again.

'Could it be that Wright's earlier transfer to the Maze frustrated McWilliams' plan?'

How frank could I be? After all it was only speculation. The governor's door was always open to members. But what would I say? *Somebody approached Charlie Conlon to know if they got a gun to him, would he take out Billy Wright?* I had already hinted as much.

Then again. Why should anyone worry! Billy Wright was away. Christopher McWilliams was away. John Kenaway was away. Charlie Conlon was away. All the bad boys were gone. No longer Magaberry's concern.

But soon, some were back.

In December 1997 Billy Wright was shot dead in the Maze. Christopher "Crip" McWilliams pulled the trigger. His accomplices were John Kennaway and John "Sonny" Glennon,

All three were transferred back to Maghaberry, and housed in the PSU for their own protection.

Chris sent word that he wanted to see me.

He was exercising in the yard with his co-accused when I arrived. Coming face to face with a man who had just murdered another man, how should I react? Would we greet each other with customarily smiles? Or, would I just hold back on the smiles on this occasion?

He proffered his hand. '*It had to be done*, Patricia,' he said, with not a flicker of the eye.

Kennaway and Glennon joined in telling me that they feared they were all sitting-ducks for reprisal. Wright's murder would be avenged. Food was their chief concern. Meals from the kitchen might be poisoned. They were surviving on tuck-shop fare. 'But to be fair to the governor and the screws,' Chris acknowledged, 'they are doing all they can to see we get fed,' The other pair nodded in agreement.

Next time I met Chris, it was in his cell. On the floor sat a stack of old newspapers. "KING RAT KILLED" the newspaper caption on the top copy.

Chris never again referred to the killing, and neither did I.

24

Given his opinion of our usefulness, I was surprised to find 'B2142 Conlon, Erne 4,' in the visits request book. Charlie was back.

I chose to see him in an interview room, rather than his cell.

Committed some weeks earlier, he had spent the customary period in inception before moving on to the wings. He had minded his own business, kept his head down. At the weekend an ordinary-class officer had reported for duty on Erne 4, saw Charlie and went directly to the SO, demanding that the prisoner be moved to another wing. The SO had acquiesced. On Monday morning Charlie was told to collect his belongings. He was moving to Erne 5.

Charlie complained at principal-officer level. There was a stay of execution, but later he was told to gather his belongings. When he requested to see the BOV the move was further delayed.

'Let me get this clear, Charlie. An ordinary-rank officer spies you, goes to his SO, and, hey presto, you're moved? It doesn't make sense, unless separation avoids occasions for trouble.

I was missing the point. Charlie pulled his chair forward. 'Right,' he said. 'How does this look to you: an ordinary-class officer giving orders to an SO? There's hostility between a lot more people in here than me and Dullis, let me tell you, but nobody else gets shifted on a class-officer's say-so. They're at their old tricks, backing one and other up. There's a clique controlling this prison that'll lie and perjure themselves to back up their own.' The Masonic Order, he claimed, ran the place.

'And maybe you'd tell me how you know?' I leaned back to listen.

Prisoners watched officers, knew every action, every gesture, every finger twist. Dullis was a bully. He was a bad egg who could depend on his back being covered.

Bells began to ring. Erne 5! the landing Charlie was destined for, had been the subject of heated discussion at a recent meeting. It functioned as a sort of sin bin for isolating persistent troublemakers. A recent innovation heralding the way forward, the regime operated a twenty-three-hour lockdown system. In effect it mirrored the PSU in intent and purpose, yet got around the rules. Those in need of a short sharp shock were now finding their way on to Erne 5.

Whatever explanation there might be for sending Charlie there, it had to have more substance than the say-so of one officer. I promised I would investigate, and get back to him.

Stripes on an epaulette distinguish rank. I hadn't twigged before asking if I might speak with the principal officer.

I *was* speaking to the principal officer.

'It's about Conlon,' I said, watching her eyes rove beyond me, following Charlie as he was escorted past the window. 'I'm querying the grounds for his move to Erne 5. Who authorised it? And, if convenient, I would like to read whatever reports are on file.'

Ordinarily, such a request would be accommodated without question. Not so today. No chair was offered. No file opened. No views shared. Conlon, I learned, was moving to the fives no matter what anyone said or thought. End of story.

'But surely …' I tried.

The subject was closed. Still, it was my duty to know why, and then justify the *why* to the prisoner.

Eventually a governor was summoned.

Like all our governors, Governor Brogan subscribed to a good tailor, and, in fairness to the man, did the suit justice. He had been briefed before joining me in the interview room.

He dispatched an officer to fetch the SO from the fours.

'Conlon was down for a move to the fives when I reported for duty to the fours on Monday morning, Boss,' the SO stated. And, no, there was no complaint on file. 'Just word he was down for moving.'

Charlie had challenged, first with the PO, and now the BOV. The SO was holding fire, awaiting instructions from the governor.

The SO went back to his duties on the fours; the officer told to fetch the prisoner.

Charlie's argument was simple. He had not transgressed. Why should he be punished?

Whether the governor's fatherly pep-talk was registering – about keeping his hands in his mits, occupying his time constructively, taking up study again – Charlie's expression gave no hint. I wanted to tell him to smile at the nice man. Even when told he might remain on the fours, he betrayed no emotion.

The reprieve was justice of a sort, I suppose. But then Charlie had not done anything wrong, had he?

Why was Charlie back in prison?

'He tried to kill his mother.' I was being accompanied to his cell by an officer. 'It was all over the *Belfast Telegraph* a few weeks ago. Did you not read all about it?'

'The charges are not to be sneezed at,' Charlie admitted, handing me the charge sheet. I glanced down the page:

THREATS TO KILL

ASSAULT ON POLICE

ASSAULT ON POLICE

CRIMINAL DAMAGE

PREVENTING THE COURSE OF JUSTICE

ASSAULT OCCASIONING ACTUAL BODILY HARM

ASSAULT OCCASIONING ACTUAL BODILY HARM

ASSAULT OCCASIONING ACTUAL BODILY HARM

But there was hope. If his mother would cooperate with his solicitor, the serious charge of 'threats to kill' might be withdrawn.

'Great,' I said.

Unfortunately the police had got around her, pretending they cared by giving her cups of tea in the station and taking her to the hospital for a check. She fell for things like that. That was the type of her.

'The fact that police showed concern. Urged her to see a doctor. You mean that wasn't caring?'

'Pretend caring.' Charlie knew their tricks.

It was Sean who later filled in the details.

On her return home from a night away, having left Charlie home alone, Maura found loud music blaring, and a neighbour with a young child complaining about the noise.

Maura confronted her son, the neighbour standing by. Charlie, high on either drugs or alcohol, was oblivious to the noise. His mother had never seen him in such a state before. She panicked, got palpitations; was very frightened. The young neighbour phoned the police.

At mention of the police, Charlie went bananas and barricaded himself inside the building, his mother on the floor above. The young girl was new to the area and did not really know the score regarding the police, Sean believed. 'Otherwise it would have got handled locally.' The police arrived and got Maura out to safety through an upstairs window and across a roof, then went back in for Charlie.

Down at the station Maura made a statement.

If Charlie was banking on his mother withdrawing that statement, Sean said, 'Charlie shouldn't hold his breath.'

After talking with Charlie I went along to Erne 5 to see conditions for myself.

The first prisoner I spoke with said he was on the verge of suicide. A non-smoker, he was locked in a cell with a smoker twenty-three hours of the day.

Terry Maguire had come back in to serve a life sentence for murder and arson. 'For fuck's sake, Tricia, it was never meant,' he confessed. 'We torched a house belonging to a fellow who owed us. Didn't know there was a squatter inside?'

And the reason he was in Erne 5?

Urinating on his cell floor. He was still urinating on the cell floor as the puddles at my feet testified. He would stop one of these days. Meantime what could I do about getting him back on the wings?

Bullying, distributing drugs . . . I took my list of complaints to the SO.

The SO corrected me. Prisoners were not locked down twenty-three hours of the day. Outside normal lockdown, they were out of their cells as regulations stipulated. Once a day for exercise, three times to collect meals, once for showers, once for telephones, once for laundry, once a week for religious services . . . Everything could be justified.

Two weeks later Charlie was transferred from Erne 4, to Erne 5. And thus began a series of incidents that would lead to solitary confinement for a very, very long period indeed.

Months into that solitary confinement I asked Charlie to chronicle events as they happened, so that I could make some sense of it.

Charlie did not gild the lily:

I came into prison on remand on the 2nd October, 1998. On the 4th December, 1998, I was housed on a 'normal' landing – Erne 4. When I went down to collect my tea-meal from the main servery in Erne House, the officer serving the chips put a small amount of chips on my plate, and I asked him for a few more, which he refused. I then went to serve myself, and the officer grabbed me by the wrist. I felt that I had been assaulted, and I said to the officer that if he ever laid a hand on me again to expect something very nasty to happen.

A short time after returning to my cell and eating my meal, the House Governor came to my cell and told me that I was being charged for using abusive and threatening language to an officer, and that I was being moved to Erne 5, a segregation landing termed the Close Supervision Unit, where prisoners are kept locked in their cells for most of the day. It is normal for prisoners on Erne 5 to be held there for a number of months before being returned to a normal landing.

I thought this was very harsh because of the relatively minor incident which led to it, and especially because this was the first bit of trouble I had been in since I came into prison. I tried to explain this to the Governor, but he said he wasn't interested. All he wanted to know was whether I was going to move to Erne 5 by myself, or he would have me forcibly moved. This particular Governor was responsible for the death of a friend of mine who received eleven broken ribs and was found dead in a cell in the punishment unit.

I told the Governor that I would move by myself and called him a murderer. I then moved to Erne 5.

The following day I was charged with using abusive and threatening language towards the Governor.

The day after that, I was adjudicated on for both charges of using abusive and threatening language. However, both charges were adjourned because of the unavailability of staff. To date, these matters have still to be dealt with, after more than three months, despite me having seen the staff involved on duty on many occasions during that period.

After some weeks on Erne 5, without any incident, I petitioned the Secretary of State on the grounds that I had my association restricted without having gone through any disciplinary procedure. I was not given any specified time for when these restrictions would end, and that it was done without the agreement of the Board of Visitors, or the Secretary of State.

A few days later, I again petitioned the Secretary of State on the grounds that I felt that I was being victimised by prison staff, and especially the House Governor in Erne House, as I know of at least three other persons in Erne House who had committed much more serious offences against prison discipline, than using abusive and threatening language, yet those prisoners weren't moved to Erne 5.

I received an answer to my petition dismissing my arguments out of hand.

After some time on Erne 5, another prisoner there began to verbally racially abuse me in the most derogatory manner. I am mixed race. After saying things like , 'does that black bastard never wash,' and 'is he real half caste, or is that just dirt,' I had a fight with this prisoner in the exercise yard, and we were both charged with fighting. This prisoner admitted to starting the fight and using derogatory language towards me. I said nothing. However, we both received the same award – 3 days CC, 20 days loss of privileges, and 14 days loss of remission.

I was despairing because of the injustice with which I had been treated, and in a moment of madness, I lit a fire in a metal bin in my cell during the first night spent in cellular confinement.

I was then taken out of the cell, and painfully moved to a bare cell by the C&R team, despite showing no aggression whatsoever, where I was stripped naked and left overnight with no food, water or toilet facilities.

The following morning I repeatedly asked to use the toilet, but my requests were ignored, so I defecated on the floor and spread the excrement on the cell door and wall in protest.

The door was opened sometime later by the C&R team, and my clothes were thrown into a pool of urine on the cell floor, and I was ordered to put them on, or else!

I dressed in the clothes and was subsequently taken to Lisburn RUC station where I was interviewed about, and charged with, starting the fire in my cell.

After appearing in court the following morning, I was returned to Maghaberry prison, to the PSU, to complete my cellular confinement.

My cigarette lighter had been taken from me for evidence and I was asking officers for lights, which were given to me.

During the evening I asked the night guard for a light, and he refused to give me it. I explained that I had been given lights all day, even by the principal officer, and that there had been no problems or incidents. The officer called me a dirty black bastard, and said that I wasn't getting a light, so I started banging loudly and continuously on my door with the plastic cup.

Some hours later the officer came back with other officers and said to me: would I give my word that if he gave me a light I would do no damage with it, and that I would be quiet.

I gave them my word, but instead of giving me a light, him and the other officers laughed at me and walked away.

I was infuriated at this, and in another moment of madness, I smashed the spy glass in my door, and continued banging all night in protest.

The following morning I was charged with lighting a fire in my cell, spreading excrement on my spy glass and smashing my spy glass.

After my period on cellular confinement was up, I was sent back to Erne 5. However, the prisoner who was charged with me for fighting was moved off Erne 5 the following day, given an orderly's job in the servery and didn't have to do his twenty days loss of privileges. Whereas I did, plus an extra fourteen days for smearing the spy glass with my excrement.

The charge into lighting the fire was adjourned because of the court case into the matter, and the charge into the smashing of the spy glass was adjourned because of the unavailability of staff.

After more weeks on Erne 5 without any further incident, I was still having my association restricted without proper disciplinary procedures, without knowing how long it would continue, and without the agreement of the BOV or Secretary of State.

On the afternoon of Monday, 1st March 1999, another prisoner on Erne 5 returned from court. His trial was ongoing at the time. He lifted the flap of another prisoner's spy glass and began conversing with him, telling him how the trial was going. At this, an officer ordered him to put the flap down and move away. The prisoner ignored the officer and continued talking through the spy glass to the other prisoner. The officer then punched the prisoner on the head and roughly manhandled him into his cell. Of course, the prisoner attempted to defend himself. All the while the officer was saying to the prisoner, it's not a girl you're beating up now. Then more officers came and the prisoner was C&R'd and taken away, presumably to the PSU.

All the prisoners on Erne 5 were outraged and incensed at the treatment which this prisoner had received and began banging on their doors, and shouting in protest. This carried on for some considerable time. Then later in the evening the prisoners smashed up the contents of their cells.

I had nothing to do with any of these incidents. That night I pressed my cell alarm because I felt sick, but no one answered it. The following morning when I saw the doctor he diagnosed a stomach virus. After seeing the doctor I requested a petition form from the Governor because I wanted to complain about my cell alarm not being answered. At the end of the day, I could have been suffering from something much more serious than a stomach virus.

For that day and the next I was denied exercise and kept locked in my cell for 24 hours per day, despite the previous incident having nothing to do with me. I saw the officer who had originally assaulted the prisoner, and called him a gobshite and a dickhead. However, the officer charged me with threatening to kill him, which was lies.

Then on Thursday 4th March, I was not allowed exercise with other prisoners as I had to go to an adjudication for allegedly threatening to kill the officer.

When all the other prisoners were out in the exercise yard, my cell door opened and there was the officer who was sneering and smirking at me, and said smugly that I was for adjudication. As I went to walk along with him, I called him a dickhead, and he attacked me.

I, of course, attempted to defend myself, but the two officers grabbed me and dragged me to the ground. The officer who originally attacked me grabbed me by the throat and stuck his baton into my neck, and said I'll run this through you, you black bastard.

Then, the C&R team came, and despite me offering no resistance whatsoever, began brutally twisting my arms and legs, causing me excruciating pain. My right arm was twisted so badly that it was in a sling for a few days after the incident.

I was then brought to the PSU, where I was put into a bare cell and had my tobacco, lighter and shoes removed from me. After a while I was given my shoes and tobacco back, and moved to a cell with a bed in it. However, my lighter was withheld from me.

I asked for my lighter back and was told that I wasn't getting it. I tried to explain that I had had that lighter with me at all times for weeks without incident, and that you couldn't just take it from me for no good reason.

However, as ever, my arguments fell on deaf ears.

The following day, I was put on Rule 32, and moved upstairs in the PSU. I again asked to have my lighter back as it was a privilege which I hadn't lost through proper disciplinary procedure. However, it was Friday evening by this stage and the duty governor came to my cell and told me that the deputy governor had ordered that I not be given my lighter, and that he couldn't overrule him. He said, if I left it with him until Monday morning he would see what he could do. I said to him, what was I going to do between then and Monday for a smoke – I was technically not on loss of any privileges at this stage. He said just to ask the staff for a light and they would give it to me, just as long as you're not up banging the door every half hour.

I agreed to be of good behaviour under these conditions.

However, a couple of hours later when I asked the night guard for a light for the first time, he said "no chance." I tried to explain to him the arrangement I had with the duty governor in a very civil tone, and said all I would want would be one more light after this, before I go to sleep and that would be it.

I passed the roll-up out the top of the door to him. He took it and said he didn't have a light.

I said, just ask the prisoner two doors up to light it for me, it's no big deal.

He said he would go and see if I was allowed a light first.

After about half an hour he still hadn't come back, so I rapped the door to find out what the hold-up was.

When he came back he said there was nothing about me having to get a light in the office, and I wasn't getting one. He was laughing as he was saying this.

I told him about my agreement with the Governor to be of good behaviour was dependent on me getting a light.

He said for me to do whatever I wanted, I wasn't getting a light.

I said to him, that you'd rather see me wreck this cell before you would give me a stinking light.

He said, laughing, go ahead wreck it.

I snapped and wrecked the cell.

Then the SO came to the flap and asked me what the problem was.

Again, I explained everything and she went away to check with the governor. When she came back she said "YOU'RE RIGHT" and the officer with her, not the one who I originally asked for a light, lit my roll-up for me and slipped it through the top of the door.

I said to him, it was as easy as that!

The following day, I was moved downstairs. I felt that I had been treated with great injustice, brutalized, degraded and humiliated, so I daubed graffiti on the walls of my cell, to protest, and to vent my rage.

To date, I have been held in conditions of cellular confinement for a week. I was charged for smashing the cell, but the adjudication was adjourned because of the unavailability of staff.

AT THE END OF THE DAY I KNOW I AM BEING VICTIMIZED BY PRISON STAFF, AND I KNOW I AM THE VISTIM OF INSTITUTIONAL RACISM NOT TO MENTION SECTARIANISM.

NO MATTER HOW MAD BAD OR DANGEROUS YOU TRY TO LABEL ME IN ORDER TO JUSTIFY YOUR TREATMENT OF ME I KNOW THAT ALL I AM REALLY GUILTY OF IN ALL OF THIS IS THE RAGE OF THE POWERLESS AND DOWNTRODDEN. IT IS THE TORMENTORS OF THE POWERLESS AND THE DOWNTRODDEN WHO ARE TRULY GUILTY!

BY THE WAY, ALL THIS BEGAN BECAUSE I ASKED AN OFFICER

FOR SOME MORE CHIPS. MAY I MAKE A SUGGESTION?

PERHAPS, YOU SHOULD INCLUDE DICKENS' OLIVER TWIST AS REQUIRED READING FOR PRISON OFFICERS.

MAYBE NOT, YOU'D HAVE TO TEACH HALF OF THEM THE ALPHABET FIRST.

CHARLES J. CONLON
Punishment & Segregation Unit
Maghaberry Prison
13th March, 1999.

25

To me, Charlie's diary revealed little that was new. I was well aware of many of the incidents mentioned, and therefore accepted his account as an accurate record – albeit from the prisoner's point of view. But I did take issue with some of his statements. Where he wrote, for example: "I, of course, attempted to defend myself"

'What do you think I should have done? Got down on my knees and begged for a light?'

'Well, calling a governor a murderer, Charlie? That's pretty heady stuff.'

'You're in a prison, Patricia. Not in your front drawing room. And let me tell you something, it won't have been the first time he was called one.'

What I knew of the other side of the story was this:

Take for instance Charlie's account of the fight with the prisoner whom he alleged used racially abusive language towards him. Earlier on, Charlie had brought that incident to my attention, prompting me to check the record of the adjudication. I found evidence to suggest Charlie was being truthful. The other prisoner did apologise: said he was sorry; said he thought he was being funny. This did not excuse them fighting. They were both equally culpable on that count, and both punished.

'But how come,' I asked the officer, 'that I see the other party on orderly duties? What happened to *his* twenty days' loss of privileges while Charlie is made to pay the full whack?'

The other fellow knew what he had to do to get back into his jailer's good books, and they showed leniency.

'I can't quibble with the fact, Charlie, that your antagonist is considered a *funny guy* around this place. Also, he knows how to play the game: to show respect where it is due. And yes, I agree, what happened would make your blood boil.'

Charlie didn't ask for leniency. He looked for justice at the adjudication and when later he found he was not going to get justice there or anywhere else, he despaired. So what did he do? He lit a fire in a bin in his cell.

By the time I got the distance of his cell, that fire had been stoked into an inferno. 'What were you thinking, to set your cell on fire? They tell me outside you attempted to burn the prison to the ground. Four officers are off duty as a result.'

What really triggered the incident was his solicitor informing him his mother would not withdraw her statement to police.

'I'd come back from an adjudication,' he said, 'and was sitting on the bed reading the papers the solicitor left, flicking the lighter in my hand. I torched the corner of a paper and dropped it into the bin. I was fascinated watching the smoke rising. I lit the next and lay on the bed watching smoke spiral up and along the ceiling, then down the wall and out through the top of the window. It calmed me down. I took the mattress off the bed and put it up against the back of the cell door to keep them ones outside from knowing. I'd have stopped when I had done with the papers.'

Either the smoke was detected on camera in the yard, or the obstruction to the flap was seen by a passing officer. Next moment, the riot squad were outside his cell door. Charlie hid under the bed. They stormed the cell and dragged him out.

'What cover did you think wire springs would provide?'

He shrugged. 'Habit, Patricia.'

It was reported at a later board meeting that four officers, suffering from smoke inhalation as a result, were sent to Lagan Valley hospital for check-ups.

'Was the prisoner sent to hospital for a check up?' asked one of our members. 'Surely he was exposed for a much longer period than any officer.'

'I am not aware, as such,' the reply.

Eleven months later, Lisburn Magistrates' Court sentenced Charlie Conlon to six months' imprisonment for arson.

The afternoon of Monday, March 1 1999, and Charlie is in trouble again, according to his diary. A prisoner is allegedly manhandled into his cell, followed by overnight disturbance on the wing. Charlie gets punished, although he has no involvement. March 4, and he is moved to the PSU.

Here I had my own notes as reference.

Alerted about a disturbance on Erne 5, another member and I had gone to the landing to see for ourselves, and to speak with officers and prisoners – provided, of course, the prisoners wished to speak with us.

The allegation that an inmate had been assaulted by an officer was on the lips of every prisoner we met.

'Could I have a word with you,' asked a female officer, beckoning us not to return to the office until she and a young male colleague had spoken with us. Glancing surreptitiously towards some officers behind glass, she explained: it was about Conlon. She was calling into question his treatment by certain fellow officers. Her colleague standing by her side nodded in agreement.

She claimed that certain officers' attitude towards the prisoner left a lot to be desired. Conlon, she said, had not been involved in the overnight disturbance some days before. The following day he was ill. He was denied exercise for no good reason. Following which, he was manhandled by officers on his way to an adjudication.

She was the only prison officer ever to cite human rights in my hearing inside that prison. She had witnessed an injustice and she spoke out. Unfortunately there was little we could do because, by then, Charlie was back in the PSU and involved in other altercations. He needed a light for his roll-up, and according to himself, not until another female officer came on the scene did he find justice.

Charlie was not the type to take too kindly to "sneering, smirking, smug" officers. Your "gobshites and dick-heads".

Of mixed race, he may well have seemed a threat to those who feared difference. He could appear formidable to those wishing to wield power over him. Often he reminded me of a young Muhammad Ali, and few smirked or sneered at the compelling Muhammad if they wanted to remain standing for long. When I first met Charlie Conlon in my classroom in Magilligan, I, myself, sat up.

If it was respect he craved, he was in the very wrong place to have his wishes fulfilled. In general, officers were regular in their day-to-day dealings with the prison population. The majority were decent men and women doing a day's work. Their job was not about boosting the prisoner's self-esteem; their job was about keeping the prisoner securely locked away. The good officer performed that task with respect.

I asked Charlie for a recent example of an altercation provoked by an officer.

'Last week,' he said, 'a group of us were assembled for court. We were filing through, chatting to each other, automatically putting our hands forward for the cuffs. A few fellows before me had their cuffs slipped on and they moved forward, but when I presented my hands the same way, my wrists were forcibly grabbed and my hands hurtfully thrust into the cuffs.'

Random strip-searching was another example. If certain officers, including Dullis, were on duty, he was invariably selected, and, according to Charlie, the search was executed in the roughest and most demeaning manner possible.

'If such be the case, and you can identify officers not acting professionally towards you, why are you aggressive towards the decent ones? I see no difference, Charlie, between you calling officers derogatory names, and them addressing you in like manner.'

We were discussing the alleged incident when an officer had stuck his baton in his neck. Had he not, in his Christmas 1996 letter to me, castigated sociologists for calling love-children anything other than bastards? 'You are selective when it suits your own purposes, Charlie. You told me in that letter the term bastard was more honest than the term love-child. You are proud of your black heritage. You lay on the language when it suits yourself.'

'There is one big difference, Patricia, between slagging oneself off, and someone attacking your character. I can say those kinds of things to you because I know the type of you.'

'But you called a governor a murderer? You can't have it both ways, Charlie.'

'The difference with the governor is he knows well enough he's not one.'

'But maybe you hurt his feelings?'

Charlie had nothing more to add.

His communication of March 13 1999, was duly noted by the BOV, photocopied and distributed to those who wished to have a copy. Matters arising would be addressed when everyone had an opportunity to digest.

One immediate outcome was that Charlie, although on a punishment regime, got access to education.

'Would you have any objection to him doing some creative writing?' I asked the governor. 'Writing about his life experience might focus his mind.'

'None whatsoever.' Moreover, he would see to it the prisoner was supplied with paper – anything to divert his energy away from his officers.

'They look for happy endings in books. They won't be getting any happy endings here. I started writing before, but I had it all said in a few pages, before I tore them up.'

'What about the African-American angle?' This question arose because a replica of the *Vietnam Veterans Memorial Wall* from Washington had been on tour in Ireland. Sean went along to view, reporting back to Charlie that he found no Charles Eason amongst the veterans commemorated.

If this man had died serving with US military forces there had to be a record somewhere. So I sneaked a visit to the internet. The memorial wall had gone online in 1996 and the search engine immediately led to links.

The 57,939 casualties were arranged chronologically by date of death. I scanned every victim within the time frame – June 1966 to February 1967. Even tweaking the spelling of Eason, I found no match.

Staying with Eason, I began searching for variations on Charles. He had always been emphatic he bore his father's name. But say his father was officially registered Albert, or Joseph - the name 'Charlie' might well have evolved in other ways?

I stopped at one particular listing:

JOSHUA WAY EASON

SSGT – E5 – Army – Regular

9th Infantry Division

27 year old Single, Negro, Male

Born on Jun 24th 1939

From MARIANNA, ARKANSAS

Length of service 4 years.

His tour of duty began on Dec 12, 1966

Casualty was on Jan 25, 1967

In BIEN HOA. SOUTH VIETNAM

HOSTILE, GROUND CASUALTY

OTHER EXPLOSIVE DEVICE

Body was recovered

Religion

BAPTIST

Had I found Charlie's father? OK, he was not called Charlie, and he was not from Texas or Kansas, but from a neighbouring state, Arkansas. He was a sergeant. Single. Negro. Baptist. And, amazingly, SSGT Eason's tour of duty in Vietnam coincided with a possible homecoming to Belfast for Maura. It all fitted perfectly.

I brought a printout to Charlie and he read it standing in his cell. Flinching, he turned 'It's him.' His next thought was to show Sean what we had discovered.

When the governor's response to his communication of March 13 came, Charlie had already spent nine months in solitary confinement.

Reading from a tabled memo, the governor said: "The case of Conlon has preoccupied board members for some time. At least seven members of the board have been involved in signing him on Rule 32. On some occasions the members knew little of Conlon, and so it might be useful if everyone knew the background to the case . . .

"Conlon is on Rule 32 because he habitually assaults staff and prisoners, to the point at which my duty of care requires me to protect them from him . . . Some members may not be aware of the extent to which Conlon preys on others . . ." This point was illustrated with a record of assaults:

September 1988 fighting with another inmate.
March 1989 assaulted four officers.
January 1990 fighting with another inmate.
March 1990 fighting with another inmate.
August 1990 assaulted an office.
August 1990 assaulted another inmate.
January 1991 assaulted an officer.
November 1990 fighting with another inmate.
January 1991 assaulted an officer.
August 1992 fighting with another inmate.
January 1993 fighting with another inmate.
March 1993 assaulted an office.
January 1994 assaulted an officer.
January 1994 assaulted an officer.
August 1995 assaulted another inmate.

He highlighted some incidents:

When in Belfast prison he broke an officer's jaw, and when in Magilligan an officer's nose. In Magilligan an officer was medically retired following an assault by Conlon.

The memo would not provide us with a record of the many charges of threatening staff, or of trashing cells and other accommodation, but would concentrate on some of the more recent incidents from reports submitted by staff since January of this year. They were:

18.1.99 Staff broke up a fight between Conlon and [Williams] in the yard. [The racist comment.]

20.1.99 Conlon set fire to his cell and barricaded the door refusing an order to remove it. [The mattress against the door incident.] A C&R team was assembled and entered the cell where Conlon was hiding under the bed. He was removed under C&R to Cell 8. Conlon refused to cooperate and lit another fire in Cell 8. Staff re-entered the cell and during a full search a cigarette lighter fell from his buttocks. He was relocated to cell 9 and placed in a canvas jacket.

The five staff involved were sent to Lagan Valley hospital, one with a gash in his hand, the others suffering from inhalation of smoke.

4.3.99 On being unlocked from his cell Conlon attacked Officer [Smith]. Two other officers went to his assistance. Three officers were injured and went off duty.

5.3.99 When being escorted he started throwing punches at the two members of staff. Conlon had the officers in the corner of the landing and was continually punching them saying, "I will kill you."

A third officer tried to restrain him and he was punched on the head. Both officer and Conlon fell to the floor and Conlon tried to bite the officer's hand and stomach. The officer suffered injuries to his right hand, neck and lower back.

'It is not in dispute,' the governor concluded, speaking to his memo, 'that Conlon has immense problems, or that he has had a very difficult background and that he needs help … An awareness of the situation does not mean that he should be allowed the freedom to act out his difficulties at the expense of others … We expect sex offenders to address their offending behaviour; those with drug and alcohol difficulties to attend courses to deal with those problems, others to attend anger management programmes and so on. I expect Conlon to address his offending behaviour …'

'Does anyone have any questions for the governor?' asked the chairperson.

I had questions. But my questions were for Charlie. When the meeting ended I lifted my papers and marched across to the PSU, slapping the governor's memo down in front of Charlie.

'Look at your record. How in God's name do you expect me or anyone else to defend you?'

Charlie scanned all four pages. He then flicked back to the incidents spanning the years 1988 to 1995. Stabbing with his finger he invited me to examine dates. 'Look at that. I've been inside since the seventies but look when all this started. If I'm as mad or bad as they're putting about, then I must have been the same before March 89 when I was spat on and then laid into by one of themselves. And count it all up, Patricia, fifteen incidences. For the abuse I've taken from them, that is a good record in its own right.'

'How's the writing coming along?' I enquired.

He'd started writing, he told me. Read it over. Torn it up.

As encouragement, I mentioned that I enjoyed scribbling for a hobby and if he would give it another go, I would join in. We could compare results. I would fictionalize my characters: himself and a few guys from the old days in Magilligan. When I noticed him warm to the proposal I asked for his preferred fictional name.

'Jude,' he said.

The response was so instantaneous, I asked, 'Why Jude?'

'Jude. Don't you know? The patron saint of hopeless cases.'

And so Jude it was.

Some weeks later we exchanged manuscripts. My three pages of fiction, his three pages of fact. Charlie introduced himself as, 'A Black Celt from a lone-parent family who grew up in the North of Ireland during the Troubles.' He wrote of the stigma attached to an Irish Catholic woman being an unmarried mother. He wrote about becoming delinquent, and his brother not. He gave details of the circumstances of his birth: being put into care, and so forth. 'I believe,' he wrote, 'that sending me to the boys' home was the major factor in determining the course which my life was to take'. Adding that, when he needed help, 'I received lies, abuse and punishment, whilst the officers and staff got big fat pay cheques, and swanned about in an arrogant hypocritical self-righteous manner. The only remorse that I feel is for the pain which I have caused my family and the dishonour that I have brought upon my parents.'

He ended with two quotations: "In 1681 Nell Butler, Irish maidservant to Lord Baltimore in Virginia, fell in love with her master's slave, Charles. Threatened with enslavement herself, Nell Butler replied, she had rather marry the negro under them circumstances than to marry His Lordship with his country."

He referenced his quote, '*Black Ivory*,' A History of British Slavery. James Walvin. *HarperCollins*, 1992, p222.'

And lastly, he quoted Malcom X. "Why should I have any sympathy for someone who has no sympathy for me?"

He signed the manuscript, Charles J. Conlon, Maghaberry Prison, 30 August 1999.

I promised that the happy ending in my fictional endeavours would come with the protagonist reunited with his African-American roots. And, indeed, it was those few pages which later formed the basis for this book.

But, there was a setback with the family tree when Charlie contacted Sean, and Sean went online. He found the listing for Joshua Way Eason and took it to his mother.

Maura was adamant. Joshua Way Eason was not his father.

Where to go next? Charlie and I pondered possibilities. Bill Clinton hailed from Arkansas. Should we phone Bill?

A phone call to the American Consulate instead, and I was directed to the National Personnel Records Centre in St Louis, Missouri. Since it was Charlie's project, Sean felt he should be the one to conduct the correspondence. But Charlie did not think it would look good communicating with high-ranking army personnel from prison. Nor did he want the reply subjected to prison censorship, so it was decided to use my home address.

He dictated, and I processed.

I was born in Stuttgart, Germany on 17ᵗʰ February, 1966. My place of birth was St. Nicholas's Hospital. I believe my father was a Sergeant in the US Army, stationed at Crailsheim Barracks in Stuttgart. My mother returned to Belfast in January 1967, where she gave birth to her second child when her partner was transferred to Vietnam. My brother Sean was born in Belfast on the 23rd of February 1967. Shortly after my mother's return all correspondence from my father ceased.

My brother and I have always understood that our father was killed in Vietnam. I understand that my father's name was Charles Eason, or perhaps Easton. He had to be stationed in Germany between May 1965 and May 1966 to account for my brother and me. We are mixed race, African-American/Irish."

I would like to find out if your records show that a person of this name was stationed there during this period, and if what I know of the circumstances of my father's death is correct information. There is always the possibility that, for personal reasons, my father did not wish to have any more contact with my mother, and that he is still living.

One way or the other I would like to know for certain.

The initial response was that Military Personnel were unable to identify a record of service from the information provided, and enclosed a questionnaire seeking more information.

Charlie completed the questionnaire, ignoring my urging to tweak in the direction of Joshua Way Eason. He would not go beyond what he had been told about his father by his mother. To the information already supplied he added only, that he believed his father's religion was Baptist, and that he was from a southern state, 'believed Texas'.

It would be November before the military were back in correspondence.

Study kept Charlie occupied during the intervening months. Finally he was working on an A Level maths course and achieving top grades. A more congenial atmosphere prevailed in the PSU, officers leaving him to get on with it. A good working relationship existed with the education staff, whom he respected, and they in turn spoke kindly of him. Yet he remained in solitary confinement.

Keeping up my calls to have him returned to normal association I noticed how, each time we inched closer to that day, a spanner would invariably be thrown into the works.

At the time, Mark "Swinger" Fulton, a close associate of the murdered Billy Wright – reportedly in charge of the LVF since Wright's murder, and allegedly personally responsible for a dozen murders – occupied a cell down from Charlie. As with Wright, Fulton was there for his own protection. A Special Protection Unit had been created in the PSU for that purpose, and since two separate regimes could not operate from one entity, privileges allowed prisoners on special protection were allowed to all prisoners. If Mark Fulton, the terrorist, was allowed a TV and posters on his cell walls, Charlie Conlon, the ODC, had equal privilege.

Charlie passed by Fulton's open cell door, and he noticed a poster on the inside: a military-style figure in combat gear and black beret.

If Swinger Fulton can have a poster on his door I can have one on mine, thought Charlie, and set to work designing one. A black power poster.

Unaware of such developments, and in light of his sustained period of good behaviour, I pressed again for his return to the wings.

Conlon, I was told, was scheduled for adjudication, charged with disobeying an order to remove material with political connotation from his cell door.

'What did the poster look like?' I asked the SO on my way through to see Charlie.

'It was a drawing of clenched fists surrounded by barbed wire,' said the SO.

'It was a drawing of two black hands joined in prayer surrounded by Celtic art,' said Charlie. Parity of esteem was all he sought. If Swinger Fulton was allowed display military type material, he would display cultural material.

'What did you do with the poster when you removed it?' I asked the SO on the way out.

It had been placed in storage with the prisoner's other personal belongings for return on release. The SO was quite happy to bring it out. As he unfurled Charlie's artwork I stood by his side giving silent but grateful thanks to Almighty God that I had never been called upon to teach Charlie Conlon fine art.

I went back to Charlie. 'I admire your artwork,' I said, 'but it strikes me, you could learn a thing or two from Swinger Fulton.

'And what might that be?' asked Charlie.

'Well, firstly. Fulton did what he was told. When asked to remove the poster, he did.

'And secondly, Fulton didn't write 'FUCK THE SYSTEM' on the bottom of his.

26

Someone hinted I should take a peek into Fulton's cell in the PSU, saying it was decked out in the colours of the Union Jack, the loyalists preferred method for staking out tribal territory. So the next Fulton Rule 32 signing I volunteered to visit him in his cell.

'Jesus, Mark, you have the place shining,' I opened the conversation while taking a chair and viewing the décor.

All his own handiwork. Officers supplied the white paint and brush, alongside the themed red bedspread and blue curtains. All that was missing, I figured, were a few kerbstones at the cell door for him to paint red, white and blue.

'Tea or coffee?' he asked, hitting the buzzer. Instantly an officer put his head round the door.

'Coffee,' I indicated, and it would not have surprised me had the officer returned with a cocktail shaker in his hands.

'Go on. Now's your chance,' I was nudged at the next meeting.

'I'm not taking the bait,' I whispered back. 'Ask the governor yourself why Fulton was allowed to decorate his own cell.'

Loath to be remembered by the Protestant people of Ulster for our role in highlighting this anomaly, we found other means of getting the governor's ear, and soon after, Fulton vacated his cell. The cell from where, earlier that year, he had allegedly masterminded the murder of the human-rights lawyer, Rosemary Nelson.

Fulton, the man linked to some of the most horrific sectarian murders during the Troubles, later committed suicide in the relocated Special Protection Unit.

The records centre in St Louis wrote back seeking more information. Charlie, at the time, was angry with everybody so I referred the letter to Sean, and we decided to contact the American Consulate again. Their person, Anne, suggested it would be best if everybody concerned come in and have a talk. 'Better still, if the mother could be present.'

Sean made the suggestion to his mother, and to our surprise she agreed. Meantime we would say nothing to Charlie as he might veto his mother's involvement.

A week later I was sitting in the lobby of the Europa, guessing it was Maura walking through the door. An attractive woman in a pale blue box-pleated suit, an ornate brooch in the lapel, and two diamanté combs securing her upswept hair, she made her way towards reception and ordered coffee before looking my way. With shoes matching her handbag, she was dressed for the occasion and exuded a warm social ease. Mother and son exchanged affectionate greetings when Sean joined us.

Maura spoke of a cross-community/cross-border education network she had become involved with. How she was enjoying her new interest, saying how her self-confidence had been boosted when she took up study.

We talked a little about Charlie. Sean could be matter-of-fact where Maura's eyes grew sad. My handbag held Charlie's account of his experience in the PSU. Sean had heard it all before. But Maura held her hand out. She stopped reading on the second page, her lips parting in a little gasp of inner pain. My compassion for this mother was heartfelt. 'That's my Charlie,' was all she could say as she handed the remaining pages back, unread.

Accepting it was she who put Charlie behind bars this time, Maura desperately wanted me to understand. Charlie had never tried to kill her. That was nonsense, and Sean agreed. They both knew he would have calmed down had the RUC not got involved. Had it not been for her heart, Maura explained, putting her hand to her breast and inhaling softly, things might not have escalated. The palpitations scared her. The police had been kind. Later, everyone advised her not to make it easy for Charlie, because she had been genuinely frightened. He needed a lesson. She didn't know what to do for the best any more, but she knew that Charlie had never tried to kill her. That was not her Charlie. The two-and-a-half-year sentence just handed down? Well, she didn't know what to say about anything anymore.

Coffee finished, and we were on our way. 'I'd love to work in a place like this,' Sean observed as we climbed the stairs to the Consulate.

Eric and Anne met us; Eric already briefed on the family history. More coffee was on offer, over which, Sean explained his motives for seeking information about his father. 'It would just be nice to know who you are,' he said, and, yes, he knew that if paternity could be established he would be entitled to US citizenship. 'Not that that bothers me,' he told Eric, 'except perhaps later on some of the kids might be interested. Who knows, maybe one day one of them might like to work in America.'

Maura, quite talkative beforehand, clammed up. Trance-like, she made the vaguest of responses when included in conversation. Sean was relaxed, at ease talking with Anne and Eric. But Maura could remember hardly anything of Germany: dates, friends' names, addresses … Sean did not press her, and neither did anyone else.

Maura relaxed when the focus switched to the general subject of tracing missing persons in the US – using social-security records, census returns, telephone directories, electoral registers. With the emphasis switched to establishing American citizenship for her grandchildren, rather than finding a missing father for her sons, she breathed easy. At which point she turned to Sean and said, Eason was definitely not his father's name. She wished she could remember but …

'Perhaps you had friends there who could authenticate that the father acknowledged the pregnancies as his?' Eric gently suggested. 'Maybe someone who was present when he visited you in the maternity hospital? Anyone who would swear an affidavit to that effect?'

Maura was equally vague about friends' names. This surprised me because even I knew the name of her companion, the lifelong friend from Belfast who was with her in Germany.

Maybe I was getting an inkling of where Charlie was coming from when he told me, 'my mother would drive you daft'. Yet it struck me as strange: Maura had not gone barmy at the mention of Charles Eason. On the contrary:

'Catch *him* getting sent to Vietnam. *He* knew how to work the system.' She was addressing Sean. 'He was back in America when you were born.' She spoke of dollars arriving. Oddly, she remembered amounts, but not the sender's name. 'That was the last time …,' her voice trailed away. She turned to me, pleading in her eyes. She wanted *me* to explain to Charlie and Sean, and to Eric and Anne. She was trying to be as helpful as she could. She was in turmoil.

'Can you remember,' I asked gently, my last try for Charlie, 'was his name Charlie?'

It was the music she remembered; the feel of the dance floor. 'He was such a gorgeous dancer, so nimble on his feet.' She became quite animated, her body quivering to a remembered rhythm.

Back to the hotel, and over lunch the three of us talked about the nice people Eric and Anne were, about Charlie, about Belfast, but we never mentioned the man-with-no-name, the beautiful dancer we were trying to track down in America.

When we finished lunch we wrapped our arms around each other on the steps of the hotel, and hugged our good byes.

'I don't think now is the right time to say anything to Charlie.' I was talking with Sean on the phone that evening. Sean agreed.

'Maybe when he gets out,' Sean suggested, 'me and him could have another go.'

It was millennium year, and sweeping changes were happening in Maghaberry. Martin Mogg had taken over as number one governor. 'You should have seen that corridor yesterday.' Carmel was describing the scene outside her office door: 'bottled-necked with trolleys, computers, photocopiers, swivel chairs … changing rooms. The number one directing operations: "You out of there; you in here".'

'Looks like things might liven up around here,' I said.

He was toying with the notion of transferring Conlon to Magilligan as a way through the current impasse, the number one said, when I raised the matter of the prisoner's prolonged segregation. Charlie would start with a clean slate in a different prison, and nobody would lose face.

The omens looked good. Charlie was filling his time with study, and getting along with staff. I tested the idea of a transfer and found him not averse to the suggestion. In fact I felt he was relieved. Finally, I thought, we are getting somewhere.

Not for very long though, did things remain all sweetness and light.

Charlie had a TV in his cell – a privilege retained since the departure of the paramilitaries to their new Special Protection Unit. No one else in the PSU had a TV. No one else was there as long as Charlie. One day he returned to his cell and found the TV gone. And all hell broke loose.

Somebody up the line, conducting an audit, noted that the current regime in the PSU did not allow for privileges, and gave an order to remove the TV.

Why commonsense did not prevail confounded me. The prisoner's behaviour had been good over a prolonged period. He was being considered for transfer to another prison. Why not phase out the privilege with the move? Unless, that is, someone wanted to provoke him?

And Charlie rose, as Charlie always rose, to the occasion.

'He went berserk. An officer lost half his face.' They were lining up to convey the news.

Needless to say the move to Magilligan was off the cards.

That episode was water under the bridge when we next met. There had been a more recent altercation.

'After feeding time last Sunday evening,' he said, 'me and Paulie Daly were slagging each other off through the cell windows. It was to kill the time. There was no harm or anything in it. It's an outlet.'

The din annoyed an officer just reported for duty. He came to Charlie's door and balled him out. Charlie could smell drink on him. 'Told me to shut up in a most ignorant and arrogant manner.'

Both prisoners knew they were breaking no rules, so they kept up the slagging.

A short time later the officer was back, a team with him. A full body search was conducted on Charlie in his cell, without, he claimed, proper medical supervision. 'Other than to humiliate and degrade me, there were no grounds for ordering that search. Searches are never done on Sundays, and Daly wasn't touched.'

I went away to check on his story.

SO Brian Clarke, a professional to his fingertips, located the file. 'If you want to go into the room next door,' he said, 'I'll bring these reports in and you can go through them without interruption.'

Reading reports from the weeks preceding the incident, everything seemed routine, until …? Disturbed, I reached for a sheet of paper, and on the spot penned a memo to the chairperson of the BOV, stating:

I visited the unit on August 10 and asked to see a record of the daily report sheets. Expecting such records to contain data relating to the prisoner's behaviour, I was surprised to find entries on the daily record sheets which carried judgements. One example: a reference to the prisoner looking 'stupid'. Another, a comment on his hair. While another ascribed motives to the manner in which the prisoner looked at officers.

In my opinion, such personal judgements should form no part of the daily recording exercise for this, or indeed any other prisoner, because such statements tell the outsider more about the one making the judgement than about the prisoner.

Of concern is an entry on the record sheet for Sunday, 6 August, entered after the report had been ruled off and filed for the day. THE REPORT HAVING STATED THAT THE PRISONER WAS QUIET ALL DAY. The subsequent entry, in another hand, and squeezed in below the day's entry, refers to a search, which led to charges and an adjudication. It involved the prisoner spitting on an officer, and damage to a unit.

I have requested information from the PSU, as to what provoked the search, and who authorised it?

I have also spoken to Conlon, and tend towards believing what he told me.

Should it emerge that his version holds true, then I will have serious questions to ask about (a) random searches, and (b) full body searches conducted on a prisoner in his cell without medical supervision.

The comments of the governor would be appreciated.

Martin Mogg made no excuses when I vented my anger at the following board meeting, accusing some of his officers of behaving like drunken rednecks.

On receipt of a copy of the memo the governor had had the matter investigated and found the situation to be as Charlie reported. He apologised. But, only to me.

Under Mogg's stewardship, the PSU got a revamp and a new name. A harsher regime might facilitate a faster throughput. Nobody would be allowed cosydown or become complacent about moving on.

All fine and dandy, until Frances phoned. Having visited the unit, she was concerned about Charlie's state of mind.

'I'm very afraid he might be losing it,' she said. 'He was jabbering like he was round the bend. Larry Hogan in the adjacent cell called me in. (Hogan, a drug dealer, with a reputation as a bully, was one of the toughest men in the prison.) Larry was on the verge of tears talking to me about Charlie's treatment,' she added. 'We have to do something, Patricia.'

Although I nursed a suspicion that Larry might well have slipped Charlie a bit of hash – drugs, Sean said, always did Charlie's head in – nevertheless, I feared that two years in solitary confinement might well have broken Charlie Conlon.

Charlie's booming voice met me as I entered the unit. *Just listen to what we have to put up with* writ large on every officer's face.

I asked to see the prisoner.

The prisoner would not see the BOV.

'I'm sure he'll see me,' I said, offering to talk to him through the door. Without waiting for clearance I walked ahead and called in through the door to Charlie.

'Yes,' I could come in. The voice through the door sounded normal. The officer by my side was twiddling the knob of a radio he had lifted from the floor.

'What were you bellowing on about just then?' I asked Charlie on entering his cell. 'I could hear you at the front gate.'

'I wasn't ranting or raving. I'll admit I was telling some of them what I think of them. I know they have me on a loudspeaker so I'm giving people something to listen to.'

I raised the question of the loudspeaker at board level. 'One would think officers heard enough from him, without putting him on air.'

'A loudspeaker in the SSU?' [Special Secure Unit – new image, new name.] What was I on about? 'A loudspeaker? Preposterous.'

I pressed my point. I had heard what I heard.

'No.' I was wrong, and beginning to look foolish, until one of our more esteemed members piped in: 'Governor, did you know that those ghetto-blasters young people carry round with them can be tuned to pick up sound? Blast it all over the place.'

'So that was why the officer hurried to pick up the ghetto-blaster from outside the door. Thank you, Roger.'

Following the meeting, Charlie went off the airwaves.

I found Martin Mogg to be a gutsy and spirited governor, and enjoyed his tenure. It was fun to sit in as an observer at his adjudications.

'Next in is A2142 Conlon,' announced the facilitating officer.

'Charlie.' I greeted him.

'Patricia.' He nodded. Today I was no McKenzie friend. We sat on opposite sides of the table.

The charges were read. 'Verbally assaulting a prison officer'.

Officer Bacon was off duty; his statement read. Charlie accepted he had used the words as stated in the officer's report, and that those words constituted a verbal assault. He would question the witness to the incident.

The witness was called.

Charlie asked the witness if he recalled hearing him say those words. The witness did recall.

'Where were we standing at the time?' asked Charlie.

'You were standing outside your cell door when those words were spoken.'

'I was returning from the exercise yard. Is that correct? You and Bacon escorted me in.'

That was correct.

'I was in good form, wasn't I? Did I not pass a joke with you and Bacon before we left the yard?' The officer half-heartedly agreed. How was he supposed to remember jokes prisoners made?

'Did I say anything derogatory as we walked down the corridor to the cell door?'

The witness shrugged.

'What did Bacon say to me as he was twisting the key in the lock?'

'I don't know what anybody else said to you. I only know what I heard you say.'

Charlie repeated the bigoted and racist remark he alleged Officer Bacon had made, including what he himself said in response. *Of course*, he had risen to the goad. He had been provoked. He was not denying that he had 'told Bacon where to shove himself, and how to do it. Else it would soon be done for him.'

It was now up to the governor to decide if Charlie was at fault. Charlie asked for time to consult his solicitor. The governor readily agreed and adjourned proceedings. The prisoner was escorted from the room, and the place readied for the next incumbent.

The SO wanted a word in our ears before he brought the prisoner in.

'Just to be warned, especially the ladies,' he said, glancing at Caroline and me. 'He has this very bad stutter, and, well, you might find the situation, you know what I mean ...'

The prisoner with the speech impediment sat down in Charlie's chair. A shrivelled-up little guy, he wasn't the size of a sixpence.

Asked to confirm his name and number, he eventually stammered a 'ye..........ss' and we all relaxed, thankful his ordeal was over.

The charges were read. The prisoner accused of disobeying an order, and using foul and abusive language to an officer.

Officer Murrell gave his report: 'Prisoner number 2750 Coots, an orderly on Bann 4, was mopping the landing floor when I walked past and noticed a spot that had been overlooked. I brought the matter to the attention of prisoner Coots. Told to do his work properly, the prisoner ignored the order.

'I issued a second order. That order was also ignored by prisoner Coots.

'On receiving his final warning, Coots responded, "If you don't move the fuck out of my road, I'll ram the handle of this mop up your hole".'

'Have you anything to say for yourself my good man?' asked the governor, using his pen to steady his jaw, while Caroline and I held our breaths, and our sides. Screwing his eyes at the prisoner, Mogg, a veteran of the English prison system, asked, 'Haven't I seen you around somewhere else? You came to us from the mainland, did you not? Maybe you haven't had a chance to find out how we conduct ourselves over here. The chappies where you came from will put up with language our chappies in this part of the world won't tolerate. Do you understand? Do you think you can accommodate yourself to our ways of doing things? Do you think you can do that for us?'

Coots, to our relief, finally stammered consent.

'Now, clear off with yourself,' said Mogg.

The ladies, for the record, never twitched a muscle.

Charlie went on hunger strike soon after. Day ten, I went to visit.

The SO was concerned. Conlon, he said, had not woken up that morning. 'No officer is willing to enter the cell to investigate in case he's faking it. The medics have been informed, and are on their way.'

'Right,' I said, 'I'll make myself scarce and come back later.'

I made the unit my last call of the morning. The news was brighter. Conlon had woken up; everything was normal. It was lockdown so I delayed leaving the prison until after lunch. Returning to the SSU, I asked to see the prisoner.

My request was referred up the line. Up the line could not guarantee my safety, or the safety of men to remain outside the open cell door while I was inside, and my request was refused.

'I want my request referred to the number one,' I said.

'The number one is on holidays.'

'Then speak to the number two, three ... or whoever is deputising.'

The PO lifted the telephone and dialled an extension. A short conversation ensued, and the answer came back. It was still no!

Uncertain which firm of solicitors were acting for Charlie – he fell out there, like he fell out with family and friends – one firm, I knew, had been loyal to him. I dialled their number, and felt happier after speaking to one of their people.

I was back in the prison within a few days, and again asking to see Conlon.

The officer leading me to the cell was chatty. 'Your solicitor lassie,' he said, 'you know the doll I'm talking about?'

I waited.

'What's-her-name? The doll in the film?'

'What film?'

'Your boy Gerry Conlon. The Guildford bombing. She was in with Conlon the other day.'

'*Gareth Pearse?*' I asked disbelievingly. '*Gareth Pearse was in Maghaberry seeing Charlie Conlon?*'

'Arrived with your solicitor boy.'

'Are you certain it was Gareth Pearse, the human rights lawyer?'

'That's her.'

No problem opening the cell door. 'Stay as long as you like. Give us a rap when you want out.' I was then locked into a cell with a man the riot squad wouldn't go next or near days before, although weakened by a ten-day hunger strike.

Charlie looked healthy and fit. 'Nice way of shedding a few extra pounds,' I complimented.

A deal had been struck between his solicitor and the governor. Dependent on him keeping his side of the bargain, within a prescribed number of days there would be a move to an upstairs cell, with a further relaxation of restrictions. And following another prescribed period, provided there were no altercations, re-integration on the wings.

'Gareth Pearse hasn't been in here?' I asked.

For a moment he was perplexed. 'Gareth Pearse? In here? The woman in here was from the *Northern Ireland Human Rights Commission*. But it fits,' said Charlie. 'The only time anyone here ever heard tell of human rights was at the pictures.'

Charlie kept his part of the deal, and the day arrived for his move to an upstairs cell. The riot squad were assembled to lead the prisoner twenty paces along a corridor, up a short flight of stairs, and twenty paces along another corridor. Charlie, his hands raised above his head, walked the distance. He was ordered to enter the cell. Face the window. With his back to the officers and his hands still raised above his head, he was told to get down on his two knees.

Charlie Conlon got down on his knees for nobody!

'Where is this all going to end, Charlie?' We were back sitting in his old downstairs cell again.

'With an AK-47,' said Charlie.

Belfast City Hall would be the venue. It would happen pretty soon. Just walk in and blast all around him. He would take out about a dozen before turning the gun on himself.

The next day he wrote me a letter.

Dear Patricia,

The last time we spoke I said something which you may have perceived as callous and insensitive, i.e. that death was part of a natural cycle.

Tact and diplomacy have never been my strong points. Speaking and acting without thinking and consequently putting my foot in it is something that I am good at! What I meant was, to quote Shakespeare, "Death will come when it will come," so it seems to me to be illogical to live in fear of death when you think about it. Obviously, however, it is something which should be avoided for as long as possible!

You are a good person, Patricia, so if there is a heaven I have no doubt you're going to it, and not for another 30 or 40 years yet at least. You'll probably outlive me. If there is no heaven or no hell, "No hell below us, above us only sky," to quote John Lennon, as I'm inclined to believe, then you're going back to the place you came from before you were born, and that wasn't so bad.

"I sometimes wish I'd never been born at all," to quote Freddie Mercury.

You have raised an outstanding family, and been involved in some of the main issues of your day. Your life has been anything but a waste.

Sincerely

Charlie.

27

No smiling face was lifted when we offered our passes to the bent head behind the desk in the SSU. We had just requested to see Conlon.

'Are you aware . . . ?' His fountain pen was capped and laid purposefully by the side of his ledger, 'that Conlon . . .'

'Yes, we are aware,' Teddy stopped him. 'We understand officers have been injured, and the prisoner has been injured, but if it's OK with you we would like to see the prisoner first. Then we will come back here and talk to yourself.'

'I will not risk men's lives taking the prisoner from his cell to meet the BOV.'

'Fair enough,' said Teddy. 'We will see the prisoner in his cell, if that's OK with yourself.'

'I see,' said the PO. 'Are you aware that extra security has been installed inside this unit? A security zone created outside the prisoner's cell? That the C&R team are permanently stationed outside Conlon's door?'

'So we've heard.'

'If Conlon is willing to leave his cell and enter the security zone, I have no objection to you speaking to him through the grille. My men cannot guarantee your personal protection in any other way. Do you still want to see the prisoner?'

'Yes, please,' we both nodded. 'Will you please ask him if he is willing to meet us?'

Word came back. The prisoner was willing to meet members of the BOV. The C&R team were waiting outside the office door ready to escort us.

'I have to warn you ma'am,' said an officer just as we were ready to fall in line, 'the prisoner is refusing to put on his clothes.'

'You mean … like he's naked?'

'Starkers?' supplied Teddy.

Teddy's face was as good as a circus. He raised a hand as if to stifle a cough, asking from behind, if I was up for it.

'I've come this far, Teddy. I'm beggared if I'm bottling out at the eleventh hour.'

'That's my girl.'

'Shall we go then,' I made the first move.

Like robots, two officers in riot gear moved into position before us. Two clones fell in behind. All six of us were on the march, down the corridor towards the security zone.

'Jesus Christ, Teddy, what am I walking myself into?' We had reached the grille with the entertainment about to commence. One of our leading men had entered the caged security zone. He unlocked the double security door sealing the cell door. 'BOV to see you, Conlon,' he called in, and then, fast as his two legs could carry him, he shot back out of the cage and locked the grille behind him. The stage was now set for Charlie's entrance.

'Are you OK?' enquired Teddy in an aside.

'I'll hold up,' I whispered.

'It's him doing likewise, worries me,' returned Teddy.

Nobody batted an eyelid as the prisoner walked through his cell door. His head high, his spine erect, no jungle cat could have managed a more impressive entrance into a circus ring than Charlie into that cage. He had donned a sharp pair of white boxer shorts for the occasion.

It was his prerogative to speak privately with the BOV. And did Charlie know it. He glowered fiercely past Teddy and me to the C&R team behind. They moved back until he was satisfied.

We scrutinised the upper part of his body for signs of injury, concerned about a gash on the side of his head. He said the doctor was due to see him in half an hour.

Business done, we indicated to the officers our intention to leave. Moving ahead while the team locked up behind us, an impatient step caused Teddy to draw aside, allowing the officer past. Then I heard Teddy shout, 'Hey you!' after the officer. Turning to the others, he asked, 'Did you see what that fellow just done? Gave me a deliberate shoulder against the wall when he was passing. One of you must have seen what happened?'

All of a sudden everybody had disappeared, leaving the two of us standing in the corridor, all on our own.

It was January 2001 when the story of the caged prisoner burst forth over the airwaves.

I had the radio tuned to the national broadcasting station of Ireland, *Radio Telefís Éireann* (RTE), and was listening to the velvet-voiced Joe Duffy, presenter of *Liveline,* promising interesting stories and coaxing his listeners to stay tuned. The afternoon papers had landed on his desk. He was reading the headlines.

'Mother of God, listeners,' he exclaimed, 'What is the world coming to? On the front page of this afternoon's *Belfast Telegraph,* the story — ULSTER'S MOST FEARED PRISONER.'

My ears pricked up. Joe's tone became more sombre as he moved beyond the headline.

'"Demand for tougher jail term for 17-stone, flesh-biting inmate, dubbed Hannibal Lecter".'

I turned up the volume. Joe's words came in soundbites.

'"Constantly locked in prison's punishment unit. Escorted at all times by four-man control teem protected by shields. Cell furniture bolted to the floor. Cell dubbed the Lecter suite . . ."'

'Mother of God', said Joe, moving on to the next item of news, 'are we safe in our beds at night?'

I had no doubt whose picture would grace the front page of the *Belfast Telegraph* when I arrived at the newsstand, and indeed, a smiling Charlie was grinning out at me. The photograph must have been commandeered from a surveillance camera.

I spread the paper on the kitchen table.

The story did not end on the front page, but continued on page six: "Shocking Insight into the life of Charles Conlon".

"Leaked Prison Service guidelines about Conlon," said Martin Breen writing for the *Telegraph*, "have revealed to this paper the measures adopted to reduce his ability to assault prison staff inside Maghaberry prison. Prison correspondence about Conlon has been seen by the *Belfast Telegraph*. Correspondence which describes him as a 'time bomb.' Saying it was 'only a matter of time before he kills someone'".

The Prison Officers' Association spokesman was quoted as linking the prisoner to "injuring 32 warders in the past two and a half years." Saying, "This latest sentence is an affront to justice considering the injuries he has caused to our members. He could be out in April but Conlon is an animal. Conlon would have been the worst prisoner in my experience.

He is the most violent prisoner we have had recently."

A sketch of the prisoner's cell was included. "Constructed at a cost of up to £20,000. The bed, stainless steel toilet, chair and sink, are bolted to the floor so they cannot be used as weapons".

Hold on a minute, Sunshine. I was talking not so much to my kitchen walls as to Mr Breen in the *Tellie*. *You are way, way, off the mark with your sketch. I have been inside that cell, sat on that bed, looked through that window. Come on, Mr Breen!*

I had petitioned the governor to provide Charlie with a study desk and chair. That furniture was made of heavy-duty cardboard, and nobody bolts cardboard to a concrete floor. The bed was the standard model for all prisoners in the SSU. The one in the sketch had more in common with an executioner's bench! The modern stainless-steel sink-unit, with drainer and double cupboards beneath, puzzled me. But, it was the light fitting in the drawing which took the biscuit. A long flex hanging down from the ceiling with a naked bulb at the end. "His bed sheets disintegrate if an attempt is made to make them into a rope, or another possible weapon?" reported Mr Breen.

But why would he need a rope, if he had a flex at the ready? I asked the kitchen wall.

"An airlock covers his cell door so food can be left and collected in a caged area without staff having to have physical contact with Conlon. A sliding grille also covers the entrance to his shower room enabling prison officers to lock him in while they search his room. Whenever he leaves the cell for exercise, court or other matters he is accompanied by four officers … They are kitted out with riot helmets, protective clothing and steel mesh gloves to prevent him from biting them."

And finally: "Disturbingly, a copy of the book *Silence of the Lambs* was discovered in his cell. He has, sources say, referred to a female prison officer as Agent Starling, the name of actress Jodie Foster's character in the serial-killer film *Silence of the Lambs*".

Next day's newspapers carried more "sensational revelations."

"It has been revealed that a file had been found in his cell." It was suspected he was using it for "sharpening his teeth".

However, the following section made more sense to me than anything else I had read.

… Prison chiefs are being sued by warders for injuries caused by Ulster's most notorious inmate. In a revelation following on from yesterday's disclosure, the [POA spokesperson] said, "Several officers injured by Conlon would be claiming compensation. Solicitors are acting for quite a number of claims. Yesterday the POA sent a letter to the Attorney General, John Morris, demanding that Conlon receive a tougher sentence after he had been handed a six-month prison term for vicious assaults on two officers. At Craigavon Crown Court he received two six-month jail terms, which will run concurrently, on charges of assault and occasioning actual bodily harm last January. One of the officers concerned is believed to have suffered brain damage after his skull was fractured with the arm of a chair ….

So that was what this was all about: longer sentences equating to greater compensation. The courts had let the prison officers down by handing down a six-month prison sentence for "a fractured skull and brain damage". What compensation might a man who had "lost half his face" reasonably expect?

Maybe the courts determined the injuries were not quite as severe as we read about in the newspapers?

The "fractured skull and brain damage" incident had occurred back in January 2000, and was recorded on CCTV. It was, indeed, a most frightening incident for the officers involved. The camera recorded the prisoner walk towards his cell door escorted by two officers. The prisoner spoke to an officer as the door was being unlocked. The officer moved out of view, returning a short time later. When the cell door was opened Charlie rushed out wielding a wooden plank. One officer grabbed a trolley that was close by, pushing it between them, but he tripped and fell to the ground as Charlie came towards him with the raised plank. A third officer came into view brandishing a floor mop. They must have been terrified. Charlie had the plank raised above the officer on the ground. As he lowered it his arm went limp. The cudgel fell to his side. He turned and walked back into the cell. The officer picked himself up. No serious injury was apparent on film. There was no voice-over.

Three times I watched the recording before I sought an explanation from Charlie.

'Did the officer say anything to provoke you?'

'No.'

'Nothing?' I probed.

'Nothing.'

'Then why did you break the arm off a chair while the man was off finding out your release date? As you had requested.'

Charlie did not know why. Other than, guessing what he was about to be told, he felt he could not take anymore any more, and he flipped.

Following the revelations in the *Belfast Telegraph* I was again visiting Charlie. Warned beforehand that I was putting men's lives at risk by insisting on my right to see the prisoner, I agreed to see him behind locked doors.

'If you insist ma'am, the door will be locked while you're inside. My officers will not guard an open door.'

Accordingly, I was incarcerated in a reinforced 6' X 9' prison cell with a man whose teeth, if I could believe what I read in the newspapers, were sharp enough to skin me. While outside stood four burly men, "kitted out with riot helmets, protective clothing and steel mesh gloves".

'What weight are you Charlie?'

'Twelve stone'.

'Not seventeen, like it says in the paper?'

'Twelve stone.'

I passed on asking him to open his mouth, and show me his teeth.

In Charlie's view the newspaper article was beneath contempt and therefore merited no discussion. His solicitor had all that in hand.

When it came time for me to leave, Charlie banged on the door to signal that intention. He shouted. He buzzed the buzzer. He banged the door again, and still nobody came.

Twenty minutes later, when someone outside reckoned manners had been put on me, the cell door was opened, and I was released.

'When are you going to get your act together and get the hell out of this place?' I said in conversation with Charlie later on.

'April,' said the governor, in response to a similar question. 'He is due for release in April.'

'What steps have been taken to investigate the leaking to the media of prisoner records and reports?' asked another member. 'Is it known who provided the newspaper with an image of a prisoner *stolen* from a prison security camera?'

'An internal investigation is underway,' we were told.

Later again. 'Has disciplinary action been instigated against any officer for passing confidential material to the media?'

'Not as yet,' we were told. And I believe it never was.

Charlie's hopes of vacating his solitary cell before his release date depended on judicial review. Two and a half years in solitary confinement had not mellowed him. It would be sweet victory to win his case. [Article 3 of the European Convention on Human Rights, provides that, "No-one shall be subjected to torture or to inhuman or degrading treatment or punishment".]

It was May 2001 before Lord Justice Kerr handed down his judgement in the matter of an application by Charles Conlon. (Ref. KERC3420)

By which date Charlie had left prison.

28

Before his release, I guessed Charlie had an inkling that the outcome of his judicial review might not go in his favour. He was incensed by the input of my fellow board members, and he wrote me another letter. This time in anger:

> *... I want you to stay out of my business and stop meddling in my personal affairs. If it wasn't for you I would never have opened my mouth at an adjudication, or had anything to do with the BOV.*
>
> *I'll never forget the way I was treated in here, 1996-1997, six months in solitary confinement for slabbering at [McGonnagle]. You agreed to a month of that solitary confinement and swore an affidavit that I needed psychological treatment. That was when you stopped inspiring me and I stopped taking your advice.*
>
> *Now you tell me that I have to work with the establishment. You are not helping me, Patricia, you are trying to undermine and control me.*
>
> *The establishment should be lined up against a wall and shot!*
>
> Good Bye
> Charlie

He added a PS, which caused a smile. He had not lost his appetite for a good old spar about politics.

In one sense Charlie was quite right to have a go at me. I had not helped by refusing to sign another Rule 32 since Christmas 1996. Had I done so, just once, I would have had an input into a dossier of evidence compiled in the prison and forwarded to the courts justifying his detainment in the SSU for such a prolonged period.

As it was, there was no voice there for Charlie. On three occasions only, had Charlie agreed to meet with anyone from the host of members who requested to see him when Rule 32 was due for renewal.

When I sat down to answer his letter, I began with the customary enquiry for his wellbeing. Continuing:

> *... I am not a bleeding heart, Charlie, nor am I likely to be conned by anything I hear from either prisoners or the establishment. In fact I am on*

record in this prison as saying that I tend towards believing your version of events, because you have no reason to lie to me. We know each other too long for that. Moreover, I do not believe that it is in your nature to lie …

Regarding the Rule 32 I signed in'96, and to a subsequent affidavit he referred to, I had this to say:

… Charlie, I do not believe you are a vindictive man, only that the enormity of your grievances overwhelms you at times. Since signing that Rule I have never ceased to raise the issue of your solitary confinement at every opportunity. I have done so to a point where my own credibility has been questioned in hurtful ways. Yet, I believe, I have made some people listen. I do not know why the most recent endeavours fell apart, only that they have, and when I went to your cell with [Frances], you did not want us there. It is your space, the only space you control in that prison, and we respected your wishes.

And then I tried my usual pep talk:

… My limited wisdom tells me we fail at many things in life. And life looked at through our failures, makes us compassionate. I would ask you to recall the happier periods in your life, Charlie, when you began to heal, and goals and hopes replaced desire for retribution and revenge. I understand that the damage done to you by years of incarceration has left awful wounds, yet you turn on people yourself, Charlie. You drive away anyone who taps on your shell.

You may sneer at what I am saying, and think, all right for her lecturing me, she got her opportunities, I never got a chance. You'll go back down that old road again, and your mother, the social workers, the police … they'll all be blamed. And yes, they failed. But, so did I. I failed, and I tried my best.

You told me once, you were owed. You wanted your dignity back. But can I tell you about a remark made to me by a prison officer as we walked through the prison gates. 'I never see anything of Charlie Conlon these days,' he said, 'I'm in transport. I hear he's giving trouble, but I always found Charlie to be a very decent type of young fellow, and that it would work out for him'.

I know that, in weaker moments you yourself have commented, that some of them are not so bad. That they try; the better ones. Remember?

I reminded him how I had once heard an officer pronounce his name in a scurrilous and defamatory manner, showing him the note in my jotter, and discussing with him my method of dealing with the matter. Then it was my turn to play the aggrieved:

… We all get weary, Charlie. Weary when we don't see results. I see your friends on the wings – not so many of the old faces around these days – and they ask about you, shake their heads and say it's not right, and we all agree that it's not right, and shake our heads. And they say that I should go and sort it out. But everything just gets worse …And, "putting people up against the wall and shooting them", is going to sort it out? Did reading Mandela's Long Walk to Freedom teach you that?

Reminding him of the *post script* to his letter, where he told me: "until Gerry Kelly tells the young people of West Belfast to join the police, they'll never join". So, wanting to finish mine on a lighter note I wrote:

… Funny! But I agree with the comment. All I'll add is: Kelly's coming pretty close baby, pretty close indeed!

I'll venture down the way to see you when I'm next in, unless you tell me otherwise …

Charlie was released before I got down that corridor again, and before judgement was handed down in his application for judicial review where, in his summing up, Lord Justice Kerr had this to say:

I have decided that none of the claims made by the applicant has been made out. The application for judicial review must be dismissed, therefore. As I have made clear earlier in this judgment, however, the continued isolation of Mr Conlon is a matter of grave concern. It seems to me that his continued removal from association requires both the governor and the Board of Visitors to scrupulously examine all possible alternatives to the present situation.

Charlie might be out, but I didn't hold my breath. And just in case he thought *he* had a monopoly on racial discrimination, I had evidence to suggest otherwise. The next letter passed to me in the prison was from a young man of African origin, and read:

> Sir
>
> Since I got in this Country and especially in this prison, I have suffered a great deal of racial discrimination, not only by other prisoners but worse in the hands of the authorities.
>
> I have been assaulted on a number of times by other inmates and worse of my assault came last month on [date]. I complained against members of staff who have performed an inappropriate search on me. I was subjected to racist jokes and mockeries about my private parts. Such, 'do let us see what a black man has.' To my surprise I was placed on report for abusing verbally a nurse who ordered this search. Which is completely non-sense, as he did report me only after my complaint against him.
>
> I then requested to see an SO. Which was denied. I was beaten unconscious, then taken by ambulance to the City and the Royal V. hospitals for two days.
>
> Since then I've been denied access to Television and segregated from other prisoners' association, and so any of my complaints doesn't lead anywhere as they are either ignored, or simply a non-sense answer …
>
> Dear Sir, I believe my human rights are violated here, therefore I would like you to clarified my situation as it is more than a month on this regime. *Please note that English is not my language.
>
> > Thank you.
> >
> > [Dowda Ojoko]

A week later I had a response ready for Mr Ojoko. First, I reminded him of when we last spoke. (In Roe House – a recently constructed block.). Earlier claims that he had been in both the Royal Victoria hospital and the City for two weeks were not substantiated. I wrote:

> … At that time I established that it was <u>two days</u>, not two weeks, you were in hospital for. I also established that you were examined by a doctor in the prison – [Dr Roden] an outside GP – who recommended calling an ambulance as you appeared in an unconscious state. I discussed with

you the diagnosis from the hospital. [Self-induced unconsciousness, and malingering.]

I had established you were sent to the City hospital for an x-ray because the equipment is located there. That there was no reported medical evidence of any injury to your body. That you returned to the prison, where you quickly fell into an unconscious state again, and remained overnight in the medical unit.

From prison records, I ascertain that your problems arose after you were involved in a "scuffle" with another prisoner. I have established that the C&R team were called to "break it up". Following which you were examined by a medical team for injuries – normal practice in such circumstances. Following this you made complaints against one member of that medical team, claiming that this person had made racial comments regarding your body parts.

I have taken your recent allegation of racism very seriously indeed, just as the staff in Roe House took it seriously when you complained to them about the racist remarks directed at you by other prisoners. I assured you at that time that "staff were looking out for you". You will recall that I told you they had spoken in positive terms about your general ability to get along with your fellow prisoners.

Far from being the all-time victim, I learned that you have, on occasion, played the racist card yourself, by indulging in good-humoured banter about the prowess of the black man.

I know that time in prison is not easy, but I would think that having a sense of humour, which staff and other prisoners tell me you appear to possess, should help you along.

If he was unhappy with this response, I asked Dowda to get back to me.

Dowda never did. And, Neither did Charlie Conlon.

Until the phone rang.

29

'Pat Convery, Belfast City Councillor, Patricia.' The voice on the line was brisk. It was also familiar.

Pre-empting his next words, 'You're looking for Seán, Pat,' but Pat interrupted.

'No. No. It's yourself I wanted. Margaret Walsh told me you'd want to know. (Margaret, another Belfast City Councillor, was a one-time member of the BOV at Maghaberry.) I'm ringing', Pat continued, the tenor of his voice growing sombre, 'just to let you know that Charlie Conlon was found dead this morning. The police have just been here talking to me.'

His words took a moment to sink in. 'Charlie dead! The police!' I sat down on the old black trunk in the hallway, the handset close to my ear.

'Sometime during the early hours. I'm afraid he hung himself. Someone out for a run early on discovered the body.' The details were scant, just what he had gleaned from the police.

'Poor, poor Charlie. Where?' I asked.

'Down by the Shore bridge.' Pat thought I knew where the Shore bridge was, but the location meant nothing.

Never for one moment did I think he would take his own life. His willpower was so strong. When I thought, what he put himself through in prison, to take his own life in the end. Attempting to come to terms with taking a rope and going out and hanging yourself on a cold dark winter's night. 'What must have been going through his mind as he fell to his death?

'Poor fellow,' said Pat.

'Poor Charlie,' I echoed. 'Why ever did he snap?'

'The police say there are marks on the body; some suspicion of foul play. A few boys in the area have been exerting muscle recently, putting the squeeze on a few fellows. (North Belfast, Pat's constituency, had had a spate of suicide reports – young men, allegedly under pressure from paramilitaries because of antisocial behaviour.) In fact,' Pat continued, 'the police had mentioned to me recently that I should speak to Charlie Conlon, saying he had gone to them recently, which was something of a turnaround.'

I learned that the evening before his death, Charlie had walked into the workplace of a former girlfriend. Told she wasn't there, he informed the two young girls who were that he had four bullets: two for them if they alerted the PSNI. One for his former girlfriend, and the last bullet for himself. This was the last anyone saw of him until his body was discovered this morning.

When I dialled Maura's number I got a disconnected tone. 'Just a second,' said the girl in Sean's workplace. She came back a few minutes later, slightly perplexed, saying, 'We saw Sean here a short time ago. Shall I ask him to call you back?'

When asked had she heard about his brother, she was at a loss. 'Maybe you would like to know,' I said, 'I have just heard the sad news that Charlie has been found dead.'

'I didn't know Sean had a brother,' she was immediately concerned.

'Perhaps Sean hasn't mentioned Charlie.' I hesitated before saying that Charlie had some problems.

'That explains the police. They were here talking to Sean, but we thought it had to do with work. (Sean had changed jobs and now worked in the care sector.) He must have left with them.' Her troubled tone indicated she wanted to talk with her colleagues, to share the sad news. To be there for Sean when he made contact with the office.

Next morning I searched the Family Notices in the *Irish News* for funeral arrangements. It was then I received yet another shock. Not until then did I realise why Maura was not answering her phone. And why there had been no Christmas cards last year from either Charlie or his mother.

Maura was dead.

> CONLON Charles (Charlie) died November 19, 2004, suddenly, beloved son of the late Maura and loving brother of Sean. His remains will leave 66 Serpentine Gardens, tomorrow Tuesday at 9.00 am to arrive at St Mary's Church Greencastle for 9.30am. Requiem Mass. Funeral afterwards to Roselawn Crematorium. Deeply regretted by his sorrowing brother, friends and family circle.
> May he Rest in Peace."

My family were equally disturbed to learn of Charlie's death. 'Will you go to his funeral, Mum?' Niamh's first question when I telephoned her in London.

'Yes, I'll go to Charlie's funeral, Niamh.'

'You and Charlie were great friends, Mum,' Ronan said on the line from Dublin. 'You'll miss him.'

'Yes,' I'll miss Charlie,' I told my son. 'But I think he's in a far better place now. At peace.' Ronan said he truly hoped he was.

I did not expect Sean to return my call. We would meet at the funeral.

Serpentine Gardens, his sanctuary of old – "my old Granny's house" – occupied now by his Uncle Jackie. Charlie's last resting place before his funeral.

Below the death announcement, friends extended deepest sympathy to the Conlon family on their sudden bereavement. Other tributes to the deceased followed: "Charlie, St Martin pray for him," a notice read. "Wherever your soul should rest I pray the keepers of it show more compassion to you than was shown to you in life. Rest in Peace, Charlie."

Padro Pio and St Joseph were asked to pray for Charlie.

And in another notice, the Sacred Heart of Jesus was implored to have mercy on his soul.

'Do you want me to come to the funeral with you?' Seán offered.

'Why don't I come instead,' said Orla, living in Belfast. 'We all felt growing up we knew Charlie, although we never met him. I'd like to come with you, Mum.'

From Brussels, Ciara echoed her siblings. 'Poor Charlie, I'm so sad to hear that he's dead.'

The curtains were drawn, and a black mourning wreath hung on the knocker of Jackie's front door when Orla and I called at the neat little semi on Serpentine Gardens, to pay our last respects on the eve of the funeral. Jackie solemnly shook our hands and brought us into the front parlour. Wreaths surrounded the open coffin. Chrysanthemums formed a guitar. Roses and carnations filled space in the small room. On the coffin lid lay mass and sympathy cards. In his open casket Charlie smiled in repose. Serene and tranquil in death.

Happy at last, I prayed, looking down on the corpse laid out in the white satin-lined coffin.

Jackie took us into the back room to sit by a blazing coal fire. Neighbours and family served us tea and sandwiches and tempted us with traybakes. Friends came and went, everyone talking about Charlie. 'Never did much harm except to himself.' Reference was made to an EXCLUSIVE in the *Sunday World* the previous Sunday. It dredged up the old Hannibal story from the *Telegraph*, scurrilously embellishing an already defamatory story with further exaggerated and unfounded mistruths, his friends believed.

Orla suggested somebody should complain to the Press Complaints Council. Her expert opinion finding immediate favour with one old mate of Charlie's.

'You're on, mate' he said, cocking his thumb to both Orla and the light bulb. 'Would you have the address of them ones on you?' He would waste no time lodging his complaint.

Maura, I learned, had died the previous year, following a short illness. Jackie talked of his exasperation getting Maura to see a doctor. 'Forgive the language,' he said, 'I don't often use bad language, but in the end I had to f…ingwell make her go. It was too late. Nothing could be done. Only sixty-four years of age. Maybe she realised herself. Maybe that's why she didn't want to go into hospital …'

Sean had taken his first break in days. 'Gone into town,' Jackie said, 'to buy a dark suit for tomorrow.'

I assured Jackie I would see Sean at the funeral. And, eventually, Orla and I forced ourselves away from the warmth inside that house, and out into the cold again.

We were amongst the first to arrive in the chapel carpark next morning. The weather clear and sharp. Low shrubs bordered the walkway leading to the plate-glass entrance. Orla pointed to the prominent notice on the door: "NO PRESS ALLOWED".

Set-in off a busy road, on the edge of a working-class interface area of North Belfast, St. Mary's is a modern, semi-circular, 1970 design. A slow trickle of mourners, interspersed with local morning-mass-goers, started to arrive. Older women muffled against the chill, the men taking their hats off to bless themselves at the Holy Water font. Orla and I joined those already in the pews. Rows of seats, tiered back towards the side walls, overlooked a central isle. Our side filled up fast, leaving seats opposite free for mourners yet to arrive. I noticed Paul Gupta walk through the door.

The solemn slow tone of church bells heralded the arrival of the cortège. Inside the chapel, the congregation rose to their feet. Sean, dignified and grave, towering above the others, walked behind his brother's coffin. Robed in white, the priest with outstretched hands received Charlie's remains, and the coffin was laid before the altar. Sean bowed to the tabernacle before moving to join his family on our side of the aisle. Across from us, empty rows filled up. Pallid young men climbed to the back pews, a few in tight-fitting suits, but most wore jeans, sober shirts and dark ties. All had made the effort. Thinly dressed young women in heavy makeup and high heels filled more seats. Some of the men remained standing against the back wall. A few huddled together. One man trembled uncontrollably.

The priest opened the Requiem Mass with the words, "Dearly beloved people, we are gathered together in God's presence …"

And what of God's plan for Charlie during his short spell on this earth?
I joined the slow-moving line of communicants advancing towards the altar, my hands cupped to receive the Sacred Host. *Sometimes God calls on a favourite to be the fall guy,* a voice inside me whispered. *Jesus didn't have it so great down here either, did He? Remember, Jesus turning to the good thief hanging alongside him on the cross with the words, "this day thou shall be with me in paradise."*

Back in the pew the voice came again. It was something Charlie said years before:

"Call me Jude".

And thus it was to Jude, patron saint of hopeless cases, I addressed my request.

'Hey Jude,' I asked, sinking to my knees. 'You'll look out for Charlie for me up there. Won't you, mate.'

'Charlie wasn't the worst by any means.' We were chatting in the chapel grounds before the hearse left for Roselawn cemetery. 'Weeks, months he went, and you never heard a word out of him.' Recent brushes with the law, I learned, were mostly driver related: insurance, driver's licence, vehicle test certificate …

'The fellow had to make a living some way or other, hadn't he?' a mate chipped in.

'According to the police Charlie had been going through a particularly self-destructive phase just before his death.' The councillor joined us as we moved closer to the family to offer our condolences. 'Loud music, all night parties, people coming and going; all the while living in accommodation close to old people, and the chapel. Drugs,' Pat said, 'are the curse of the area. Last week saw the funeral of a young overdose victim from this very chapel.' Someone else said the priest had some very strong words with the congregation as a consequence.

When the crowd thinned, we moved towards the family group to commiserate. We shook Jackie's hand. He wholeheartedly thanked us for coming, repeating the words, 'I know. I know …'

Tracy, Sean's partner, and his three children stood with Sean, other family members close by. I was meeting Tracy for the first time. Restrained in dress and makeup, wearing a dark business suit, her hair soft and loose, she smiled while she placed her arm around her little son. The children were all crying, one child setting the other off. They were clinging to their parents, their little faces bereft with grief. It is heartbreaking to witness children cry at funerals.

'Charlie had gone past the point of return weeks before he died,' Sean said, when we finally got to speak. 'You know yourself what he was like, Patricia. His life had broken apart again. No one could help him anymore.'

Not knowing his mother had died until I saw the death notice, I apologised for not being in contact. 'Me and Charlie, we had this little tiff,' I explained. 'We always made up, and I thought we had all the time in the world.'

Sean wanted to have a longer chat but this was not the right time or place. In a few days, when life settled back to normal, he would give me a call.

Although Charlie had been back in Maghaberry serving time on the wings, our paths had not crossed. Privately, I felt the message had gone down the line to certain officers to stop taunting him, and I wanted to leave good enough alone. He was in and out before I even knew he was back.

When Sean phoned a few days later he confirmed that Charlie had interpreted my non-communication as wanting to keep my distance. And since I was Charlie's friend Sean believed, like his family before me, I might well have given-up-on Charlie.

But that was just half our conversation.

What he said next truly floored me. And I suspect Sean took delight anticipating the impact his news would have on me.

'Did you know that Charlie found his father before he died?'

'You have to be kidding?' I was literally dumbfounded, wanting to ask a thousand questions.

'Where? How? Tell me everything.'

'In America. He was alive all the time.'

Sean explained that mother and son had been reconciled before Maura died. How, on her deathbed, she had finally told Charlie why his father had not been part of his life. 'You were right, Patricia,' Sean said, adding yet more surprising information. 'Charlie and me. We're not full brothers. We have different fathers.'

'What's Charlie's father's name?'

'Eason,' said Sean. 'Charles Eason.'

'And he wasn't killed in Vietnam?'

'No. Charlie was talking to him on the phone a month before he died.'

'Charlie was right all along about the name. I knew it!' I exclaimed. 'I just knew he was right.'

'Yes,' said Sean, 'except we were searching for a dead body when we should have been looking for a living one.'

'More fools us?'

'It was only a half hour before she died she told Charlie. I didn't make it to the hospital in time, and didn't get to hear about my own father, but she freed up Thelma (the friend who had been in Germany with her) to talk to us and tell us the whole story. Thelma had kept her secret for her all those years.' Maura had also shared her secret with another friend she had made through the education network, and, it appeared, she freed her up as well to talk to Charlie and Sean.

Sean, in the most matter of fact way, but clearly relishing his role, told me how Sergeant Charles Eason was called back to the US to engage in training new recruits. 'That affair seems to have finished early on, because my mother appears to have fallen for a friend of his – the one who ended up as my father. When she fell pregnant she was afraid to tell Charlie's father because she thought one would kill the other. They said Charlie's father had a quick temper.'

'So Charlie didn't lick the quick temper off the floor then,' I laughed, fascinated by the tale.

How sad, I though, that Maura could not have told those boys the true facts from the start. The stigma attached to being an unmarried mother must have cut deep, and more especially an unmarried mother with two black kids. Maura was no "Nell Butler who would rather marry her master's slave Charles than Lord Baltimore".

I asked Sean had he made contact with his own father.

'No, not yet.' He was in no rush.

For the first ten months of his life in Germany, Charlie had been looked after by nuns. Sean believed that it was his mother's intention to put Charlie up for adoption when she returned home. Her plan was to join Sean'a father who had recently returned to the United States. But things did not work out. When Maura's mother first saw Charlie she believed Thelma to be the mother. She bonded with the baby and thereafter nobody would countenance adoption. So Charlie stayed within the family, and when Sean was born, Maura was actively discouraged in her plans to join his father in the US. And so it never happened.

'What my mother done I believe,' Sean said, 'was when talking to Charlie she told him things about *his* father. Charlie was the one always wanting to know. I was never that interested. That day in the American Consulate she must have felt she should be talking about the one that was *my* father because I was the one there. She was never any use at lies.'

'If you think about that day, Sean, she didn't deny the name Eason. She just said that it was not *your* father's name. And it appears she was telling the truth.'

'So, how did Charlie make contact when he finally found out?'

'The internet. A website for contacting American military personnel.'

'And what state was Charles Eason from?'

'Arkansas.'

'I don't believe you. The same state as Joshua Way Eason.'

'Aye, and Bill Clinton,' laughed Sean.

Charles Eason had responded immediately to the hit on the web, and had been in regular contact, phoning Charlie at his girlfriend's place. "Sergeant," Charlie called his father when they spoke. 'I have all the correspondence here, photographs as well,' Sean continued. 'I'll let you see his letters any time you want.'

Charlie had been invited to visit the US at his father's expense. 'There was talk of his father coming over here as well. But his father got sick and that trip had to be postponed. This was all happening when the break up between Charlie and his girlfriend happened. And then Charlie's head just went. A lot of this may have preyed on his mind when he went out and done what he done.'

Sean and I shared our thoughts as to why Charlie had "done what he done". I had witnessed before, as had Sean, him take a project to a certain point, only to turn round and blow the whole thing apart when uncertainty entered, unable to embrace what lay beyond. Charlie had no confidence in the real world. Sean's *take* was, as always: 'Charlie always knew he was going back to prison, no matter what.'

I asked if Charlie had told his father about his past. Sean believed he had. His father knew he had been in prison, but Sean did not know to what extent he was aware of Charlie's record.

Charlie had two half brothers in the US.

I read the letters. Loving letters from a father to a new-found son. A father who, for thirty-seven years, did not know of his son's whereabouts. A man saying he would travel anywhere in the world to meet him. How everyone in his family back home in the US wanted to meet him. "Charlie," he wrote in one poignant sentence, "My Dad was the best man I have ever known, and when I'm gone, I want my three sons to feel that way about me." And as I read on, the tears rolled down my face.

In photographs, the striking resemblance between father and son was obvious. Charles Eason, with some friends on the golf course in Hot Springs, Arkansas. It was how Charlie Conlon might have looked in twenty years time had his life taken a different course. Had he wised up.

How sad this dear man must have felt when he learned of his son's untimely death so soon after getting to know him.

Sean wholeheartedly encouraged me when I said I would like to write to Charles Eason, and tell him a little about the Charlie I knew.

And so, one day in February 2005, I wrote a letter to Charles Eason in Arkansas. I started by offering commiserations on the death of his son:

> … *I was a teacher in Magilligan Prison in the early 1990s when Charlie was serving a sentence there. I will enclose a copy of a letter Charlie wrote me back then which tells of a relationship sustained almost to the end of his life. His letter tells it much better than anything I can say in this short letter to you. I'm sure you know that Charlie's life was not an easy one, and I pray that he has found happiness now.*

> *We have a system here, where the Government appoints independent lay people to act as monitors of our prisons. I served in that capacity until just recently. For twelve years I visited Maghaberry Prison regularly and kept up contact with Charlie when he returned to prison on a number of occasions.*

> *Through Charlie I met his mother Maura, and his brother Sean. Although Maura and Sean loved him dearly they were exasperated on many, many occasions, as was I. At one point I encouraged him to trace his father; a father Charlie firmly believed had died in Vietnam. It is ironic that the internet yielded one; Joshua Way Eason, born '39 from Arkansas, died Vietnam '67. Religion: Baptist. Details which, except for the name Charles, corresponded with what Charlie believed. He was adamant, though, that his father's name was Charles, and that he had been called after him. He was also adamant that Sean was his full brother, although I had suggested to him that physically they did not look remotely alike. They were very alike in their personalities. Charlie was very intelligent, very handsome, and just a very nice guy.*

> *Charlie and I talked about writing a book about his life. I have quite a lot of material and have sketched out a rough draft – in a sense I was waiting for Charlie to 'grow up' before I could give it the happy ending we were all looking for, although Charlie warned me not to rely on him. I was working on a chapter this evening, and that prompted me to write this letter to you. If you would like to see some pages, I would be happy to send them. Even if the book is never finished, or published, you might like to see my take on Charlie.*

> *I don't know how much Charlie told you about his prison career. There were un-savoury parts. I need to warn you of this before reading. But despite everything, Charlie was a dignified, gracious fellow, whom any father would*

have been proud of had life gone better for him, and this is what I want for him in my writing.

And, sending greetings from Ireland, I finished my letter and posted it to Arkansas.

In March I was hospitalised, therefore not at home when Charles Eason called from Hot Springs, Arkansas. He talked with Seán, who delighted in telling me, in my hospital bed, about their conversation. Immediately I felt better I called back, and since then there have been other long telephone conversations, letters and cards, and promises to visit each other.

'You know something, Patricia,' Charles said, referring to the past. 'Back then I was a very young man. Maura? Why, Maura, she was twenty-six, twenty-seven years old. I was just, I guess, twenty years old back then. But I never would have left Charlie behind. You understand. I was posted back to the United States before he was born, and I never did get to see him. Charlie, he was with the nuns all this time I was gone, but I always sent dollars each month to that place for his care. And then all of a sudden, Maura was gone, and she had taken Charlie with her. And the nuns, they wouldn't say where she was gone to . . .'

He talked of subsequent endeavours to trace his son.

'I knew it was Great Britain someplace Maura was from. I figured England. That's were I looked. I never did think to look to Ireland. All my life I never stopped thinking about Charlie. My wife, she knew all about Charlie; and my other sons too. They knew. Let me tell you something, Patricia. It was a bad time back then. A very bad time, with Vietnam and everything going on. You know something about Maura. She always had my mother's address in the United States. She always knew how to contact me, but she never did.'

'Out of curiosity, there is something I want to ask you.' I was again speaking on the phone with Charles Eason. 'Are your family part Native-American?'

'Let me tell you something. My father's grandmother, I guess that must be my paternal great-grandmother, she was one hundred percent pure native-born Cherokee Indian.'

I learned more about Charles Eason, and about his family. Since his army discharge, he had worked for a company for many years, rising to a senior position before his recent retirement. About Charlie's troubled life, he had this to say: 'You know something, Patricia. If Charlie had been with me he would not have got in trouble. I would have looked out for him. Maura and me? That was all finished before I left Germany. I knew there was something else going on there. But Maura, she knew I always wanted Charlie. She could have got in touch with my mother. She always knew my mother's address.'

Those long conversations on the telephone between father and son – his father phoning Charlie on a regular basis, setting the phone on loudspeaker in his living room so all the family could join in – was the honeymoon period for both. Perhaps Charlie did not want to spoil the illusion, spoil his mother's reputation in his father's eyes, and that was why he never mentioned he had a brother. Charles Eason had no notion of Sean's existence until a friend of Charlie's telephoned him following Charlie's death.

Charlie had promised to send photographs. None were sent. No recent shot had turned out well enough to satisfy Charlie, so his father was still waiting.

I went hunting, but finding a photograph was easier said than done. 'They don't do studio portraits *inside*.' Pablo Delaney reminded me. 'Only mug-shots of mugs.'

Pablo and I sat lamenting Charlie's tragic demise.

'Tell me the truth, Pablo. Was Charlie dealing drugs?'

'Nah,' he dismissed the notion, 'them ones would never let Charlie Conlon handle drugs. Never let him handle money. They had him sitting around with them, using him as the strongman. His reputation was all them ones was interested in, And the more of that he had the better for them. If he was dealing drugs, he wouldn't be out driving a taxi without a licence and getting lifted. The fellow was trying to make a few bob for a living. Nah, Charlie was never dealing drugs. Charlie was just *saft*.'

Charlie? Just soft? That was an interesting angle?

'Which reminds me, Pablo. You know I met your niece, Kerry-Marie in Maghaberry. How is she these days?'

'You should just see that wee girl today. You should just see that same wee girl. Her own business. Driving her own four-wheel. Her own flat. Excuse me. Her own *a-port-ment*. Business suits, the whole works, just like auld Maggie Thatcher. Remember the craic back in the old days in Magilligan?' He buried his head in his arms, and surfaced a moment later. 'She learned her lesson, that same wee girl. She's not stupid.'

'Have you heard anything of Joe McCoy?' I enquired.

'Joe's a heroin addict on the streets of London.'

'Brad Pitt, to play you in the movie when I write *your* life story? Wind your neck in Pablo! Have you ever seen yourself in a mirror? Brad Pitt is blond, fair.'

'What the hell odds, can't they always rub a bit of boot polish on him?'

'One last thing, Pablo, and I swear to God, if you tell me the truth I won't put it in the book. Was it you carried off the Northern Bank robbery? The twenty six million heist before Christmas?'

'Lean closer to me, sweetheart, till I whisper in your ear.'

It is four in the afternoon of September 26, 2005. I lift the phone, 'Charles,' I recognised the voice.

'We've just been talking about you over there,' I said. '*Katrina*, such devastation in New Orleans, it's been all over the TV.'

'And we've been looking at developments over there on TV as well.' Charles explained why he called. 'I think it's a good thing. This giving up arms. I think it's a very good thing, this IRA decommissioning of arms.'

Then, as always, we talked about Charlie.

'You know something Patricia. We've been talking some more over here about what you've written. Those recent pages you sent me. And what we can't understand is why Charlie didn't just move on, you know?

'You know something else, Patricia. I never so much as stole a candy bar in my whole life.'

It is almost midnight that same day. The phone rings.

'How's about you sweetheart?'

'Pablo! Will you GET OFF THAT BLOODY MOBILE PHONE, or do you want the PSNI battering down my front door in five minutes time?'

'Never worry your head about the likes of them ones. *Happy days, kiddo.*'